# Mission by the People

# Mission by the People

Re-Discovering the Dynamic Missiology of Tom Allan
and His Scottish Contemporaries

Alexander Forsyth

PICKWICK *Publications* · Eugene, Oregon

MISSION BY THE PEOPLE
Re-Discovering the Dynamic Missiology of Tom Allan and His
Scottish Contemporaries

Pickwick Publications
An Imprint of Wipf and Stock Publishers
199 W. 8th Ave., Suite 3
Eugene, OR 97401

www.wipfandstock.com

PAPERBACK ISBN: 978-1-4982-3269-2
HARDCOVER ISBN: 978-1-4982-3271-5
EBOOK ISBN: 978-1-4982-3270-8

*Cataloguing-in-Publication data:*

Names: Forsyth, Alexander, author.

Title: Mission by the people : re-discovering the dynamic missiology of Tom Allan and his Scottish contemporaries / Alexander Forsyth.

Description: Eugene, OR: Pickwick Publications, 2017 | Includes bibliographical references and indexes.

Identifiers: ISBN 978-1-4982-3269-2 (paperback) | ISBN 978-1-4982-3271-5 (hardcover) | ISBN 978-1-4982-3270-8 (ebook).

Subjects: LCSH: Allan, Tom, 1916-1965 | Church of Scotland—Clergy | Missiology.

Classification: BV2065 F65 2017 (print) | BV2065 (ebook).

Manufactured in the U.S.A.                                      08/09/17

For Joy, Eilidh and Katie, with much love.

St. Bernard once said: 'A mission suggests the heavy labour of the peasant rather than the pomp of the ruler. For if you are to do the work of a prophet you need the hoe rather than the sceptre.' It is the sceptre that the Church in Scotland holds that is to many the offence. For they see in it not the symbol of recognised authority nor the symbol of loving service, but rather of privilege and dictation. To wield the hoe is to be content to serve in love. It is to get down to the roots of life, even though the stones be many.[1]

—Ralph Morton, 1954

1. Morton, *Evangelism in Scotland*, 54.

# Contents

# Acknowledgments

I WOULD LIKE TO THANK my academic doctoral supervisor, David Fergusson, for all his support, insight and encouragement. My thanks also to Maggie Boulter for donating the papers of her father (Tom Allan) to New College, University of Edinburgh; to John Harvey, Bill and Betsy Shannon, Andrew MacGowan and Allan Clark for kindly providing access to papers and recordings in their private possession; to Maggie and John for their great friendliness, kindness and assistance; to Frank Bardgett for additional extracts from D. P. Thomson's diaries; to Kenneth Roxburgh for quotes relating to "Tell Scotland" from the Billy Graham archive at Wheaton College, Illinois; and to Will Storrar, David Smith and Doug Gay for their analysis, all opinions and errors ultimately being my own.

I greatly enjoyed the research of archives in Edinburgh, New York, and Geneva. For all of their help in doing so, my thanks to the staff in the libraries of New College, University of Edinburgh; of Union Theological Seminary, New York City, and in particular to Betty Boden; and of the World Council of Churches, Geneva, especially to Hans von Rütte.

My thanks as well to the Arts and Humanities Research Council and the Hope Trust for financial assistance.

Passages from my doctoral thesis and two journal articles previously published on Tom Allan under my name, as set out in the bibliography, have been included.

# Abbreviations

AA.6    The Papers of Tom Allan, New College Library,
        University of Edinburgh

CSWC    Centre for the Study of World Christianity, New College,
        University of Edinburgh

EC      *Evening Citizen* newspaper, Glasgow

NLS     National Library of Scotland, Edinburgh

RGA     Reports to the General Assembly of the Church of Scotland

# 1

# Introduction

## The Lay Apostles

There is, however, confronting us in the church to-day a mighty problem. How is this Good News to be communicated to men and women, the vast majority of whom regard the church as irrelevant, unconnected not only with the pressures and demands of ordinary life, but even with the vague stirrings after God within their own hearts?

—Tom Allan, 1950[1]

FROM A DISTANCE THROUGH the settling darkness, a solitary figure in dog-collared shirt, long coat and flat cap can be seen quietly closing the side door of St George's Tron Parish Church in the centre of Glasgow. He turns, walks along the street in the brisk winter breeze, and is soon lost into the arms of a city at night: merging into the bustle of the nightlife and the clamor of the traffic.

The actions of Revd Tom Allan in those few seconds that ended the BBC Television programme in 1961 on his work were symbolic of much of his ministry and mission.[2] Closing the door on the comfort of the safe and familiar structures and stepping outwards into a direct encounter with people on the street. A movement designed to bridge the gap between Christianity and society, to reconnect the institutional church to the world. His focus was a critical engagement with the triumphs and tragedies of everyday, lived existence; seeking to re-establish a Gospel of meaning and relevance to the everyday experiences of ordinary men and women. He anticipated a

1. Allan, *The Secret of Life*, 14.

2. AA6.7.1, BBC Television, *Meeting Point in a City Centre*, broadcast on 26 March 1961, DVD held in the Papers of Tom Allan, New College, University of Edinburgh.

revolution to occur within the church in its implementation. From Allan's viewpoint, what was needed was a departure from self-regarding piety and a culture of expected norms and behaviour. In his view, this was a mindset which had for too long prioritised social status and an intrusive, prurient morality over the daily physical and spiritual needs of people in broader society, and the uplifting of the downtrodden and the poor.

The mission of Tom Allan sought to re-engage by the empowerment of lay church members as individuals and in community, to witness to Christ in word and deed where they lived, worked or gathered socially. The language of liturgy and evangelism would be of the street and the context would be the life of the world. The message would thus find a synthesis between the Gospel as proclaimed in word and as expressed in action.

The key then was authenticity, presence and dialogue, to meet what Allan saw as the "three primary problems . . . [of] contact, communication and consolidation"[3] with those outwith the church, in particular those who were far distanced from it.

Allan's model of mission was, therefore, focused on a vigorous, tangible Christianity of depth and purpose, exercised at ground level through a re-discovery of the "apostolate of the laity." As he expressed early in his ministry:

> It is becoming clear that there is one way before all others to which God is calling His church to-day: and that is to reaffirm the Apostolate of the Laity. So that ordinary folk who know in their own lives something of the transforming power of Christ go out as His ambassadors into the workshop, the factory, the market-place, the community. If the secular world will not come to us, then we must reach out to it, bearing in our lives the image of Christ, and translating our faith into terms of active and decisive witness.[4]

Ordinary Christians would be in the vanguard, inspired towards a selfless empathy for others, seeking the transformation of the individual and of society in Christ. Ian Henderson later wrote: "Tom Allan was different. He had got the message. Christianity has to do with love."[5] As Allan told his Glasgow congregation in a sermon in 1949:

> The only road to true fulfilment of life is through our self-giving sacrifice to others, through a love that reaches out to

---

3. AA6.5.7, *EC*, "Rescue the Fallen," Article 5.

4. Allan, *The Secret of Life*, 14.

5. Henderson, *Scotland*, 50–51.

them irrespective of our own comfort or our own desires, a love which knows no limit in its scope, a love which gives without asking for any reward . . . a constant self-offering.[6]

## Content of This Study

This book primarily considers the writing and actions of Tom Allan in expressing that missiology. Allan was a minister of the Church of Scotland, evangelist and theologian of particular public prominence in Scotland and beyond in the period from 1946 to 1964. His ideas on the basis of Christian mission were drawn from diverse, rich sources in Scottish and European theology and tradition. His gift was to collate and then apply those influences to two working-class parishes in Glasgow, and to set out both his inspirations and the practical outcomes in his seminal book on parish mission, *The Face of My Parish*. He further contributed significantly to the development of a theology of evangelism at international level through the World Council of Churches.

From 1953 to 1955, Allan was the leader of the "Tell Scotland" Movement, which sought to implement his ideas on a national scale through an audacious, ecumenical plan to evangelize the nation. The decision, at Allan's instigation, to invite Billy Graham to conduct the "All Scotland Crusade" of 1955 diverted attention from Allan's focus on the lives and witness of ordinary people, split the Movement by alienating those who disagreed with Graham's methods, and deeply affected to this day both the public perception of Christianity in Scotland, and the concept of Christian mission within the churches. On stepping down from the full-time leadership of "Tell Scotland" in 1955, Allan implemented his ideas on mission in a significant city center ministry in Glasgow until his forced retirement from ill-health in 1964.

The key to the implementation of Allan's missiology was the organic growth from "bottom up" of church and community in a complementary evolution, each reshaped and revitalised by the other. Its fulcrum was the formation and development of a lay "congregational group," a dynamic cell to be trained and activated through Bible Study and prayer as the forefront of mission in the parish. Their purpose was to carry out constant oral witness and social service to those around them, whose content would be contextualised to the local situation. The institutional church would face

6. Sermon 23 October 1949, *The Congregational News Review*, North Kelvinside Parish Church, vol. 1 no. 1 (December 1949) 6.

upheaval and re-modelling as the vitality and energy of the "congregational group" combined with the raw enthusiasm of the new arrivals into the wider church community, counter-balancing and diminishing the strength of the institutional conservatism that was inherent amongst the diehard members. The new arrivals would replenish the "congregational group," creating a rolling cycle of further development and growth. The church thus renewed with increased vigor would demonstrate the signs of a true New Testament *koinonia*, and consequently radiate the Gospel within the parish. In this manner, Allan's goal was the regeneration of a static institution towards the creation of a lasting "missionary parish" with the church at its heart.

The dynamic post-war Scottish missiology of which he was at the forefront thus sought a continuous engagement at every level of the whole Gospel for the whole of life. It was a concept of mission which embraced in full both personal salvation and social justice, refusing to be typecast as "liberal" or "evangelical," seeking ecumenical unity for the ultimate goal of the implementation of the Kingdom of God by every method possible.

The book, therefore, begins with an in-depth consideration of Allan's concepts of mission and their implementation in the local parish, at national level and in global terms. Focus will then turn in chapter 3 to examining the reasons why Allan expressed mission in that way, considering the social and church context in Scotland of the post-war period, and Allan's personal inspirations and his theological sources, which all influenced the development of his model of mission.

The following chapter will then analyze the causes of the model's "success" or "failure," by examining the tensions within the model which contributed to its outcomes. In particular, inherent tensions are considered between aspects which were of an older era and those which were forward-thinking and innovative for his time. The focus here will be, firstly, upon the centrality of the position of the church in Allan's missiology and the extent to which that impeded potential growth; and, secondly, on the contrast between Allan's promotion of the lay development of Christian community at a local level and his later support of the blunt instrument of mass evangelism. The effect of the social revolution from the late fifties onwards on Allan's model and the Scottish churches is then addressed, including an examination of whether the steepness of the decline in the Scottish churches was, to any extent, directly related to methods of mission in the fifties such as the "All Scotland Crusade."

Thereafter in chapter 5, consideration of Allan's work is broadened by looking at several other dynamic attempts in Allan's time to "contextualize" Christianity to the surrounding culture, in ways which were both through and for ordinary people, being: the "Mission of Friendship," industrial witness and House Churches of the Iona Community; the incarnational ministry of presence of the Gorbals Group Ministry in Glasgow, inspired by the East Harlem Protestant Parish in New York; and the ecumenical drive of Robert Mackie, Ian Fraser and Scottish Churches House. Although bearing marked similarities to Allan's focus, their initiatives diversified in the extent of the role given in mission to the church, and the method in which to express the Gospel appropriately, particularly alongside the urban poor.

In seeking the connections of the models of Allan and his contemporaries to the present day, important filters are then added at the start of the concluding chapter 6. The lens of a current global, missiological framework is set out, including the need to view all mission in a Western nation such as Scotland as a "cross-cultural translation," and applying an overarching concept for the ethos of mission of "prophetic dialogue."

Thereafter, accounting for the reasons why the models of mission of Allan and his contemporaries succeeded or foundered in their time; the changed social circumstances in which we live; and viewing their work in the light of current global missiology, in the concluding section of chapter 6 conclusions are made and principles are derived for Christian mission now, in seeking a model in the present that would serve the goals which they represented.

The life and work of Tom Allan and his contemporaries offers hope today to a church divided and in decline, for its lessons in the priority of mission to all Christian expression, of acting in mission through ecumenical unity beyond narrow theological cliques, and, centrally, of the residual potential of the ordinary people within the institutional parish church, in times when mission becomes increasingly focused on separate and distinct "Fresh Expressions" or "emerging church."

The central kernel of the book is a recovery through their work of the "apostolate of the laity," in the belief, like them, that the primary way in which institutionalised Christianity can look to exercise mission in the present climate is through the lives and witness of ordinary Christians. It is an affirmation of the mission of the whole people of God entailing the closing of the lay/clergy divide, the recognition of diverse gifts and ministries, and an overhaul of the church and the forms of mission which it produces.

## Motivation and Purpose of the Present Study

The overriding concern is the result of universal questions, whose quest for answers is perhaps the outcome of all reflection on mission: how is Christ speaking now, in this time, in this place, to those who profess Christian faith, so as to engage with the people with whom they interact, in the society and culture in which they live, in order that they might fully exercise in the world the work of God through His Word?

David Smith quoted the Dutch missionary theologian Johannes Verkuyl, to the effect that Christ's promise is to be with the church "all of her days," and so "the church must forever be asking "What kind of day is it today?" For no two days are alike in her history."[7] This book seeks to further engage in that essential task, through a like process to what Paul Ricoeur termed "the hermeneutics of retrieval."[8] It seeks to retrieve the theology and practice of missiology in Scotland in the immediate post-war period, as a case study in the broader Western Reformed context; to re-discover "for this day" the mode and means to communicate the Gospel in the public arena, in order to relate faith to the lives of ordinary people, in the context of the cultures around us.

In seeking the answers, a direction of travel which is rooted in the practicalities of lived experience, and a determination to seek practical outcomes from historical and theological reflection, is central. Can that process of historical "retrieval" offer bold insights for the future of church and mission in times of institutional decline? My contention is that Allan's work, in conjunction with that of the Iona Community, the Gorbals Group Ministry and those at the forefront of a golden age of ecumenism in that period, offer a vital story on the centrality of lay witness which echoes resoundingly in the present day.

In the halcyon period of dynamic modes of mission in Scotland during the two decades following World War II, many of the key issues that now also perplex the late modern church were addressed and confronted in theological reflection and in practice. It was a period where a buoyant Christianity in Scotland acted as a "petri dish" for the experiments and trials of missiological innovation, in an arc between Europe and the USA, implementing international influences as the ink dried on the published pages. Action was precipitated by the restless theology of Bonhoeffer, Bultmann and Ellul, or from international practice such as the incarnational sacrifice of the French worker-priest Movement; the social and political protest of the storefront churches of the East Harlem Protestant Parish; ecumenical co-operation inspired by the World Council of Churches; and even the mass revivalism of Billy Graham. Scotland thus acted as a crucible for the

7. With reference to Matt 8:20, Smith, *Mission after Christendom*, 133.

8. As quoted by Gay, *Remixing the Church*, 20, in the context of the recovery within the "emerging Church" conversation of pre-Reformation liturgy and ritual.

simultaneous implementation of rapidly evolving strands of missiology, in all their glory and conflict, with the drama of the success and failure of such models being played out. It is hoped that through that window we might not only recognise the sources of the legacy passed to us in the present, but also glimpse a view of the future.

## Potential Scope and Relevance in Broader Missiological Perspective

All the models met the criteria of the five "headings of an agenda" for future cross-cultural mission in the West, by which the great ecumenical missiologist Lesslie Newbigin concluded an article some thirty to forty years after the period we will consider:

a. "the declericalizing of theology so that it may become an enterprise done not within the enclave . . . but rather within the public sector";

b. "the recovery of the apocalyptic strand of the New Testament teaching" of hope for the world;

c. "that witness . . . means not dominance and control but suffering," with "a radical break with that form of Christianity which is called the denomination";

d. "the need to listen to the witness of Christians from other cultures"; and

e. "the need for courage."[9]

The urgency of achieving those goals to maintain the very existence of the church in Scotland as an institution has been a clarion call of leading commentators for decades. As long ago as 1990 within *Scottish Identity: A Christian Vision*, Will Storrar called for the abandonment of the Church of Scotland's claim to national, territorial ministry, which for Storrar expressed a "view of its identity which looks increasingly shipwrecked in the secular tides of the late twentieth century."[10] That identity as a Church *of* Scotland required radical adjustment to a Church *for* Scotland, displaying a "distinctive life from the rest of the secular community, and yet with an overriding sense of responsibility for that nation in mission, social criticism and service."[11]

9. Newbigin, "Can the West be Converted?," 7.

10. Storrar, *Scottish Identity*, 134.

11. Ibid., 223.

As well as an overhaul in vision and structure at national level, that urgency translates at local level to the vital need for the re-thinking of the nature of the parish church, and a re-activation of the relationship of its members and elders to mission in the community. Peter Neilson, the principal author of the Church of Scotland's ground-breaking 2001 report "Church Without Walls," put it this way:

> The parish potential is vitiated when the area is seen as fodder to sustain the church, rather than the field into which the church is called to sow, plant, serve and harvest . . . either the parish is a legal entity to be protected, or a sign of the calling of the church of Jesus Christ to make known the grace of God to every nook and cranny of the nation—in every neighbourhood and every network.[12]

The hope from this book is that a realization may occur that models of mission and church which sought to meet those goals were, in fact, implemented in this country in the recent past. The theology and practice of mission that was put into place by Allan and his contemporaries invites key parallels and principles to be drawn for the church in the present day in Scotland, at parish and national level, which might provide hope and inspiration for addressing such vital concerns. However, if this is not to remain solely an exercise in local mission drawn from recent Scottish church and social history, can the ideas of Allan and his contemporaries be potentially broadened out? Can they offer guideposts for future direction not only in Scotland but also beyond?

In making a claim to a broader application, perhaps the most resounding concession to be made of the place of Western Christianity ought to be that it is no longer the center of the Christian world, and cannot claim to speak from any position of power, privilege or authority. The extraordinary shift to the global South of the locus of Christianity in the past half-century with the growing demise of any residual Christendom model in Europe, means that this study, and that of any Western theologian, must be read contextually and can only claim universal appeal insofar as such a contextual reading elsewhere might allow. There can no longer be a defining global culture through which to read theology.

Thus tentatively stepping forward into the arena, insofar as the present study does not reflect what Stanley Skreslet describes as "the highly variegated nature" of the field of missiology, this is due to the perspective from which it is written, and a recognition that its outcome will initially be

---

12. Neilson, *Church on the Move*, 49–50.

grounded there.[13] Nevertheless, with Scotland being a nation with a Presbyterian tradition which has spread worldwide, and a long history of global missionary endeavour, this story and its conclusions might be seen as a case study and illustration with parallels across the Western nations.

Posing the challenge "Can the West be Converted?" in his compelling article of that name, Newbigin enquired: "why is it that we have a plethora of missionary studies on the contextualization of the gospel in all the cultures of the world from China to Peru, but nothing comparable directed to the culture which we call "the modern world"?[14]

This book is intended more broadly as a contribution to the missiology on the contextualization of the Gospel in the West at the heart of an ongoing transition between "modern" and "postmodern" sociological outlooks, which might be described as a period now of "late modernity." It acknowledges the well-trodden distinction that the present Western world has formed, in Newbigin's words, a "modern scientific worldview" whose "most distinctive and crucial feature . . . [is] the division of human affairs into two realms—the private and the public; a private realm of values where pluralism reigns and a public world of what our culture calls facts."[15] Thus religion resides within the private "heretical imperative," whereby unfettered free choice can be applied to beliefs and values, all outcomes being equally valid. Only within this realm is it acceptable to raise the question "why"? By contrast, in the public sphere there is a rational search for consensus on unadulterated "fact," by exclusively considering issues of "what"? and "how"? Once established, it is then expected that such "fact" will be accepted unstintingly by all.

The present study looks to engage with realizations for "contextualization" in mission which begin to emerge from the exercise of models of mission in the past which met Newbigin's "headings for an agenda"; through a sense of "bridging the gap," not only between the cultures of church and world, but also between private and public realms.

The realizations thus include, firstly, that exercising mission in the present-day West entails a cross-cultural journey, just as it did for the nineteenth century missionary in encountering pre-modern culture abroad in the global South. Secondly, there is the realization that the cross-cultural journey, is not, as it was then, from the modern, church culture towards premodern traditional societies, or one of literal translation between "mother tongue" languages. Instead, the "cross-cultural translation" which we face in

---

13. Skreslet, *Comprehending Mission*, 2.

14. Newbigin, "Can the West be Converted?," 2.

15. Ibid., 4.

present times in the West is from the remains of the church as institution towards increasingly distinct late-modern cultures in society, and further to cross the divide between belief and rationality which society has established.

Thoughts of Christian mission have to cope also with the realities of diminishing levels of Christian institutional adherence; the end of the Christendom era in which the public voice of the institutional churches as moral guardians was assumed; a changing face of society through increased social mobility and movements of mass migration; and the necessity to express Christianity in a manner which recognises vital inter-faith respect and dialogue, in the light of the presence of militant factions of Islam and recurring terrorist atrocities in the West.

The task of imagining Christian mission in those circumstances is undoubtedly complex. Mission needs to be not only a horizontal movement to establish relationships with surrounding cultures, but also to respectfully interrupt the public assumptions, as Newbigin described them, of "a society which has no public beliefs but is a kind of neutral world in which we can all freely pursue our self-chosen purposes," thus including if we so wish "an enclave of religious experience."[16] Crossing such a private/public divide, is "without possibility of question, is the most challenging missionary frontier of our time."[17]

Christian mission thus lies at the friction point where it seeks to dialogically engage within differing cultural viewpoints, and also to meet the public realm at a level beyond its assigned compartment; a movement towards a place where Christianity might offer a critique upon pre-supposed public "fact."

The conclusions to this book are thus offered as the basis of a model in our times of an expression of Christianity which is not restricted to a private enclave, but crosses over to the public realm. It does so by emphasizing that ordinary people should be equipped to develop faith communities with or without reference to the institutional church from the starting point of the "micro-cultures" which they already inhabit; through an expression of their faith which bears authentic witness to the Gospel by not only the intentional voicing of beliefs, but also a humble open-heartedness for all in the broader community. Such mission must be respectful and dialogical, but be prepared to stand up to injustice in word and deed. The goal is a meeting and interaction of Christianity and culture, such that both will be changed for the better as a result, to the benefit of all in wider society.

16. Ibid., 7.

17. Ibid.

# Foundational Concepts—the Laity,
# the *missio Dei*, and Contextualization

## The Laity

If importance is to be place on the role of the "laity," some definition of that term is required, recognising its potential ambiguity. Hans-Ruedi Weber, long-time director of the Department of the Laity of the World Council of Churches, took care to point out that the term "laity" is not derived from the biblical content of *laos tou theou*, "the people of God," but instead from biblical translation and ecclesiastical use from the third and fourth centuries AD onwards.[18]

Baptism is the central uniting factor in all *laos tou theou*, holding in unison those ordained and those who are not, those paid by the institutions to exercise leadership and those who volunteer, and those who lead worship and those who participate.

In the strictest sense, "the laity" therefore encompasses the whole people of God, both clergy and all others. However, for present purposes the convenience is adopted of the negative definition of "laity" as it is commonly understood, being as "non-clergy." They are categorized by Weber into three sections: (a) professional workers for the church, not being ordained clergy; (b) those relatively few lay people who play a very active role in church activities; and (c) the majority of Christians who regularly worship, but spend most of their work and leisure time outwith the church environment in the world.[19] It is to groups (b) and (c) that much of the consideration is directed here. However, given that there is a focus on the dissolution of the clergy/laity divide, the recovery of the notion of the "laity" as indeed forming "the whole people of God," both ordained and non-ordained, is also a key consideration.

To set the ground for what lies ahead, a brief discussion is also appropriate also of fundamental concepts which underpin present day missiology, and are taken to be sitting in the background of all that will be considered. The first concept is the *missio Dei*, that all mission is rooted in the trinitarian person of God. The second is of "contextualization," sometimes interchanged with the term "inculturation," which presupposes that all theological expression is necessarily rooted in its local context within a two-way dialogical conversation in mission between Gospel and culture, rather than the Gospel being transplanted as an immutable object no matter the surroundings.

18. Weber, "On Being Christians," 32–33.

19. Ibid., 34.

## The *missio Dei*

For the past sixty years, the concept of the *missio Dei*, that mission is not a creation of the church but instead "God's activity, which embraces both the church and world,"[20] has brought about a fundamental reconsideration of the church's relationship to the world outwith its boundaries, aptly summarized in this way: "It is not the church of God that has a mission in the world, but the God of mission that has a church in the world."[21]

As mission emanates from God and not the church, there is a realization that the role of the church is formed by identifying the presence of the God in the world, as James Torrance states: "The mission of the church is the gift of participating through the Holy Spirit in the Son's mission from the Father to the world."[22]

In such participation, there may be a recognition of a "relational perception of God—a God in whom interpersonal love is active," with mission as a fundamental constituent of God's existence and purpose: "the mission of God flows directly from the nature of who God is . . . God's intention for the world is that in every respect it should show forth the way He is—love, community, equality, diversity, mercy, compassion and justice."[23]

Secular society is then no longer viewed as a hostile enemy to be overcome in battle, with those outside the church as prospects to be won. The theology of church as conqueror of the world becomes church in solidarity with the world. *Missio Dei* involves the abandonment of the geographical and territorial outlook on mission, and the adoption of domestic and pannational mission based on faith, love and reconciliation.

The concept of the *missio Dei* is not, however, without its pitfalls, principally the danger that it can become "more of a slogan than a defining phrase."[24] The difficulty for the concept of *missio Dei* as a tool for missiological analysis, as John Flett has pointed out, is that "*missio Dei* is a trope. It satisfies an instinct that missionary witness properly belongs to the life of the church without offering any concrete definition of that act." Thus, reducing everything to the concept of "sending," the "vacuity emerges," creating a "trinitarian illusion behind which all manner of non-trinitarian mediations operate with sanctioned impunity."[25]

20. Moltmann, *The Church in the Power*, 64.

21. Tim Dearborn, "Beyond Duty: A Passion for Christ, a Heart for Mission," quoted in Church of England, *Mission-Shaped Church*, 103.

22. Torrance, *Worship, Community and the Triune God of Grace*, ix.

23. Kirk, *What Is Mission?*, 28.

24. Ibid., 25.

25. Flett, *The Witness of God*, 8–10.

Despite its inherent uncertainties, there has nevertheless been a central benefit as "a theocentric focus on mission as the *missio Dei* replaced the former church-centric focus"[26] that had prevailed for centuries. There is a freedom in the realization that individual motivations for mission are, as Karl Barth expressed it, "mere representations of a motive which one can neither describe or assume, because it is identical with the current will and order of one person, namely the divine person, the Lord of the church."[27] Michael Amaladoss concurs, writing that: "To contemplate the Trinity, our mission in the world is a freeing experience, so that we can carry on our own mission without aggression and anxiety, conscious that we are making a real contribution to the realization of God's plan for the world. We learn to be sensitive to what God is doing in the world and to coordinate our own mission with God's mission."[28]

The church is, therefore, in Jürgen Moltmann's words, "one element in the power of the Spirit and has no need to maintain its special power and its special charges with absolute and self-destructive claims," nor any need "to look sideways in suspicion or jealousy at the saving efficacies of the Spirit outside the church; instead it can recognize that the Spirit is greater than the church and that God's purpose of salvation reaches beyond the church."[29]

Where then does this locate the members of the church in their focus towards mission? If church, mission and the world are inseparable, then involvement of the laity of the church in the mission of God in the world must also be fundamental. Mission becomes a founding core of the church.

Therefore, in David Bosch's words, "there is church because there is mission, not vice versa."[30] Or as the Church of England's *Mission Shaped Church* report sets out: "[it] is therefore of the essence (the DNA) of the church to be a missionary community . . . this sets the standard by which the church tests all its activity."[31] Indeed, if the church is subsumed within God's mission, it is wholly subject to God's sending, and thus, as Stuart Murray concludes for the church, "mission is not an agenda item—it is the agenda."[32]

How then can the *missio Dei* be more fully realized in the relationship of the church to the Kingdom of God and the world? The secure judgment is, in my opinion, the middle ground that the church can be viewed as "the

26. Thomas, ed., *Readings in World Mission*, 103.

27. Karl Barth, "Theologische Fragen und Antworten," as quoted in ibid., 104.

28. Amaladoss, "The Trinity on Mission," 106.

29. Moltmann, *Church in the Power of the Spirit*, 64–65.

30. Bosch, *Transforming Mission*, 390.

31. Church of England, *Mission-Shaped Church*, 85.

32. Murray, *Church after Christendom*, 137.

only self-conscious agent of the kingdom,"[33] whilst not being equated with the realization of that Kingdom. Therefore, whilst God's mission is carried out both within and outwith the church, it is advanced to a greater extent in the knowledge and exercise of a missionary purpose, as well as occurring without the church in the secular world.

The church's role is thus succinctly summarized by Andrew Kirk as follows: "In its preaching and teaching, the church is an advocate of the kingdom; in its worshipping life it is an emissary of the kingdom; in its work for reconciliation, peace and justice it is an instrument of the kingdom."[34]

The churches and their members therefore "need a missional ethos, expressed in their core values and nurtured in their corporate life," by the development "at translocal level of a shift from institution to movement."[35]

For such a shift under the *missio Dei* from "institution to movement," in Phillip Potter's view there are four processes of change that the church and its members need to initiate: (a) as the church is not the center but a means of mission, it must work to "adapt its forms and structures to God's mission today"; (b) they must "take with radical seriousness what is happening in the world . . . listen to the world's agenda"; (c) they must realize "the whole world is the mission field"; and (d) they must be "renewed to be the sign of the new humanity."[36]

In doing so, there is an inevitable deflection of the concentration of energy away from the plans of church people for the salvation of the unchurched, or as Bosch amusingly described it, mission as "more than calling individuals into the church as a waiting room for the hereafter."[37] The movement is instead towards a demonstration of the plans of God for all in the visible implementation of His love. As Bosch explains:

> The primary purpose of the *missiones ecclesiae* can therefore not simply be the planting of churches or the saving of souls; rather, it has to be service to the *missio Dei* representing God in and over against the world, pointing to God . . . in its mission, the church witnesses to the fullness of the promise of God's reign and participates in the ongoing struggle between that reign and the powers of darkness and evil.[38]

33. Kirk, *What Is Mission?*, 35.

34. Ibid., 36.

35. Murray, *Church after Christendom*, 137, 142.

36. Philip Potter, *Life in All Its Fullness* (Geneva: WCC, 1981), quoted in Thomas, *Readings in World Mission*, 114–15.

37. Bosch, *Transforming Mission*, 377.

38. Ibid., 391.

Mission of the church through the *missio Dei* must, therefore, divert from inward strategies of re-organization: a trench-building mentality aimed at self-preservation which is in denial of its true purpose as called by Christ. Its focus instead should be living and sharing the Gospel in engagement and action, serving people contextually in their social, economic and pastoral realities.

## Contextualization

Of importance for the present and future is to seek to recover the process of "contextualization" of the Gospel in the missionary encounter. Although they did not use such terminology, it was that process which informed the grand missiological designs of the dynamic Scottish practitioners and theologians emerging in the post-war period, with Allan at the forefront.

It is "contextualization" which "captures in method and perspective the challenge of relating the Gospel to culture."[39] In mission theology over the past half-century, there has been a recognition of a journey away from a past "adaptation" or "accommodation" in relation to culture, which was common in the Western global missionary era. This was a "kernel and husk" approach, by which the only concession to local culture was in the outward dressing of the message, without altering the theology or cultural assumptions underneath.

Instead, in the realization that all theology, including that of the missional donor, is culturally conditioned, "contextualization" seeks to strip away the cultural baggage of the donor in mission to allow the Gospel to be fully heard and connect deeply within the local context, in a process which Stephen Bevans has called "kenotic apostolicity."[40]

In his classic work *Models of Contextual Theology*, Bevans identified five models by which cultural context may potentially be accounted for in theology and mission:

- The "translation model" assumes only an adaptation to the local in form and language, under a pre-supposition that the message will remain the same;

- The "anthropological model" seeks to preserve local, cultural identity;

- The "praxis model" seeks transformative social action in the local context;

39. Whiteman, "Contextualization," 2.
40. Bevans, "Mission in Britain Today," 170–71.

- The "synthetic model" seeks dialogue between faith and culture; and

- The "transcendental model" looks towards the mindset of the recipient of the Gospel, rather than the surrounding context, to aid him/her in an understanding of faith.

Bevans argued in a 2011 essay that such models of "contextual theology" take account of two realities in which there is a "mutually critical dialogue": both in the "experience of the past" from Scripture and church tradition, and the "experience of the present," or a particular context, which has one or more of at least four elements: "personal or communal experience, secular or religious culture, social location and social change."[41]

For Bevans "It is the honoring or testing or critiquing of experience that makes theology *contextual*."[42] Thus thinking "contextually" creates a "dialogue that tries to articulate my context, my experience . . . with the experience of Christians down through the ages that we find in Scripture and Christian tradition."

Bevans argues that "contextual theology" not only offers the church new agendas and outcomes depending on the local, but more fundamentally "it offers the church a new look at *itself*."[43]

An over-reliance on "contextualization" is not, however, without its criticisms and dangers, some of which could be levelled at those within our journey who travelled deepest into the local social, cultural and political context, namely the Gorbals Group Ministry and the East Harlem Protestant Parish. David Bosch identifies six such risks:

- If mission as contextualization is confirmation that God has turned around the world, there is a danger that God is simply identified with the historical process and not as God;

- If it is a construction of a variety of "local theologies," there is a danger of relativism with many mutually exclusive theologies and no coherent message;

- There is a risk of absolutism, with the insistence that one brand of contextualized theology is absolute truth to the exclusion of all others;

- If it is "reading the signs of the times," they can often be misread from a claimed special knowledge;

41. Bevans, "Contextual Theology," 3–17.

42. Ibid., 9.

43. Ibid., 17.

- Praxis cannot be the only authority for theological reflection, as there needs also to be a "critical theology of mission"; and

- There needs to be not only praxis and theory, justice and truth, but also *poiesis*, as in piety, worship, mystery, with a need to hold these dimensions together.[44]

Whilst recognizing such misgivings and potential pitfalls, some of which were lived out in practice, the journey of increasing "contextualization" in the developing Scottish models described and analyzed in this book, was centered on a belief that for faith to flourish its communal expression had to become, in the longer term, wholly indigenous to the culture in which mission had taken place. As Sunquist expresses that necessity:

> Contextualization must come out of the lives and experience of a local community of faith. Outsiders can and should be able to dialogue about what is appropriate, but God's Spirit is more than able to guide the local Christian community without outsiders imposing what may well be the exact opposite of what they are trying to promote.[45]

In its essence, this involves a dialogical engagement of the Gospel with culture which, whilst wary of syncretism, acknowledges that, in Heard's words, "the Christian faith is never transmitted in a culture-free or culture-neutral cocoon: it needs to be incarnated in the heart of each culture." For such a dynamic to occur by moving deeper beyond a sheen of passing recognition, "attention to language, level of education, social dynamics, cultural idiosyncrasies, and the history of the parish is essential."[46]

The desire to make faith come alive in this way, as authentic and genuine to the lives of ordinary people, lies at the heart of the journey undertaken by Tom Allan and his contemporaries. They all sought to live out what is described by Whiteman as one of contextualization's principal functions:

> Contextualization attempts to communicate the Gospel in word and deed and to establish the church in ways that make sense to people within their local cultural context, presenting Christianity in such a way that it meets people's deepest needs and

---

44. Bosch, *Transforming Mission*, 420–32. For further criticism of over-reliance on "contextualization" in mission, see for example Jione Havea, "The Cons of Contextuality . . . Kontextuality."

45. Sunquist, *Understanding Christian Mission*, 256.

46. Heard, "Inculturation," 77.

penetrates their worldview, thus allowing them to follow Christ and remain within their own culture.[47]

## Conclusion

With that background, to avoid Christianity in mission and evangelism being lost in translation between the ecclesiastical world and the language and rhythms of the street, in my opinion a re-acquisition is necessary in mission of a prophetic voice of Christianity which can, in the phrase of Lamin Sanneh, identify and exude in its engagement a "dynamic equivalence" to the cultures of the nation.[48]

In seeking to do so, the intention in what follows is not to offer a dewy-eyed hagiography of the remarkable people who sought to do so and their achievements or failures. It is instead hoped that, through the triumphs and many pitfalls of the recent past in efforts to contextualise Gospel and church to the lives of ordinary people, an appreciation might emerge of the direction of the road ahead.

Of particular note is the crossover effect—the manner in which these voices and projects though distinctive and particular, were also interwoven and respectful of the other. For example, Tom Allan could at once be inspired by Abbé Godin and the French worker priests towards a notion of the local, organic growth of Christian community through the laity, and yet be central in the invitation to Billy Graham to conduct the "All Scotland Crusade" of 1955. Does this render such work fatally flawed and incoherent; or does it offer a glimpse of the hybrid nature of all mature missiology, in a combination of the old and the new, of priorities dimming and emerging, between generations in faith of differing theological hues, seeking to bring together all possible modes and considerations in an attempt to relate the Gospel?

It is a meeting of the "modern" and the "postmodern" elements that they represent, of both "Tell" and "Serve," seeking whatever new creation results from an unconditional self–offering to the people, speaking in their language, in the place where they are. It is a confluence which alerts us to the need for "making Christianity real" by crossing boundaries, seeking a hybrid Christian community which reflects both donor and recipient, but is very much of the street and of the world.

---

47. Whiteman, "Contextualization," 2.

48. See Sanneh, *Translating the Message.*

# 2

# The Ministry and Mission of Tom Allan
# from 1946 to 1964

> Tom Allan was not only one of our greatest preachers, he was
> one of our greatest Christians. His life and his preaching had a
> compassion, an authority and an urgency that characterised the
> Apostle Paul.

—Billy Graham, 1965[1]

T HE PRESENT CHAPTER CONSIDERS the content and practical outcomes
of Allan's model of mission by lay evangelism through the church; by
considering what Allan did and said in the period from 1946 to 1964 in parish ministry, at the forefront of a national campaign, internationally through
the World Council of Churches, and in the books and articles that he wrote.

## Allan's Missiology in Action in Scotland

### North Kelvinside, 1946–1953

In the last years of the 1940s, it was all very heady and exciting.
One came away with the impression that if [North Kelvinside]
was what the post-war church was like, it was going to go places.
*Ian Henderson, 1969.*[2]

---

1. *The Christian*, 17 September 1965, AA6.11.7, 8.
2. Henderson, *Scotland*, 49.

Following war service in the RAF, Tom Allan completed ministry training in the Church of Scotland at Trinity College, Glasgow in the summer of 1946.[3]

He was ordained and inducted into his first charge of the parish of North Kelvinside, in the west end of Glasgow, on 4 September 1946, at the age of 30. It was then a high-density, tenemented, working-class area. At his arrival, the communicant membership of North Kelvinside Parish church numbered around four-hundred people from a parish population of about ten-thousand.

Allan's student connection with Rev. D. P. Thomson, Evangelist to the Home Board of the Church of Scotland, had grown stronger as a leader of the latter's summer Seaside Missions to Scottish holiday resorts in 1946 and 1947.[4] In autumn 1947, Thomson was considering how the enthusiastic young Seaside Missioners might be engaged during the winter. The course of the next decade of evangelistic activity in Scotland was embarked upon from a phone call by Thomson to Allan in early autumn 1947. Thomson suggested that the missioners might go round the doors of Allan's new parish in North Kelvinside.[5]

In late September to early October 1947, fifty student volunteers under Thomson's direction carried out an extensive parish survey and initial door-to-door visitation over two weeks. In his sermon in the Sunday service at the end of the first week, Allan reflected with foresight on what had occurred: "during the past week, we have passed through an experience which will affect the life not only of this congregation, but an experience which may have repercussions throughout the length and breadth of Scotland."[6]

The final figures after ten days of visitation indicated around 36 per cent of homes without a church connection to any denomination.[7] It was, said Allan that Sunday, a "staggering fact" that so many were entirely distant from organized Christianity, indicating a "desperate need on our own doorstep." It brought upon Allan the realization of the scale of the task before him and the urgency required in his response. As he later wrote:

---

3. On Allan's life until 1946, upbringing and personal influences, including D. P. Thomson, see chapter 3.

4. Allan took a six-month sabbatical from North Kelvinside from 1 April 1948 to organize Seaside Missions for the whole of Scotland: North Kelvinside Kirk Session Minutes, 30 December 1947.

5. Thomson later recalled the detail of their conversation in *Personal Encounters*, 113.

6. AA6.2.3, Sermon 5 October 1947, "Sermons on Matthew."

7 Allan, *The Face of My Parish*, 24.

> Above all we learned that for a vast number of people on the
> doorstep of a church which had been established for over 50
> years, that church might as well not have been there. They were
> not hostile to it, or antagonistic. They were merely indifferent,
> apathetic, impervious, both to the existence of the church and
> the message it existed to proclaim.
>
> It was a startling discovery to make; but an essential one.
> At the very beginning of my ministry I was compelled to face
> up to the fact that my church in Glasgow was in the middle of a
> missionary situation, no less than the church in Africa or Latin
> America.[8]

That realization, whilst rather obvious in the present context, set Allan
apart in his time. The parish system of the Church of Scotland was embed-
ded in a normative "attractional" model. It was based the entrenchment
of a territorial ministry throughout every corner of the nation and the assumption that the Christianization of the country had been long achieved.
Protestantism, and the Church of Scotland in particular, retained a strong
social and political influence in education, local government and ordinary
working life. In lieu of a Scottish Parliament, the voice of the annual General
Assembly, which represented over one million adults who were members
of the church and their families, exerted substantial influence on the moral
compass of the nation and the direction of legislative and political pathways.

Therefore, at a local, parish level, the mere presence of the church in
the locality, and its performance of the ordinances of religion, were taken
to be sufficient to bring those in the parish to the church doors from duty,
loyalty and social habit, without any necessity to consider the parish as a
"mission field." There was thus little perceived need for the local church to
devise any concept of what mission might entail if applied on its doorstep,
because the position which the church believed it had established in Scottish society over the centuries would safely ensure its continuance.

At the start of his ministry, what set Allan apart as a distinctive missionary thinker and practitioner was not only the stark realization of the
identification of the problem, but the source of the intended solution. He
understood the failure of the local church in any way to relate to working-
class lives, in contrast to the assumption of self-importance within the hierarchy. He further recognized that the potential answer must lie beyond a
dutiful repetition of what might have gone before, perhaps performed with
an exaggerated vigor. Instead, Allan sought to imbue the streets of North
Kelvinside with fresh and radical ideas on mission that were emerging from

8. AA6.5.11, *EC*, "My Week" c.1959, (vi), 4.

Europe, applying those insights into action in his local context as soon as English translations of such texts came off the press in the late forties.

Allan called for a "congregational group" to be formed, being lay people dedicated to the outward expression of their faith in prayer, mission and service to the people of the parish, and amongst their families, friends and colleagues.

As for the method for the "congregational group" to initiate contact with those in the parish who were outside the church, "visitation evangelism" was now wholeheartedly adopted by Allan and Thomson. All of Thomson's many mission endeavors throughout Scotland from 1948 to 1958 were short-term expressions of that method, being campaigns of a brief duration and "hit-and-run" in nature, often involving the engagement of visiting young people as the missioners rather than local parishioners.[9] What Thomson's brief campaigns gained in impact they lacked in the permanence of Allan's application of a model of development by slow growth through the lay witness of local people in the parish setting.

With the "congregational group" fully engaged in "visitation evangelism," the mission in North Kelvinside began in earnest, as did the influx into the church. Within three months, a hundred new members were added to the existing four hundred. Within two years, the congregation had doubled. In the year 1951 alone, there were one hundred and ninety-six new members, one hundred of them by first-time "profession of faith." Eight hundred people attended six "congregational socials" in the winter of 1952. At the first Sunday communion service lead by Allan on 15 December 1946, three hundred and seven people attended, but by his final service on 19 June 1953, the communicants had more than doubled to six hundred and twenty-two.[10] At Allan's departure in September 1953, the membership had tripled over seven years to around one thousand three hundred.[11]

Allan realized that the key in North Kelvinside was the development of a sense of Christian community at grassroots level, interacting with the everyday lives of the people, as he reflected to his members in 1949 "I am

---

9. See Bardgett, *Scotland's Evangelist*, chapters 7 to 11.

10. North Kelvinside Parish Church, Kirk Session Minutes.

11. *The Congregational News Review,* North Kelvinside Parish Church, vol. 4 no. 8 (December 1953). As of December 2006, the communicant membership of North Kelvinside was a mere 62: Blakey, ed., *The Church of Scotland Yearbook 2007/8,* 364. By December 2014, the congregation had united with the neighboring parish to form Ruchill Kelvinside, with a combined membership of 79: Galbraith, ed., *The Church of Scotland Yearbook 2015/16,* 435. The Church building at North Kelvinside is now demolished.

convinced that in North Kelvinside we are being drawn together as members of one united family under God."[12]

Efforts in maintaining the "congregational group," embarking on "visitation evangelism" and seeking to serve the community were continuous. Buoyed by the possibilities of the recruitment and inspiration of the laity as the vanguard of a missionary church, that focus became the center of Allan's model of mission at parish and national level for the following seventeen years of his ministry.

And yet, despite the numerical success and the gradual re-alignment of his church towards mission, Allan viewed the concrete results of the North Kelvinside mission, and its portents for the future, as comparatively poor. Writing in mid-1953, Allan reflected on the past six years: "it has been a painful business. Perhaps if we had known what lay ahead we would never have undertaken it."[13]

## The Face of My Parish

An immensely moving document, springing from a passionate personal concern and bearing on every page the hallmark of integrity . . . an authentic word of the Lord for minister and layman alike, and for the church at large as it girds itself for its essential task in this generation.

—James S. Stewart, 1954[14]

The literature of evangelism is seldom so candid or so modest in its claims, and seldom so searching in its challenge.

—James Whyte, 1984[15]

Ronald Gregor Smith, then editor of SCM Press, encouraged Allan to bring to wider attention his experiences in North Kelvinside. The practical implementation of the mission would be set out, along with its inspiration from Allan's broad knowledge of post-war European missiology. Gregor Smith was to edit the book *The Face of My Parish*, published in 1954; a classic in lay evangelism which Allan wrote in his manse on Clouston Street in North

12. *The Congregational News Review*, North Kelvinside Parish Church vol. 1, no. 1 (December 1949) 2.

13. Allan, *The Face of My Parish*, 18.

14. Stewart, Review of *The Face of My Parish*, 63.

15. Whyte, Preface, i.

Kelvinside, in between extensive parish duties, radio broadcasts, involvement with the World Council of Churches and both seaside and parish missions.[16] *The Face of My Parish* became a bestseller with widespread influence
in Britain and the USA, and was translated into several languages.

Allan was candid in the Preface to *The Face of My Parish* in his overall
assessment of the practical success of the model for mission which he had put
into practice: "I have no success story to tell. Rather the reverse. Anything I
have to say arises, not from the success of the work in North Kelvinside, but
from our failure to do anything more than touch the fringes of the problem
of serving a predominantly working-class parish in a Glasgow suburb."[17]

His early months at North Kelvinside had been a "period of questing . . .
for a pattern of congregational life that would be vital and relevant, questing
for a method of evangelism that would succeed in breaking through the
barriers in the church and in the world."[18]

The model of mission that Allan devised and implemented that was to
dominate the rest of his ministry was summarized by him thus in *The Face
of My Parish*:

> Gradually three principles became articulate for me and I began
> to hold them with increasing conviction. The first is that the
> solution to the vast problem of communicating the gospel to
> the masses who live outside the sphere of Christian fellowship
> is inextricably bound up with the local church—that the key
> to evangelism lies in the parish. Secondly, that the church can
> only fulfil its function, and penetrate the secular world when it
> is exhibiting the life of a genuine and dynamic Christian com-
> munity . . . And thirdly, that in all this the place of the layman
> is decisive.[19]

The keystones to a contextual expression of the Gospel were, therefore,
the local, parish church; the re-vitalizing of that church to approach the
marks of a genuine Christian community; and the recognition that lay
people were the start and end of any missionary ideal.

To fulfil these goals, shortly after the initial visitation Allan called in
late 1947 for the "congregational group" of the dynamically motivated to be

---

16. Compiled in June 1953 as Allan was preparing to depart for the "Tell Scotland"
Movement and published in 1954, drawn from twelve articles published in *The British
Weekly* from October 1952 to January 1953.

17. Allan, *The Face of My Parish*, 7.

18. Rev. David Orrock, in MacDonald, ed., *A Fraction of His Image*, 5.

19. Allan, *The Face of My Parish*, 66.

formed, who would be what Allan described in *The Face of My Parish* as the "overwhelming minority."[20]

Allan set out in *The Face of My Parish* that the functions of the "congregational group" which was then formed were threefold: as "a training school in Christian discipleship" through biblical study and discussion of the relevance of faith to the world; as "an attempt to restore the parochial community" of the immediate post-Reformation; and, finally, as "an evangelising agency . . . an outlet in which its members can find the opportunity to express their faith in terms of service," in the congregation, in the community and in places of work, business and leisure.[21]

The essence was that "such a community must be an organic growth . . . The community cannot be established by decree. It must discover its own existence."[22] From his North Kelvinside experience, Allan wrote that he "began to realise that here in the group there was the nucleus of a dynamic community, a 'church within a church,' which bore at least some traces of that first *koinonia*" of the New Testament.[23]

Allan believed that the group would initiate radical change in the church, but in so doing be its savior: "The work will be ultimately effective if the group of volunteers becomes, through the reality of its experience in the mission, a true *koinonia;* if what began as a parish mission becomes, in effect, a missionary parish; and if the mission of friendship is a prelude to a constant mission of service. These things will not take place overnight. And they will cause upheaval in the church."[24]

In seeking through the group a "missionary parish" through "a constant mission of service," internal "upheaval" was thus anticipated and, indeed, occurred. Rapid church growth caused the wholesale revision of the church's priorities, and the engagement of ordinary folk, particularly the young. The new and unfamiliar faces had little concept of the formalized church behavior that was expected of them.

Those forces of change and youthful exuberance, and the new members that were their product, were confronted by an existing church which struggled to cope. Recognizing a gap of around six hundred people between the number of new members as compared to the resulting additional communicants, Allan lamented in *The Face of My Parish* that:

20. Ibid., 78.
21. Ibid., 69–70.
22. Ibid., 68.
23. Ibid.
24. Ibid., 98.

> I was in fact in danger of becoming a minister of two congrega-
> tions, worshipping in the same building . . . There were those
> who had grown up in the church and had worshipped in it
> all their days. And there were those who had been brought in
> by the campaigns of visitation . . . Tragically we had to watch
> many of these people drifting away as the months passed from a
> church which appeared to have nothing for them and which was
> incapable of assimilating them into its life.[25]

Allan diagnosed three reasons for the failure in assimilation: firstly, the attitude of the old members; secondly, the absence of a vital and living community to join; and, most importantly, a "much deeper malaise" which Allan identified from his principal influence in the work of Henri Godin and Yvan Daniel,[26] being "a cleavage between the church and the world."[27] He concluded that "the main reason for our ineffectiveness in combating the secularism of the world is that we ourselves in the church have capitulated to secularism of another kind."[28]

The "secularism" which had captured the church was the expression by churchgoers of "social distinctions which have divorced the churchgoing people among the working-classes from their neighbours living in the same tenement." Therefore, for the incomers to the church to be accepted and integrated they had to become, as Allan expressed it, "'respectable,' different from the people among whom they lived, and separated from them, not by their Christian profession, but by their assimilation of a super-imposed middle-class culture."[29] For Allan, what was ruining the church's ability to relate to the world was the presence of "an enclosed community . . . domi-nated by a set of values and characterized by a range of 'activities' whose only authority or justification is that they are traditional."[30]

Thus, the church had rendered itself unwelcoming as a social gath-ering point for those outwith its structures, so that remaining within the church for them would amount almost to a desertion of their own kind. Furthermore, in confrontational language, Allan diagnosed that the cleft affected the church's very credibility, as "the church is separated from the

---

25. Ibid., 33.
26. Godin and Daniel, "France a Missionary Land?"
27. Allan, *The Face of My Parish*, 37.
28. Ibid.
29. Ibid., 39.
30. Ibid., 41.

working-classes by its subservience to a *bourgeois* culture . . . it has transformed the revolutionary ethic of Jesus into an inoffensive prudential morality."[31]

How was this chasm between church and world to be bridged, such that the laity and the church might be redeemed from its "subservience to a bourgeois culture," and the "revolutionary ethic of Jesus" be restored? Allan set about to implement radical reform within the church.

The "first priority" was "the need for the development of a new pattern of life within the congregation," so that it might become "a redeeming influence on the whole community in which it is set."[32] This meant the inspiration and empowerment of ordinary people, but also retaining the importance of the development of a faith community itself, recognizing through the work of Jacques Ellul that "a true lay apostolate presupposes the existence of a community in which and through which the Holy Spirit may speak."[33]

Allan wholeheartedly adopted as the solution to impact upon the parish the concept of *rayonnement*,[34] or the radiation of Christianity as mission from all actions of a church glowing with the Holy Spirit, by which "evangelism is . . . a permanent element in all church activities, and . . . the evangelising agent is not the ordained minister, but the whole Christian fellowship." Allan wrote that "the congregational group exists, then, to translate this idea of *rayonnement* into a practical reality."[35]

In the "congregational group," Allan placed his trust "that this group in fact points the way forward towards a new pattern in parochial life which will supply at least some answer to the problem of bringing the message of the gospel to bear on the lives of those masses around our doors who regard the church as a harmless irrelevance."[36]

However, as in the assimilation of new members, Allan further wrote that in North Kelvinside "I would like to be able to report that the congregational group has been a tremendous success. It has not. It has raised more problems than it has solved. But we believe that they are the problems not of decay but of growth."[37] That growth potential arising out of a dynamic cell of church laity was recognized in the qualified success of the group in North

31. Ibid., 42.

32. Ibid., 48.

33. Ibid., 62.

34. Set out in the report of the World Council of Churches from the founding Amsterdam conference of 1948, and published as *The Church's Witness to God's Design: An Ecumenical Study.*

35. Allan, *The Face of My Parish*, 70.

36. Ibid., 78.

37. Ibid., 72.

Kelvinside, through which Allan could assert: "My own experience has been that when we begin to see the power latent in that inner group of committed men and women who exist in all our congregations, and direct our energies towards the task of making that group a disciplined and trained spearhead for evangelism within the community, then we may begin to see the positive results for which most of us long."[38]

Only by 1953, after all the apparent numerical gains that others lauded, could Allan report that, "we are beginning to see the restoration of a genuine parochial community, in which differences of background and training are being transcended, and which is making real both to the group members themselves and the people around the power of the Christian fellowship."[39]

However, the tensions apparent in Allan's model were to likewise hinder Allan at a national level, as the influence spread of his missiological ideas and practice. There remained an unresolved friction between, on the one hand, the dynamism of the Gospel demonstrated at local level within the broader community in word, deed and example by a dedicated and inspired nucleus, often consisting of the young; and, on the other, the reticence of its recipient institution to adapt a culture of stolid tradition to allow the integration of those whose imagination had been caught, so as to create some form of purposeful re-generated church that may have better withstood the coming storm of the sixties.

## "Tell Scotland," 1953–1955

The immense privilege of unfettered access which the Church of Scotland enjoyed in the post-war years to the major media of press, radio and television is now almost unimaginable. Melville Dinwiddie and Ronald Falconer, two Church of Scotland ministers, were in charge of the BBC in Scotland. From 1933 to 1957, Dinwiddie was the regional director for the BBC in Scotland, and from 1945 to 1971 Falconer was responsible for the output of all religious television and radio programs.[40]

Determined to fully utilize their media resources for effective Christian evangelism, Dinwiddie and Falconer took initial steps in their Radio Missions of 1950 and 1952. The startling events in North Kelvinside had caught their attention at the BBC, then based in Queen Margaret Drive, Glasgow on the doorstep of Allan's parish. Allan became a popular broadcaster in the

---

38. Ibid., 79.
39. Ibid., 78.
40. See MacLean, "Marvellous New Trumpets," 414.

Radio Missions, given his clarity of language, easy-going use of anecdote, and his warm baritone voice.

In an ominous reflection of what might follow, Falconer believed that both Radio Missions foundered through lack of organized follow-up by the churches: "ninety out of every hundred sat back and did nothing . . . In proportion to their inactivity, so were the results in their parishes."[41]

Nevertheless, encouraged by the experience of the Radio Missions, Dinwiddie and Falconer corralled the Reformed churches into considering a fully coordinated national evangelistic campaign, to be directed in conjunction with the mass media.

The movement that came to be known as "Tell Scotland" was born at a Joint Conference of the Home Board of the Church of Scotland and the BBC on 30 October 1952, with a national launch on 4 March 1953. In anticipation of developments, Tom Allan had offered his services to the Home Board for a period of five years as a full-time evangelist. At its first meeting on 2 April 1953, the Steering Panel of "Tell Scotland" were "unanimously and cordially of the opinion that Mr Allan was the person to lead the "Tell Scotland" movement."[42] He assumed the post of Field Director in September 1953.[43]

Representatives of all Reformed denominations were invited to join later that year.[44] The parent Joint Committee of "Tell Scotland" consisted of senior church figures such as George MacLeod, James S. Stewart and John Baillie. A subordinate executive Steering Panel was formed to plan the detail of the mission and decide organizational issues as they arose. The Iona Community was initially supportive of the Movement, as can be seen from the participation of MacLeod and of its Deputy Leader, Ralph Morton, at a high level.[45] The Movement quickly encompassed the support of virtually all non-Roman Catholic denominations: The Church of Scotland, the Scottish Episcopal Church, the United Free Church, the

41. Falconer, *Kilt*, 72.

42. Minute of Steering Panel, 2 April 1953, "Tell Scotland" Archive. See also Small, *Growing Together*, 55–9 (compiled from the minutes *inter alia* of "Tell Scotland").

43. Small, *Growing Together*, 55.

44. The Roman Catholic Church in Scotland did not take part in ecumenical groups or initiatives until the formation of Action of Churches Together in Scotland in 1990.

45. MacLeod was a member of the Joint Committee of "Tell Scotland," and Morton of the Steering Panel. Morton also wrote under its auspices "Tell Scotland" booklet No.2 on *Evangelism in Scotland Today*, and James Maitland, then Warden of Community House, wrote *Caring for People—the Church in the Parish*.

Congregational and Baptist Unions of Scotland, the Churches of Christ and the United Original Secession church.[46]

The description of Ron Ferguson is thus apt: "Tell Scotland" was indeed a "broad-based liberal ecumenical movement."[47] Given its breadth and vast scale in its drive to evangelize the whole nation of Scotland, "Tell Scotland" was, in Peter Bisset's words, "perhaps the most important movement of mission that Scotland had seen in the course of the century,"[48] and indeed has seen since then. Its presence "dominated the churches' thinking and action for a decade."[49]

The statement given at the founding press conference for "Tell Scotland" on 9 September 1953 set out the reasons for its founding:

i. We are recognising the inadequacy of traditional methods of Evangelism.

ii. We are conscious of the apparent failure of the conventional life of the church to respond in compassion to the needs of the world.

iii. We are convinced that the only word for a bankrupt world is the Word of the church's Lord.[50]

As Frank Bardgett comments, "this confession of failure . . . was as much a challenge to the Kirk itself as to those outside. "Tell Scotland" called on ministers and congregations not simply to attempt new campaigning methods but, more radically, to renew their common life, structures and programmes."[51]

It was Allan's focus in the "Tell Scotland" principles on the local, the ordinary and the everyday, with the church laity at the heart of mission, which once more set the missiology apart. Allan stated the goal of "Tell Scotland" to be "to bring the Gospel to bear in the whole life of the nation at every level,"[52] envisioning an engagement in every corner of society.

When it came to drawing the campaign map for doing so, there were two assumptions that went undisputed. The first was that the foundations of

---

46. For a full list of all those involved from the different denominations on the Steering Panel, see Falconer, *Kilt*, 76–7. Only the Free Presbyterian Church and some Free Church of Scotland ministers dissented.

47. Ferguson, *George MacLeod*, 271.

48. Bisset, *Kirk and Her Scotland*, 9.

49. Falconer, *Kilt*, 75.

50. Minute of Steering Panel, 9 September 1953, "Tell Scotland" Archive.

51. Bardgett, *Scotland's Evangelist*, 299–300.

52. Allan and Meikle, *"Tell Scotland" Movement*, interview recorded at Aberdeen on 31 October 1954.

the mission were to be laid in the purging and re-invention of the existing church within the parochial structure, not by experimental or exploratory forms of mission, or towards para-church lay communities outwith its supervision. As Allan departed North Kelvinside, he left the congregation in no doubt that he intended to confront the largely dormant membership of the national church, and to rouse them towards dedicated action on the street in mission and the service of others. Thus the key for Allan at this initial stage was not so much the "telling" of Scotland as its "serving" through a renewed and re-invigorated parish. He told his parishioners at his Farewell Social at North Kelvinside on 22 September 1953: "I become more and more convinced that only a revolution in the conventional pattern of the church's life will do in the situation today . . . I believe that God is calling his church in Scotland today to new fields of service, which will demand from us a new level of consecration, a willingness to study the faith at a deeper level, and above all, a new readiness to serve our fellow men in love."[53]

The second assumption was also highlighted by Allan at the same occasion: "Mr Allan pointed out that this congregation has the opportunity of profoundly influencing the life of the whole church in Scotland. Anything which he has to say to the church today comes direct from his experience of what happened here in North Kelvinside. He is going to tell Scotland that the Grace of Christ still makes men new, and that God still uses ordinary people to work his miracles."[54]

Despite the mixed success and ongoing challenges that he had expressed in *The Face of My Parish*, Allan as Field Director of "Tell Scotland" thus sought to transpose the North Kelvinside model of mission into the national movement, with the emphasis remaining on the creation of an insurgent cell of local laity to begin the journey towards "missionary parishes" across the nation. As Bisset later commented:

> It had been the congregational group at the heart of the church's life which [Allan] had seen giving new authenticity to the meaning of the church. It would be such groups throughout Scotland committed, convinced, and caring, who would make the Gospel count once more within the life of the land. It was they who would bridge the dichotomy between those who saw the essential expression of the Gospel either in caring deed or in saving word. Throughout Scotland, the Gospel would be incarnated in

---

53. *The Congregational News Review*, North Kelvinside Parish Church, vol. 4 no.8 (December 1953) 4.

54. Ibid.

the lives of men and women who in word and deed would make Jesus known.[55]

The founding principles of "Tell Scotland" which were maintained throughout its thirteen-year existence were therefore:

i.  ... effective evangelism is not a sporadic encounter with the world but a continuing engagement at every level.

ii.  The agent of effective mission is the church itself, the redeemed community ...

iii.  If the church is to become the agent of mission in its own situation, then every effort must be made to encourage the layman to recognise his calling to the apostolate, and to train him for the task of witness.[56]

A three-stage programme was set out to reflect the central emphasis on the laity:

> Phase I: September 1953 to June 1954: To encourage and stimulate general discussion on the theme of mission among ministers and office-bearers.
>
> Phase II: September 1954 to June 1955: To recruit and train the lay forces of the church for the task of witness, through congregational or area groups meeting regularly for prayer and Bible study, and seeking together concrete forms of service in their community, at their work and in their leisure.
>
> Phase III: Beginning September 1955: The outgoing mission, in continuing engagement with the world, of a community exhibiting the marks of genuine "koinonia," and witnessing to the Lordship of Christ in a unique and striking way in word and deed.[57]

Much of the general principle could have been written by George MacLeod rather than Tom Allan. MacLeod had adhered to the crucial detail: that the focus would be on the recruitment and enabling of the "congregational cell," first specifically proposed in a Committee meeting of 4 June 1953.[58] This focus replaced a draft model of three mission phases that had specific content more akin to the "Iona" model of mission based on MacLeod's "Mission of Friendship" to his earlier parish in Govan in the thirties:

55. Bisset, "Kirk and Society," 56.

56. RGA 1954, 220.

57. Ibid.

58. Small, *Growing Together,* 59.

by the intensive preparation of the congregations, special media broadcasts and then follow-up with integration.[59]

By contrast to this earlier "Govan" draft, the precise content of the mission within Phase III was deliberately left undecided by the Steering Panel, in a nod to the important recognition of what would now be called "contextualization": "The Steering Panel has consistently sought to avoid drawing up a 'blueprint' for mission, believing that the local congregation, or group of Congregations, must discover the method best suited to the local situation."[60]

Whilst an admirable strength at local level viewed through present-day eyes, a complete absence of agreed purpose, content and method of mission as starting points, even in the form of general principles or permissible alternatives, served to open the door to conflict between those whose model was one of service and integration with the struggles of the world, and those for whom oral proclamation and calls to decision ought to take priority. That absence then also permitted the justification of adopting one of those approaches at national level over the other, as occurred with the later invitation to Billy Graham, further exacerbating discontent at the highest level, and leading to confusion and inactivity on the ground. A failure to fully identify goals or principles might be unnecessary in a unitary parish such as North Kelvinside where decisions could be taken swiftly *ad hoc* and special events might easily be related back to the local and the everyday. However, on a national scale of over two thousand parishes in the Church of Scotland alone, it begged the questions, "what are we meant to do?" and "to what end?"

If "Tell Scotland" was to significantly progress Christianity under this model nationally, the key would be for the hierarchical structure to step back from any "top-down" initiative at all, and adhere to their promise not to impose any blueprint for mission. It required Allan, the Joint Committee and the Steering Panel to fully permit each locality to dictate the direction of mission, where for example the creation of an organically developing Christian community in high-density urban tenements ought to markedly differ from a dispersed farming community.

At all costs, therefore, what the Movement had to avoid at national level under Allan's model was any temptation to centralize and focus the message and mode of mission upon one prominent individual or theological hue, or to create the public perception that such a decision had occurred.

59. Ibid., 56.
60. RGA 1954, 221.

The first recorded dissension of George MacLeod within the Movement came at the Committee in early 1954. MacLeod was beginning to realize, before an invitation to Billy Graham was considered, that at such an important stage his cherished integration of a "communal evangelism," by the interaction of faith with the daily struggles of life and concurrent social protest and witness, might be in danger of being relegated to the background.

George S. Gunn had produced a memorandum encouraging the Committee to define not the content of mission, but instead to set out the broad purposes of the Movement in missiological terms, as:

1. An endeavour to bring individuals to a personal acceptance of Jesus Christ;

2. A building up of the converts into the fellowship of the church;

3. A challenging of the conscience of the people to disorders of community life . . . [and]

4. A presentation of all this by a penitent church . . .[61]

Gunn identified that although most missions might achieve (1), many foundered at (2), most were hesitant of (3) and all failed at (4)!

The Committee again decided to come to no definite conclusion on purposes, as "this could best be worked out existentially." George MacLeod complained in a letter to Falconer that the Panel had "'sidetracked' Gunn's proposal, particularly in the third part as it related to addressing the social needs of society."[62]

As he wrote his letter to Falconer, MacLeod may have had at the other side of his desk his notes for The Cunningham Lectures that he delivered in early 1954 at New College, Edinburgh, later published as *Only One Way Left*. His suspicions were aroused that Allan might divorce the marriage of faith and social action. In a lecture entitled "The Darkness of Mission," he stated categorically: "the disembodied Word is not enough. Even correctly stated it is not the Word at all."[63] In an obvious allusion to "Tell Scotland," he continued:

> 'Scotland,' you say, 'is embarking on a rounded Mission of the church, with the church as the community in the forefront.' But be careful that we do not still embrace the darkness . . . Is the

61. George S. Gunn, "Tell Scotland," within the "Tell Scotland" Archive.

62. Minute of Steering Panel, 4 March 1954, "Tell Scotland" Archive; and Small, *Growing Together*, 63.

63. MacLeod, *Only One Way Left*, 42.

> [danger] not the deeply rooted conviction that all [political] is-
> sues are the periphery of our work, a distant derivative of our
> Faith whose main engagement lies elsewhere? Is it not a con-
> tinuing conviction that the Message stands consistent within
> itself: and that the church can become revitalised within the
> borders of its own domain: from which domain, at some date
> always projected into the future, it will seriously close with the
> claims of Christ in society?[64]

Perhaps Macleod's fears were allayed slightly by the terms of a "Tell
Scotland" Pamphlet on the lay group in evangelism, written by Allan
and published in mid-1954. Allan emphasized engagement in "fields of
service."[65] The first field of service would be wholeheartedly engaged by the
later Billy Graham Crusade:

> The Group must keep the ultimate objective of all mission in
> view—which is to lead men to a saving knowledge of God
> through Jesus Christ.[66]

The second field of service, that of MacLeod's concentration, would
founder somewhat along the way: "Assuredly a group which has come alive
to the needs of the time will be as much concerned with the political and
economic witness as it will be with preaching at the street corner: it will be
as much concerned with the bodies of men as with their souls."[67]

It would have come as no surprise to Allan that if he sought to pursue the first field of service without the second, MacLeod's vocal judgment
would be that by projecting "political and economic witness" into the future, "Tell Scotland" was now "embracing the darkness." In the event, that
was precisely the course that Allan chose.

The first full year of "Tell Scotland" in 1953–1954 was filled with hope.
Allan travelled the country extensively in pursuit of Phase I; the education
and recruitment of presbyteries, clergy and congregations.[68]

Allan's unceasing work and national media exposure made him well
known in the public consciousness. As the popular magazine, *The People's
Journal*, reported in an interview in early 1955, "it has suddenly made
Scotland aware that the neat, tireless, polite, cultured, 39-year-old son of

64. Ibid., 55–56.

65. Allan, *The Agent of Mission*, 9–15.

66. Ibid., 15.

67. Ibid., 14–15.

68. His pocket diaries at AA6.9 reveal an astonishing workload and distance
travelled.

an Ayrshire butcher is a religious superman. Other ministers describe him
as the greatest pulpit orator of the century." It noted that: "his capacity for
work is phenomenal . . . he works 16 hours a day—travelling, lecturing,
discussing, broadcasting, writing, and always indulging in what he likes
most—meeting people."[69]

Allan's encouragement in that period to the lay people of the churches
came in radio broadcasts such as the following. He set out a call to arms in
words that were to become somewhat contradicted by subsequent events,
where he sought to empower the ordinary to seek the extraordinary, and
appeared to firmly distance the depth and theological foundation of the
movement from any "old-style" mass evangelistic campaign, such as Graham might conduct:

> What is the "Tell Scotland" movement anyhow? [It] is a move-
> ment of the major Protestant churches in our land to carry the
> message of the New Testament into every branch of our national
> life. *It is not a spectacular campaign with banner head-lines. It's
> not a tip-and-run raid into enemy territory.* It is based on the
> solid conviction that the best method of winning Scotland for
> Christ . . . is through the *quiet, patient, consecrated witness of the
> local congregation* to the Truth by which it lives and for which
> it stands. That witness will mean different things in different
> places—at least in detail. But one thing is certain. *The key to the
> whole Movement is with the laity—with you.*

It could not be a powerful witness, said Allan, "unless its members are
prepared to take their Faith seriously." He explained the degree of obligation upon ordinary church members: "what does all this mean in concrete,
practical terms?" Three things: "we've got to learn to pray"; "we've got to get
to know more about our faith; that means study"; and "we've got to translate
all this into terms of service: going out to men in compassion and love to
serve them for Christ's sake who died for them."

Therefore, Allan said in his broadcast, there was a key to "Tell Scotland" getting off the ground: "the very first objective of the 'Tell Scotland'
movement is to see the emergence of groups of lay people in congregations
throughout the country . . . we begin there."[70]

In 1953 to 1954, Allan had succeeded through such efforts in creating
a national air of anticipation, filled with potential for an ongoing mission

---

69. Alan Dunsmore, "Tom Allan Doesn't Pull His Punches," *The People's Journal*,
26 February 1955, within the Papers of Jessie Margaret Strathdee or Johnston, Box 31.

70. AA6.3.2, all at Tom Allan radio talk, "The Missionary Church," 6–8 (my
emphasis).

based on the local formation of Christian communities centered on expressing love, dedication and service. Allan reported in an interview in October
1954 that "I've been deeply moved over the past twelve months . . . by the
universal acceptance of these fundamental principles of mission."[71] Allan
was, however, by then a worried man from his travels around the country
as to whether that reception could be transferred into practice, saying: "I
am more and more convinced that the church is not yet ready for what we
are asking it to do."[72] In other words, he feared that a lackluster response to
the formation of congregational groups would characterize Phase II, and
therefore cause the whole project to fizzle out before Phase III got started.
Allan concluded that "some fire has to be kindled before the 'Tell Scotland'
Movement becomes incandescent."[73]

Allan believed that the Holy Spirit had led him to the solution. He had
attended a Billy Graham rally at Harringay, London in early 1954. According to Falconer, he had been "strangely moved" and "had come to believe
deeply in its efficacy."[74] The conviction formed in Allan's mind that Graham
should be invited to lead an "All Scotland Crusade."

Allan reported to a meeting of the Steering Panel of "Tell Scotland" on
22 April 1954 that he had met Billy Graham and the leaders of his Crusade
in London, after attending the rally: "It was Dr Graham's wish to come to
Scotland but he would only come by the invitation of the church. Mr Allan
felt that if this were separate from the "Tell Scotland" Movement it could
do irreparable harm . . . He felt that Dr Graham might spark off something
within the church which was really necessary to start 'Tell Scotland.'"[75]

Very quickly at that initial meeting, the lines of schism caused by
Graham that would later fatally split "Tell Scotland" were drawn. Ralph
Morton of the Iona Community voiced his opposition: he did not doubt
Graham's sincerity but "felt he was shelving all the crucial problems wor-
rying people today."[76]

In answering Morton at the meeting, Allan made his hopes clear that
a Crusade would be complementary to the lay focus of "Tell Scotland," dependent on the response of the church:

71. Allan and Meikle, "Tell Scotland" Movement, interview recorded at Aberdeen
on 31 October 1954.

72. Ibid.

73. Allan, The Agent of Mission, 21.

74. Falconer, Kilt, 77.

75. Minute of Steering Panel, 22 April 1954, "Tell Scotland" Archive.

76. Ibid.

It was felt that the general conception of what "Tell Scotland" was trying to do might be lost if Dr Graham were invited to co-operate with it, but Mr Allan said that [Graham] would be regarded a prelude for "Tell Scotland"and that the real work of the movement would begin in 1955. He felt that Dr Graham would not have a long-term influence unless the church followed it up.[77]

The departure from the local and the personal was immediately obvious and sat in apparent direct contradiction to the "Tell Scotland" principles, themselves based on Allan's prior missiology. The decision was referred to a meeting of the parent Joint Committee on 3 May, for which MacLeod prepared a memorandum entitled "Should Billy Graham Tell Scotland?"[78] MacLeod opposed the invitation to Graham under "six propositions," including the following grounds:

a. a warning on mass evangelism: "By asking Graham do we not lay ourselves open to asking all such as the spearpoint of a mission to Scotland?";

b. a call to Scottish tradition, writing that if this method was best, "why is it not the mark of our own missionary endeavours? Do you employ this approach in your own congregation? Do you call for decisions at the end of any service?";

c. a reminder of the purpose of "Tell Scotland": "I don't doubt Graham would 'succeed.' Where then does our 'congregational mission' come in? I thought our congregations were to be the agents of mission. We must be careful that the congregation does not become merely the 'follow-up' of mission."; and

d. a strong rebuttal of Graham's separation of conversion and social action: "Is the theory that we must get a sufficient number to Christ . . . and then someone will blow the whistle and we will all get down to social action? Is so, who is to blow it and when?"

With MacLeod's paper before the members of the Joint Committee, Falconer's later recollection of the meeting of 3 May was that "most of us were against having anything to do with the 'All Scotland Crusade.'"[79] D. P. Thomson's contemporaneous diary entry, however, suggests a rather differ-

---

77. Ibid.

78. Folder 254, "Tell Scotland" Campaign 1953–9," National Library of Scotland, NLS Acc. 9084, MacLeod of Fuinary and Iona Community.

79. Falconer, *Kilt*, 77.

ent course: of general agreement amongst the Committee on 3 May, with Ralph Morton being unable to find a seconder for his opposition.[80]

A delegation of four, including Tom Allan and Ralph Morton, was sent to London on 6 May to meet with Billy Graham. At a subsequent meeting of the Joint Committee on 14 May, the invitation to Graham was passed. According to Falconer, it was only the personality and leadership of Allan that won the day: "We were hopelessly divided; yet unwilling to throw overboard such a devoted and charismatic brother as Tom. We held him in deep affection and respect; in the end we closed our ranks and went with him."[81]

In the same month, the Church of Scotland at the General Assembly then backed an overture to support the invitation to Graham. They did so in the wake of the endorsement of Tom Allan and the "Tell Scotland" Joint Committee and in the reverberations of the Harringay Crusade, recognising too that by now a rejection of Graham would fatally split the whole "Tell Scotland" Movement, no matter the warning signs that an acceptance of him may also do so. Many had also experienced Graham's preaching during his prior visits to Scotland with "Youth for Christ" in 1946 to 1947, with positive recollections.

MacLeod valiantly opposed the invitation to Graham at the Assembly, albeit it had already been made. Describing the "speech of the week" by "George MacLeod at his oratorical best," as he "went into action with all guns firing," David Read reported the core of MacLeod's argument in the *British Weekly*. MacLeod presciently recognized that the damage to be caused by Graham's presence was not necessarily his method *per se*, but the effect this would have on the prior focus of the mission of "Tell Scotland" at a local level: "dare we give the impression to well over a million souls who are our charge and responsibility that the methods of Dr Graham should form the spearpoint of the 'Tell Scotland' campaign?"[82]

As was raised above, in the absence of any clear message otherwise from the hierarchy of the Movement at national level, the danger was that only one "spearpoint" would become indelibly associated with the meaning of "Tell Scotland." However, as Falconer later recalled: "George MacLeod fought us, tooth and nail. But George lost the day, as he so often lost gallant

---

80. "Diary of My Life," 4 May 1954, quoted in Bardgett, *Scotland's Evangelist*, 189. The full minute of that meeting is suspiciously missing from the "Tell Scotland" Archive, as with those for the further meeting of 14 May 1954, and of 10 June 1954 when Billy Graham was invited to be present, the only such missing minutes from its decade-long history.

81. Falconer, *Kilt*, 78.

82. Read, "British Churches," 7.

fights in that Court. The Fathers and Brethren cheered him to the echo for his passionately brilliant speech—and voted overwhelmingly for us."[83]

With hindsight, Falconer recalled that this was the beginning of the end: "We were persuaded to change our strategy, thereby sowing the seeds which were to choke a promising movement."[84]

Allan bravely attended a gathering of the Community on Iona in June 1954, where he was left in no doubt as to their opposition. As Morton reported in *The Coracle* of October 1954, echoing MacLeod before the General Assembly: "The general opinion of the Community was that the message and methods of Dr Graham were inadequate and even dangerous in that his campaign would be likely to disrupt the serious and long-term work of the 'Tell Scotland'Movement, with its emphasis on the congregation as the agent of mission."[85]

In mid-August 1954, Tom Allan received the acceptance of Billy Graham to conduct the "All Scotland Crusade" and his confirmation that it would be based in Glasgow in Spring 1955.[86] At the request of Billy Graham, Tom Allan was appointed Chairman of the Executive Committee of the Crusade.

## The Crusade and its Aftermath

The numbers exposed to the Gospel through Graham's preaching at rallies in the Kelvin Hall, Glasgow and in football stadia, and by the skilled utilization of radio relays, were astounding. As Allan noted afterwards:

> Between the 21st of March and the 30th of April, 1955—the six weeks of the Crusade—a total of 1,185,360 people in Scotland attended meetings of one kind or another directly connected with the Crusade. Of these, 830,670 were at the nightly meetings in Kelvin Hall and at the closing rallies in Ibrox Stadium and Hampden Park; 217,700 were at services of the Relay Mission in various parts of the country; and 136,990 were at other meetings addressed by Dr. Graham and Team members during the

---

83. Falconer, *Kilt*, 78. Falconer suggested that their victory was depressing: "I felt sick inside about it all . . . But the die was cast. We must make the best of it."

84. Ibid., *Kilt*, 77.

85. *The Coracle* 25, October 1954, 3.

86. Graham had chosen Glasgow because of its reputation as "the most sinful city in Britain." *Time*, 4 April 1955.

Crusade. And the total number of enquirers in Scotland during these weeks was 26,457.[87]

For six weeks, Graham preached in front of a volunteer choir at the Kelvin Hall of one thousand two hundred people. Capacity crowds attended each night of eleven thousand in the main arena, with a further three thousand five hundred people in the adjacent circus arena to which the rally was relayed.

Following the last rally at the Kelvin Hall, closing meetings were held at Ibrox Stadium with an attendance of around fifty thousand, and at Hampden Park where "the congregation numbered close to a hundred thousand—the largest congregation ever to assemble in Scotland's history."[88]

"Relay Missions," organized by Bill Shannon, were conducted in the week of 10 to 17 April. In thirty-seven centers throughout Scotland, the Crusade rally from the Kelvin Hall was relayed by radio across the country, to groups gathered by local "Tell Scotland" committees.

Graham's delivery was ecstatic, rousing and dramatic. Preaching then in his prime, he was undoubtedly an electrifying orator. His sermons were lengthy, at around fifty minutes each night, and repetitive in the texts employed and the metaphors used. There was a concentration on fear, sin and death—of substitutory atonement in the bloody sacrifice of Christ for our sins and our implication within it, and the need for immediate repentance and redemption to avoid hell. As Allan recalled: "invariably the last quarter of an hour of his sermon dealt with the way of salvation—repent, believe, receive Christ, obey."[89]

On Good Friday, the Kelvin Hall rally was broadcast live on television and radio throughout the United Kingdom by the BBC, to an estimated audience of thirty million people. Graham preached on Galatians 6:14 and Revelation 3:16, imploring the United Kingdom that it is the indifferent person that "makes Christ sick," they being people who "will forever be separated from God unless they repent of sin, accept by faith the depth of Christ and then bend their will to do the will of God."[90]

The conclusion of the rally was the "altar call," the invitation by Graham for individuals to come forward to be saved in Christ, as the massed

87. Allan, *Crusade in Scotland,* 8.

88. Ibid., 15. During the residency at the Kelvin Hall, Graham also addressed large crowds at Tynecastle Stadium in Edinburgh, Pittodrie Stadium in Aberdeen and in Inverness. He spoke to soldiers at Redford Barracks in Edinburgh, at Barlinnie Prison and at John Brown's Shipyard in Clydebank.

89. Ibid., 14.

90. Burnham, *Billy Graham,* 36–38.

choir sang "Just as I Am." Teams of "counsellors" were employed to then take each "enquirer" to Counselling Rooms.[91]

Allan was in no doubt as to the effect of the Crusade: "for thousands, Kelvin has proved to be the very gates of heaven. This hall may prove to be the turning point in the religious history of Scotland."[92] The Report of the Home Board to the General Assembly of May 1955 echoed that proclamation: "We are living in a day of most manifest grace when those who do not thrill with a new awareness to the conquests of Jesus must be blind and deaf."[93]

Others were not so convinced that Graham and his methods would have any lingering effect. Respected Glasgow journalist Jack House was aggressively critical in the *Evening News*, writing that "Billy Graham did not impress me in the least . . . after an evening as boring as any I have ever had in any hall, the final scene (when the converts came) nauseated me."[94]

This was nevertheless the most widespread exposure of the Gospel of Jesus Christ to the people of Scotland in the history of the nation. So did it work in its goals not only of "winning souls," but crucially for the purposes of "Tell Scotland" of Phase II recruitment of the laity in readiness for Phase III mission?

The demographic of "enquirers" at the main meetings was set out as follows:

> Of the 19,835 people coming forward at the Kelvin Hall, Ibrox, and Hampden, 5,819 were men and 14,016 were women—29 percent against 71 percent. 79 percent indicated that they were making a first-time decision for Christ . . . 34 percent signified that they were communicant members of some branch of the church, and 62 percent that they were regular attendees at public worship. The age-groupings were as follows: under 12: 11 percent; age 13–29, 62 percent; age 30–49, 19 percent; age 50 and over, 8 percent.[95]

Why were there were so few "converts" if the crowds were so large? Of note is the high proportion of churchgoers in attendance and also amongst

91. A "Decision Card" was made out on the nature of the commitment being made. The follow-up involved initial contact from the "counsellor," then correspondence and Bible materials being sent out in Billy Graham's name. A local Church follow-up was initiated by the "Decision Card" being sent to the minister of the Church to which the enquirer belonged, or had chosen.

92. Quoted in Burnham, *Billy Graham*, 68.

93. Report of the Home Board, RGA 1955, 233.

94. Quoted in Burnham, *Billy Graham*, 49.

95. Allan, *Crusade in Scotland*, 108.

the "enquirers," a statistic which was reflected in Allan's later rallies in the parish at St George's Tron. Presumably, their "decision for Christ" had already been taken.

Callum Brown also makes a cogent case that "the real success was in its role as spectacle."[96] It was showbiz at its best, in an era of Hollywood glamour and a yearning for the "thrill of the new." The rallies held the most allure for youth and women, replicating the Harringay Crusade of the previous year. The low percentage of overall "converts" and their primary demographic amongst those groups was also the outcome there: "of those who 'came forward' in London in 1954, 65 percent were women and over 50 percent were under 19 years of age."[97] The departure of these constituencies in the social revolution of 1958 onwards was to prove costly for the church. So too was the failure to translate the sharp, initial hike in attendances and membership in the immediate aftermath of the "All Scotland Crusade" into any lasting effect on church connection, or alteration in the church's inherent ethos, the two perhaps being closely linked.

In terms of evaluating the potency of the Crusade as an example of mass evangelism, it was unreservedly superb. It was brilliantly organized by those at the top of the structure, such as Allan and Shannon, and the thousands involved at a more local level. The presentation of Graham and his team was near faultless. Religion, for a while at least, was back at the forefront of public life. There is no doubt that the Crusade generated vast publicity. As the *Evening Citizen* wrote, Graham "has made religion news again . . . bequeathed to our native clergy a legacy of renewed interest in God's word, a legacy for them to exploit when he has gone."[98]

Graham achieved his primary purpose, as he claimed himself prior to his departure: "people are no longer indifferent about religion, and the greatest problem facing the clergy is indifference."[99] The buzz in the air was palpable: "the most popular topic of conversation—on the streets, in night clubs, shipyards and civic luncheons—is Jesus Christ and Billy Graham."[100] There are many stories of faith being kindled or renewed by Graham's preaching. In the longer term, some church people found a firmer grasp of faith. Many considered forms of Christian ministry whose commitment had been insipid.

96. Brown, *Religion and Society in Twentieth-Century Britain*, 205.

97. Colquhoun, *Harringay Story*, 232–33, quoted in ibid.

98. Burnham, *Billy Graham*, 60.

99. Ibid., 73.

100. Ibid., 41.

Billy Graham did his job. Scotland was aware of what he did, how he did it and what his purposes were. When he was invited, no-one in Scotland could have been under any illusion that the package would differ from the call to an individualist salvation that had been heard on Graham's prior visits to Scotland, and demonstrated so publicly at Harringay in the previous year. Nor could they have doubted that the presentation of the message would involve a wreaking of emotion on a wave of mass excitement. As MacLeod had warned before Graham arrived, there was no expectation that any "social gospel" would be preached. Despite criticism of the message, Scotland got exactly what it asked for, on an unprecedented scale. However, as Allan had argued, the Crusade was designed not as the culmination of "Tell Scotland," but as the end of the beginning.

In the immediate aftermath of the Crusade, Allan anticipated an intensive mobilization of the laity as the visible expression of Phase III of the "Tell Scotland" Movement, writing: "the outgoing mission will be expressed in many ways—in personal work, in house-to-house visitation, in cells for witness in factory and shop and office, in public meetings, and in other ways yet unexplored. And it seems to me that the full significance of the All Scotland Crusade will be seen in what happens in Scotland in the next twelve months."[101]

What then of that litmus test of Graham's intervention within "Tell Scotland"? In the initial year after the Crusade, there was a considerable amount of visitation activity in parishes, with estimates of around 600 such campaigns from 800 congregational groups.[102] However, insofar as the Crusade was charged with enabling the widespread recruitment of the laity under Phase II of the plan and thus inspiring the outward mission of Phase III, it failed to do so to a sufficient and lasting degree. Those local "Tell Scotland" committees who implemented Phase III mission did not experience long-term benefit in the numerical composition of their churches, or the depth of belief in the Gospel amongst their communities.

There was no longer-term resurgence of mission in Gospel witness and social service, or sustainable increase in membership or attendances. The problem was summed up by Allan in the following year: "In hundreds of Congregations not even a beginning has been made. No lay group is in being. No permanent mission has been established. No bridge-head to the world, however rudimentary and perilous, has been built."[103]

---

101. Allan, *Crusade in Scotland,* 127.

102. RGA 1956, Report of the Home Board, 233.

103. AA6.2.18, "Broadcast on "Evangelism," c.1956.

Billy Graham's biographer wrote: "The "All Scotland Crusade" . . . had created immense expectancy throughout Scotland. The heather seems dry, Graham had lit a fire and departed, his part done. And the heather did not blaze."[104]

Despite the beneficial conditions, the brilliant organization and unremitting zeal on the part of Allan and others, the Crusade was a long-term failure in terms of implementing the empowerment of the laity, the missionary church, or the conversion of the unconnected masses. The slow decline of the impact and response to "Tell Scotland" in the late fifties and early sixties coincided with the gradual but unremitting diminution in the membership and public influence of the churches in Scotland, in the rapid onrush of secularization.

Writing in 1960, the church historian J. H. S. Burleigh claimed a direct correlation between Graham's Crusade, further evangelistic activity and long-term benefits to the church: "It is certain, in spite of the doubts of some, that the church did gain from the "All Scotland Crusade" of Billy Graham. Never in its history has there been more of a missionary spirit in the church expressing itself in an active churchly evangelism."[105]

The work of the University of Glasgow sociologist John Highet proves those assertions to be wrong, at the least in relation to any degree of positive effect that it may all have had in the longer term.

On the one hand, Highet acknowledged that "the ten years following the Second World War have been marked by Protestant evangelistic activity on a scale unprecedented in Scottish ecclesiastical history."[106]

However, on the other hand, Highet concluded from surveys throughout the fifties in relation to such activity that: "It cannot be denied that at least one hope in the minds of missioners was that their efforts would result in adding appreciably to the numbers of committed and regularly worshipping Christians. If we are right, this hope has not been fulfilled."[107]

Any consideration of the overall effect of "Tell Scotland" and the All-Scotland Crusade on church and nation in the period to 1960 is indebted to Highet's figures, within his three most prominent publications: *The Churches in Scotland Today* in 1950; "The Churches" in 1958; and *The Scottish Churches* in 1960.

They revealed, firstly, an initial post-war growth in Christian affiliation. In 1950, Highet reported that "there has been an over-all increase of

104. Pollock, *Billy Graham*, 198.

105. Burleigh, *A Church History of Scotland*, 413.

106. Highet, "The Protestant Churches in Scotland," 101.

107. Highet, *The Scottish Churches*, 111.

12,785 in the membership of six Protestant denominations in the period
1947 to 1949, and a probable increase in the Roman Catholic population
of some few thousands."[108] The gains that have been considered in the work
of Tom Allan in North Kelvinside were thus contributory to a more general
trend of a numerical rise in this initial post-war period.

Secondly, Highet's research demonstrated a temporary surge in church
attendance in the wake of the "All Scotland Crusade," followed by a significant dip, tending to indicate that any numerical effect upon religious
observance was transitory. As he set out in his 1958 publication, a team
under Highet's supervision carried out surveys in 1954 to 1956 in which
they sought to identify any significant differences in church attendance in
Glasgow caused as a result of the "All Scotland Crusade" of 1955. Numbers in the non-Roman Catholic denominations were counted over three
Sundays in three periods: in April and May 1954, then in the immediate
aftermath of the Crusade in May 1955, and again in May 1956.[109] The three
Sunday average rose from 56,503 in 1954, to 67,708 in 1955, and then fell
in 1956 to 62,224 (all around 30 per cent of membership and 8 to 9 per
cent of the city's population). The average in 1956 was therefore below the
1955 "Crusade" levels, but above the 1954 levels prior to the Crusade i.e. at
a rough midpoint.[110]

Thirdly, Highet's 1960 book supported the veracity of his 1954 to 1956
figures which tended to suggest that the gains from the Crusade and "Tell
Scotland" were less that might have been expected. His 1960 book further
surveyed whether at least the ethos of the churches had altered as a result
of "Tell Scotland" or the "All Scotland Crusade." He carried out a survey of
Scottish ministers of non-Roman Catholic Christianity, with three hundred
and twenty-six responses.

There were three main issues posed:

### 1. Effect on attendance

Of two hundred and twenty-six Church of Scotland responses where
higher attendances had been reported, only thirty-one indicated that the
Crusade or "Tell Scotland" had "some effect" and sixteen a "very slight"

---

108. Highet, *The Churches in Scotland Today*, 229. The six denominations were the
Church of Scotland, the United Free Church, the Scottish Episcopal Church, the Methodist Church, The Congregational Union, and The Baptist Union.

109. Highet, "The Churches," 729.

110. Ibid., 730 and Table CL1, 731. The peak attendance was 72,079 on Sunday 1
May 1955 (the Sunday following the end of the Kelvin Hall rallies). Within three weeks
in May 1955, this had fallen to 61,620.

effect on the increase, with a variety of unrelated causes being otherwise attributed.

### 2. *Effect on membership of large-scale or local campaigns*

In the Church of Scotland, 93 per cent replied that on membership there had been "little effect or none at all," or a "slight effect," with only 7 per cent indicating a "decided effect." The same result occurred when all denominations were combined. Of the respondents in the first category from the Church of Scotland, 56 per cent reported "none at all."[111]

Stated otherwise, if this sample of three hundred and twenty-six churches in all denominations in 1959 is taken to be representative, any appreciable impact on membership from "Tell Scotland" *or* the Crusade occurred only in 7 per cent of churches.

### 3. *Whether "the activities under consideration had had any impact,* *apart from membership and attendance, on their congregation"*

In the Church of Scotland, 47 per cent replied "none," 13 per cent "little" effect and 40 per cent "some" effect, with a similar distribution when all denominations were accounted for.[112]

Stated otherwise, if this sample is taken to be representative, there was little or no impact on the basic activities of the congregation, and therefore on mission (!), from "Tell Scotland" or the Crusade in around 60 per cent of the churches in Scotland.

In other words, viewed overall the re-orientation of the congregation towards mission had abjectly failed in the majority of parishes.

As a cross-check, the later figures of Wolfe and Pickford in their 1980 book, *The Church of Scotland: An Economic Survey*,[113] appear to corroborate Highet's numerical findings in relation to church adherence and membership: being an initial burst of increased activity following Graham's Crusade of 1955, an all-time high in membership in 1956 and thereafter the effects of rapid decline. Again, Wolfe and Pickford's results tend to suggest, as in Highet's 1960 survey, that the impact in the longer term of both "Tell Scotland" and Billy Graham was minimal. Dealing with statistics for membership and Professions of Faith, they stated that "a very pronounced peak was reached in 1955, co-inciding with the year of the Billy Graham crusade, followed by a sharp decline, especially from 1964 onwards."[114]

111. *The Scottish Churches*, 105.

112. Ibid., 112.

113. Wolfe and Pickford, *The Church of Scotland*.

114. Ibid., 82.

Therefore, instead of the anticipated rapid acceleration of Christian adherence and the evangelisation of the nation, the statistical results suggest a rollercoaster effect of a short, sudden lift, followed by a rapid descent down the precipice on the other side, even in the short term after 1956, but especially in the longer term from the sixties onwards.

Graham's Crusade had thus been a diverting "flash in the pan," if not more seriously damaging. In place of revival came not only stasis but the decline of the churches: "1956 was the end of a dream."[115] Since then, "the religious crisis which emerged during the second half of the twentieth century has been unprecedented."[116]

As early as 1957, the cracks began to show within the upper echelons of "Tell Scotland." A meeting was called at Troon to discuss the future, partly due to "certain reservations about the value of the All Scotland Crusade."[117] The Steering Panel member, Charles Duthie, expressed a growing undercurrent of regret that must have inspired a loud "I told you so!" from George Macleod and Ralph Morton, reporting "a widespread feeling that the "Tell Scotland"Movement is in danger of losing its power and direction, perhaps of disintegrating [due to stressing] a personal evangelism which has no social dynamic . . . an exaggerated trust in mass meetings . . . with a limited intellectual content."[118]

"Tell Scotland" tried to maintain the momentum through "Kirk Weeks" in Aberdeen and Dundee, which were intensive local events and conferences based on the German *Kirchentag*, with initial success in refocusing the momentum of "Tell Scotland" on the laity, but diminishing returns. It drew a number of influential and forward-thinking ministers to the four Commissions set up in the late fifties on "Evangelism," "The Bible," "The Laity" and "The Community."

However, as a national movement "Tell Scotland" slowly declined, until eventually being subsumed within the Scottish Churches Council at its inauguration in December 1964, as did the congregational groups and the hope of an evangelized, Christian society. In May 1958, the first full conference of "Tell Scotland" conveners was organized for Wiston Lodge, Biggar. A mere three years after the Crusade, the parlous state of the "Tell Scotland" movement at local level on the ground was reported:

115. Bisset, "Kirk and Society," 58.

116. Brown, *Religion and Society in Scotland since 1707*, 158. The number of communicant members in the Church of Scotland as of 31 December 2014 was 396,422 (Galbraith, ed., *The Church of Scotland Yearbook, 2015/16*, 294), as compared to 1,061,706 in 1974, a decline of 62.6% in forty years.

117. Small, *Growing Together*, 78.

118. Ibid., 84.

It was clear that, as far as the church at large is concerned, "Tell Scotland"is not a success story . . . In many places, the local committees failed to carry anything like all the ministers with them. Reasons given were: this was another stunt: men in parishes are already overwhelmed with their congregational responsibilities: if "Tell Scotland"is to be taken seriously then ministers are faced with the unenviable task of reorganising their whole approach to ministry.

Some ministers, who might be willing to attempt something, had reservations about the value of the "All Scotland Crusade," and as a consequence their allegiance was lost.

Through Visitation Campaigns a number have been brought into the church, but these did not remain, because the church is not ready to receive them and the church had nothing that really gripped them.[119]

In its final stages, the exasperation of its then Field Organiser, Ian MacTaggart, at the failure of congregations to come near to implementing Phase III is apparent. The "Tell Scotland" report which he presented to the General Assembly of 1961 all but serves as its obituary: "Large tracts of the country . . . have been untouched by the Movement . . . It would be idle to pretend that the imagination of the church has been deeply and permanently stirred by the trumpet call to present the 'Good News' to every man, woman and child in the land."[120]

So why did the failure occur?

The first obstacle after the Crusade to the implementation of Phase III was the immediate departure of Allan as Field Organiser of "Tell Scotland." He accepted a call to St George's Tron, Glasgow in September 1955, the very month that Phase III was due to begin. Without Allan at the helm, a lack of direction and simmering disunity that had been suppressed by the charisma of his leadership came to the surface: "The Crusade and Tom Allan's subsequent departure did leave the Movement 'hopelessly divided' not only at the level of the Executive Committee, but also throughout the country. Scotland did see 'the church fragmented' as never before."[121]

It transpired that it was a man of his almost unique caliber, and ability to transcend and ameliorate theological divides who was required to direct such an uneasy alliance at the national level. The unfortunate consequence

119. "Notes on Wiston Lodge Conference for 'Tell Scotland' Conveners, May 7–9 1958," 1, "Tell Scotland" Archive.

120. RGA, 1961, 255. The year afterwards MacTaggart resigned without direct replacement; Colin Day taking on the role of Field Organiser in conjunction with other tasks in the Movement.

121. Ibid., 13.

was that "none of those who succeeded him had his personal charisma, however hard they tried."[122]

That, however, can only be part of the story. Billy Graham arrived in Scotland at a period in its history when the ground for the transmission of the Gospel was more fertile than it ever had been, or perhaps ever will be. It was an era, as Highet wrote, when the "just 'not interested' form a minority among the unconnected."[123] In Callum Brown's words, in the mid-century period "a vibrant Christian identity remained central to British popular culture."[124]

Yet, despite the beneficial conditions, the Crusade and thereafter "Tell Scotland" were failures in terms of implementing the empowerment of the laity, the missionary church, or the conversion of the unconnected masses.

As the death of "Tell Scotland" became certain, competing theories emerged as to the cause:

> Inevitably, there were recriminations, especially from those who had bitterly opposed the coming of Billy Graham, and had seen the steady progress of "Tell Scotland" seemingly eclipsed by the apparatus of Mass Evangelism. But there were others who had shared in these shining years of advance, who with varying degrees of enthusiasm and doubt had embraced or at least accepted the 'All Scotland Crusade,' and who now wondered in their hearts whether it had not all been a terrible mistake.[125]

Why did Allan's visionary missiology set out in the heady early days of "Tell Scotland" ultimately fail to evangelize the nation after the Crusade? It would be easy to offer a one-line solution, of which the preferred candidate would be Graham himself, pointing to the chronological co-incidence of rapid institutional decline. Was an otherwise promising grassroots movement simply crushed under the weight of the Billy Graham juggernaut?

In weighing up the Crusade with the pre-1954 missiology that he and Allan had implemented, D. P. Thomson was later in no doubt which would have been the better course: "The putting of the same time and effort, and of even a fraction of the money spent, into parish and regional work of evangelism in which the local forces were being both trained and used at every stage, would have proved far more effective and fruitful in the long-run."[126]

---

122. Falconer, *Kilt*, 82.

123. Highet, "The Churches," 749.

124. Brown, *The Death of Christian Britain*, 169.

125. Bisset, *The Kirk and Her Scotland*, 12.

126. Thomson, *Dr Billy Graham*, 36.

Whilst this is a potent, partial explanation of the decline of "Tell Scotland," and rightly maintains a validation for the "pre-Graham" local, lay model, it is not fully coherent as an explanation for the failure of "Tell Scotland," nor is it wholly transferrable to the decline of the churches in Scotland more generally. The failure of both is somewhat more complex, involving an unfortunate co-incidence of intertwining factors, some peculiar to the Crusade and its after-effects and therefore attributable to the decisions of individuals, but others, perhaps more conclusively, centered on the surrounding ecclesial and social conditions in the country. Whether a diagnosis can be made after the *post mortem* that the decline was due to individual blame, or carried a degree of inevitability no matter what, may remain somewhat elusive. As Peter Bisset argues: "Whatever truth there was in the criticisms, and the proponents of Crusade Evangelism cannot ignore the simple evidence of the ski-slope of decline which immediately followed the Crusade, it is probable that blaming Billy is in itself an insufficient answer to the question of that went wrong during these critical years."[127]

As to the immediate effect after the Crusade in the mid to late fifties, three factors could be cited that were particular to the ""All Scotland Crusade" or the use at that point of "mass evangelism," as being contributory to the failure. They were the focus on the powerful personality of Billy Graham drowning the central significance of lay witness in the Scottish church mindset; the vacuity of some Crusade "conversions"; and the fragmentation afterwards of a loose ecumenical alliance of disparate strands of Christianity due to Graham and his methods.

There were, however, two longer-term and more deep seated factors of more general application, which served to undermine the efficacy of the initial "pre-Graham" model itself, and, perhaps irrespective of Graham's contribution, cast doubt on whether it stood any chance of significant long-term gain. One is missiological and the other sociological: inaction and reaction in the churches, and the onrush of secularization. In chapter 4, they shall be examined in greater depth, along with Allan's "reversion" to the mass evangelistic method, when assessing the struggles in Allan's time of implementing his missiology as a whole and its relevance today.

For now, it may be sufficient to emphasize one conclusion in relation to the longer-term picture. The Billy Graham Crusade may not of itself have been primarily responsible for the rapid decline of the Church of Scotland, but it did play a crucial part in destroying the potential of the "Tell Scotland" campaign, and with it the initial promise of the contextual re-orientation of

127. Bisset, *The Kirk and Her Scotland*, 13.

the church to the community, at what transpired to be a vital time for such a change immediately prior to major social ruptures in Scottish society.

It furthermore eradicated for generations the development that had begun of a conception of mission in Scotland based solely on local, lay witness and the organic growth of Christian community through dedicated cells.

Finally, the Crusade proved that mass evangelism, due to its inherent nature, is incapable of successfully acting as the inspiration and empowerment of the laity, whom in my view now hold the key to the future of mission.

In other words: (a) Tom Allan, in inviting Graham as the spark for lay empowerment, was profoundly and admirably motivated, but was wrong; and (b) mass evangelism as a means of mission in Scotland has had its day in missiological terms, even setting aside the vastly different social climate.

As regards the factors peculiar in the short term to the "All Scotland Crusade" of 1955, despite the astonishing scale of attendances and the concurrent volume of public impact, key questions were being voiced in the popular media even in the immediate aftermath. The editorial of the *Glasgow Herald* newspaper on 1 June 1955 asked:

> How much . . . of the new wave of religious disputation . . . has centred around the personality and methods of Mr Graham and how much around the larger verities? How many of the "decisions" were the result of a temporary emotional stimulus and themselves, accordingly, likely to prove impermanent?[128]

The first issue was the power of Graham's personality focus and professionalism. The message of the Crusade trampled on the ideas of local, organic growth, which simply got lost. There was an immediate identification of "mass evangelism" and Billy Graham with "Tell Scotland," due to the blaze of publicity and public awareness.

The concepts became blurred of gradual local empowerment of the laity, and the importance of ecumenical unity: "The central significance of lay witness, and the creative alliance between contending aspects of Christian witness appeared to have been destroyed by the high focus upon Crusade evangelism."[129]

As Allan's later Assistant Minister Bill Shannon puts it, "the 'do-it-yourself' evangelism of inarticulate church members was stopped in its

128. "World Council of Churches, IMC, Miscellaneous Papers," World Council of Churches Archives, Geneva, Box 26.19.10, File 10.

129. Bisset, "Kirk and Society," 57.

tracks by the slick professionalism of the Graham Organisation."[130] By comparison, the humdrum of everyday, local church life and their attempts at mission were cast in shadow, such that "for not an insignificant number of ministers, the Crusade was an elephant tramping heavily across their own gardens."[131]

The second factor was the potential vacuity of Crusade conversion. The churches may have started from a weak base, as it was clear in many cases that the nature of the "Graham buzz" for individuals was transient. The conclusion drawn after a passage of time was that the "conversion experience" induced might be so confused and paper-thin as to be not only meaningless but counter-productive. Those being brought in by the Crusade to ostensibly be at the forefront of Phase III mission were not up to the task.

That is the powerful message not of a cynical outsider, but again of the man at the very heart of post-war evangelism in Scotland. D. P. Thomson had received duplicate decision cards for all "enquirers" outside Glasgow. When visiting each area of Scotland, he went through every card with the local minister, to check on whether contact had been retained with each "enquirer" and concluded: "on the whole, the results were disquieting in the extreme. I ended the enquiry more convinced than ever of the dangers of 'mass evangelism.'"[132]

As to the Crusade itself, Thomson believed that many were misguided and unaware of what they were doing in answering Graham's call: "Afterwards in the counselling rooms it was sometimes only too obvious that many of those who had come forward just did not understand either what they were doing or why they did it. The results of this can be tragic."[133]

Thomson reported that a number of others later felt that they had been duped: "I had to live and work with some who had taken a step of this kind, and who bitterly resented it afterwards, believing that they had been forced into a false position under stress of mass emotion. I know what a heartbreak this has been to me and to so many of my clerical brethren."[134]

Even assuming their genuine enthusiasm, what expectation of church did the Crusade impose on new "converts"? The thrill of the spectacle of the mass event, and the brilliance of Graham's oratory simply could not be replicated on the hard pews of a Sunday morning. There was a naive assumption

130. Shannon, *Tom Allan*, 12.

131. Bardgett, *Scotland's Evangelist*, 310.

132. Thomson, *Dr Billy Graham*, 35.

133. Ibid., 18.

134. Ibid.

that someone drawn to Christianity by the "Kelvin Hall" experience would be equally drawn to the "damp church hall" experience.

Some embarked on a vain search for local "Billy Grahams,"[135] reproducing the "pernicious cult of the "popular preacher" so disparaged by Allan in *The Face of My Parish*.[136] Others departed the mainstream for evangelical groups "whose preaching and theology they found more in keeping with Graham . . ."[137] Most just fell back to disinterest or disillusionment.

The third factor specific to the Crusade was the fragmentation of a loose alliance. The "Tell Scotland" Movement was *de facto* distanced from the Crusade, perhaps because of the extent of division as expressed by Ralph Morton and George MacLeod of the Iona Community. It was agreed at the meeting of the Steering Panel on 9 September 1954 that the Movement would not be organizationally involved, nor mentioned in Graham campaign publicity.[138] As Graham's biographer John Pollock notes "the unity was . . . not as deep as it looked," often based on loyalty alone: "Those who would not have supported Graham but being committed to "Tell Scotland"were loyally behind a crusade of which they did not fully approve . . . deeper still lay a fundamental cleavage on the meaning of the Cross and the nature of the Gospel. The long term effect of the Crusade would depend on these hidden tensions being resolved."[139]

As long as Tom Allan remained in control and Graham's Crusade was successful, all factions might remain buoyed by a spirit of optimism and leave their differences aside. On the other hand, in the absence of either, when recriminations began the coalition was likely to collapse.

Allan had executed an apparent *volte face* in his views on mass evangelism and its ability to integrate with the concept of the "apostolate of the laity" in a parochial structure.

It was Allan's belief that one should seek personal conversion as a matter of decision and consent *before* considering the local, communal implications of the Gospel that inspired him to invite Graham, as a provider of the former only and not the latter. That belief led Allan to justify Graham's evasion of social and political issues whilst in Scotland. This crucial departure alienated MacLeod, and contributed to the demise of the Movement.

---

135. Pollock, *Billy Graham*, 199.

136. Allan, *The Face of My Parish*, 100.

137. Highet, *The Scottish Churches*, 106.

138. Small, *Growing Together*, 65.

139. Pollock, *Billy Graham*, 194.

Despite their unity of eventual purpose, "Allan versus MacLeod" became the battle of competing theological emphases, with Graham as the catalyst. Not only at a local level, but within the upper echelons of the "Tell Scotland" Movement, the Crusade created an irreparable rift. The decision to invite Graham thus "was a crucial decision, since it provoked opposition and criticism, and as one of the key factors in the eventual breakup of the shaky coalition."[140]

As his biographer Ron Ferguson explains, the bottom line was that MacLeod "was utterly opposed to mass evangelism, which he saw as a tempting, glamorous short-cut which would turn out to be a divisive diversion from the genuine congregational missionary task."[141]

MacLeod denounced what he saw as Graham's evasion of social issues, commenting that if he could not commit to a position, how could his converts be expected to do so? Graham had been asked about Senator McCarthy's "witch-hunts" in America and had replied "I have no views on that, my message is spiritual."[142] MacLeod criticized his fence-sitting as unbiblical: "If by 'spiritual' he refers to some ethereal controversy between man and his Maker which somehow continues independent of the historic process, then Graham may well have an interesting religious theory to present to men, but it is not the religion of Abraham, Isaac and Jacob."[143]

Thus MacLeod asserted that "anyone who escapes these issues through a hatch called the "spiritual" is not teaching Bible Christianity but nineteenth century pietistic escapism."[144] As the popular Christian writer Cecil Northcott had written of Graham at The Greater London Crusade of 1954: "What Graham omits from his evangel is the deadly corporateness of sin, and the infinitely intricate involvement of all of us in it . . . It calls for more than personal conversion, and more than a personal response."[145]

Yet it is clear that the confrontation which Graham induced had a profound effect on Graham's later ministry. From the vantage point of 1966, his biographer John Pollock wrote: "If Graham left his mark on Glasgow, Glasgow influenced Graham, and in no way more than his thinking about the social implications of the Gospel."[146]

---

140. Ferguson, *George MacLeod*, 270.

141. Ibid., 271.

142. Ibid., 273.

143. In *Ariel*, the Winchester College magazine, as quoted by Ferguson, ibid.

144. "Should Billy Graham Tell Scotland?" NLS Acc. 9084, MacLeod of Fuinary and Iona Community: Folder 254, "Tell Scotland" Campaign 1953–9."

145. "The Greater London Crusade: Harringay Not the Right Method for Today," World Council of Churches Archives, Geneva, Box 26.19.10, File 10.

146. Pollock, *Billy Graham*, 194.

Indeed, the criticism of MacLeod and others appears to have stung Graham almost immediately, and initiated a gradual departure from the fundamentalism with which he was associated, towards a more "expansive evangelicalism" incorporating social justice. This, in turn, found a place at the heart of Graham's vision, as its founder, of the international evangelical Lausanne Movement in 1974. With Lausanne, "Graham was creating an alternative not only to the WCC but to American fundamentalism and its missionary sensibilities."[147]

Much to the chagrin of his right-wing backers, two years after the All Scotland Crusade Graham accepted an invitation from liberal Protestants to conduct his New York City Crusade of 1957, at which Tom Allan spoke on parish evangelism. He invited Dr Martin Luther King to give the opening prayer, introducing him as the leader of "a great social revolution going on in America today."[148] Passing beyond his later dalliance with the politics of Richard Nixon, Graham went on speak out about global poverty, the arms race and in praise of Pope John Paul II.

Whilst his experiences in Scotland in 1955 may have been formative in changing Graham's direction, and thus have influenced the historical realignment of global evangelicalism towards a more purposive social agenda, it is unfortunate for Scotland's sake that Graham's position was not more fully formed when he was here.

## St George's Tron, 1955 to 1964

> The new minister, Reverend Tom Allan, was the first great man I ever met . . . an evangelising Christian socialist, he took the old church by the scruff of the neck . . . New people poured into the church from all over the city. Lives were started afresh.[149]
>
> —Bill Paterson, actor, 2008

Before Billy Graham had even arrived, Tom Allan had confided in D. P. Thomson in October 1954 that "he feels like giving up 'Tell Scotland.'"[150] He had first met with those at St George's Tron Parish Church, situated on Buchanan Street, Glasgow, in late February 1955, the month before the "All

147. Rice, "Cape Town 2010," 52.

148. Ibid.

149. Paterson, *Tales from the Back Green*, 94–95. He is the son of Allan's Session Clerk at St George's Tron, Jack Paterson.

150. Thomson, "The Diary of My Life," entries 19 May 1954 and 6 October 1954, by kind permission of Frank Bardgett.

Scotland Crusade" began.[151] Allan had felt bereft when distanced from his calling: preaching and parish mission. Allan preached as sole nominee of St George's Tron on 24 April 1955, prior to the end of the Crusade. He was inducted into the charge on 7 September 1955.

Allan exhibited in his eight-and-a-half years of city center ministry an unflagging dedication towards encouraging a core understanding of the missionary basis of Gospel and church, to be expressed in the preaching of the Word and the service of those in the parish community. It was here that Allan, more than any contemporary, was able to implement the "Tell Scotland" model of parish and mission; of absolute dedication to the people through self-giving, a living presence on the streets and a contextualized Gospel, with the laity of the church at the heart of it all. As he had envisaged, the re-vitalized institution came to life as the hub of a missionary parish of constant witness and service.

As far as worship and church membership were concerned, the effect on the dormant "preaching station" was dramatic. Speaking in New York in early 1957, Allan recalled how it had been intended to demolish the church prior to his arrival for a car park. Instead, eighteen months on, he informed them: "About 50 came to my first service. Last Sunday I preached to 800." In these days of heady optimism and opportunity, Allan told his audience in New York that he attributed this dramatic resurgence to, firstly, the fact that "our young people are responding to the tremendous adventure the church can offer," and, secondly, a yearning and desire for the Gospel in the social climate:

> What we are fighting against is partly the aftermath of the world
> wars' disillusion, the collapse of old conditions that people had
> supposed would last forever. Now there's hunger for something
> real. For the first time in history we are living in a one-dimen-
> sion world, a world of vast and unprecedented breadth but little
> or no height, a world where the divine dimension is no longer a
> reality. We want to bring back that dimension . . . I believe that
> here and in Scotland and other parts of the world a spiritual
> revolution is underway. People want it. That's what the world is
> hungry for.[152]

The internal activities of the church were re-vitalized with a rapidly growing congregation, a weekly congregational group meeting, house

151. AA.6.9, Diary.

152. "Youth Role Stressed by Minister, Scot Here Points Up Revival Need," by Sally MacDougall, Staff Writer, a cutting from a New York newspaper, possibly the *New York Times*, early 1957. Papers of Jessie Margaret Strathdee or Johnston, Box 31.

visitation, and business contacts. The activities of the church were summarized in the BBC Television programme on Allan's ministry, broadcast on 26 March 1961:

> Five years later, St George's Tron is a going concern. On a Sunday evening the church is near-full; on a Wednesday night, people meet in the church for bible study; on other week-nights, in various parts of the city, house groups meet to follow up their bible study and apply their findings to their own lives as laymen ... The church is no longer waning; it's got bulk, body and ... serious evangelical and social purpose.[153]

Allan initiated pre-work morning services with attendances of around three hundred people, and opened the doors of the church for the city to come in during the day. On Saturday nights, he went out with the youth group to speak and preach to those on city center streets that were full of revelers, and gave an open invitation to return to the church for prayers.[154]

Monthly evangelistic youth rallies were overflowing beyond capacity. The *Daily Express* reporter, one Magnus Magnusson, witnessed a rally held in March 1956, a mere seven months after Allan's induction. His report was written under the dramatic headline "3,300 Queue to hear a sermon: By the man who clears up after Billy Graham." Magnusson wrote: "He is doing it by a series of monthly Saturday evening rallies in the heart of Glasgow. Suddenly, since the New Year, attendance figures have bounced." In January 1956, he reported, there were 900 people, in February 1,600 people, "and on Saturday there were 3,300 of them—1,500 at St George's Tron and the rest listened to relayed broadcasts in two other churches."[155]

Externally, Allan undertook short-term Canadian Crusades in 1958 to Toronto and Calgary, in 1960 to Hamilton, Ontario and Winnipeg, and in 1961 to Halifax, Nova Scotia. Allan's Canadian rallies were in churches and large arenas, often backed by choirs and soloists, and delivered in like style to Graham. The scale of attendance was not dissimilar—the final rally in the Calgary Stampede Corral being before ten thousand people, with twelve thousand on the concluding evening in Halifax.[156]

As regards the church's relationship with Glasgow and its people, Allan set the tone for his congregation to engage in and replicate. He was driven

153. *Meeting Point in a City Centre*, Editing Script at AA6.7.1, DVD of broadcast at AA6.7.14.

154. *The Bulletin*, 15 November 1957, Papers of Jessie Margaret Strathdee or Johnston, Box 31.

155. Newspaper cutting in Papers of Jessie Margaret Strathdee or Johnston, Box 31.

156. MacDonald, ed., *A Fraction of His Image*, 20.

by a commitment to demonstrate that the church cared. A banner was raised outside announcing "The Church at the Heart of the City, with the City at its Heart." Allan wrote influential columns in the *Evening Times* and *Evening Citizen* newspapers from 1955 until 1963. One such article from 1959 encapsulates the strength of his social commitment and his perception of the responsibilities of ordinary Christians in his congregation:

> What is the need in Glasgow today? First, an informed and compassionate public opinion . . . We need to have our eyes opened to see the city with the eyes of Christ and our hearts broken with the kind of love which sent Him to Calvary . . .
>
> Second, we need a body of committed men and women in every Congregation who are prepared to put the teaching of Jesus into positive and concrete action, and tackle the social problems on their own doorstep with consecrated understanding and common sense.
>
> So long as there is a man without a chance in Glasgow or a girl looking for a home, none of us who call ourselves Christians can be at peace.[157]

The social responsibility of Christian witness and action would be paramount to his model of forming true Christian community. A committed Socialist in his politics, Allan had been invited to stand as an MP in 1946, and had considered doing so in preference to a life in ministry. His writing was highly critical of apartheid[158] and of racism in the workplace,[159] and supportive of the Civil Rights Movement in the USA.[160]

Allan thus vigorously defended the locus of the church to speak out on social issues: "it is not only a right. It is a clear, inescapable duty. If the Christian faith has nothing to do with the ordering of man's life in this world, then it has completely broken with its Founder."[161]

The impetus was theological—an all-embracing love of God for all people within the parish, no matter their social standing or religious belief, to be exercised by all those within the Christian community. He repeatedly emphasized the vital importance of Christianity as a "week-day religion," with the power of Christ becoming evident "as much at the bench or the desk as it does at the Communion Table."[162] In that light, he told the congregation

---

157. AA6.11.7, *EC*, 31 October 1959.
158. AA6.11.3, *EC*, 15 May 1960.
159. AA6.5.11, (iii), 10.
160. AA 6.11.7, *EC*, "The biggest social challenge facing the West," 15 June 1963.
161. AA6.11.1, *EC*, 14 May 1960.
162. AA6.11.8, *Evening Times*, 26 January 1957.

of St George's Tron of the expectations upon them as the laity of the church in mission and service:

> First, we're a parish church, with a God-given responsibility for every living soul in the parish 24 hours a day . . . it means the respectable and the dissolute, the rich and the poor, the good and the evil, the young and the old, Protestants, Roman Catholics, Muslims, Jews, Communists—there are no labels to define our responsibility. It is to all men all the time.
>
> Second, we are part of the church of Christ. This is what the church exists in the world to do. Its Gospel is not for some privileged handful of people. It is for the whole world. Its compassion is not limited to the lovely and the loveable. It extends to the unlovely and the lost. Only then can we be true to Christ.[163]

Allan had immediately recognized the need of the people on the streets directly outside his church building, situated as it was at a key junction geographically in the center of the city. Allan wrote to the congregation, "Round the coffee stalls, pubs and cafes of the city center where thousands spend their leisure, is centred one of the greatest social problems of Glasgow. Together with lay people, we are going to these coffee stalls trying to get alongside the broken, hopeless despairing wreckage of humanity with which we are challenged there."[164]

As Allan set out on many occasions in his weekly newspaper column, he initiated contact and in some cases an ongoing faith and church connection with alcoholics, prostitutes and criminals.[165] Allan talked in the newspapers about the connections made with those who would not normally attend church, those in city center at night and in the "model lodging-houses" for the homeless: "we've seen some pretty miraculous conversions here . . . We've had ex-convicts, ex-Borstal boys, street walkers . . ."[166]

The key for Allan was to inspire the congregation into outward action, by confronting them with life as it was lived on the church's doorstep. As member Angus MacDonald wrote in the parish newsletter in June 1964:

163. AA6.5.7, *EC*, "Rescue the Fallen," 1959, Article 1.

164. *News Review* of St George's Tron, June 1964, from Angus MacDonald, "A Wonderful Partnership," Papers of Jessie Margaret Strathdee or Johnston, Box 31, File 31, TD1800.

165. For example, AA6.5.2, *EC*, "The Black Abbot Finds God," and "Down-Town Parish," 30 August 1958.

166. Cutting from the *Evening Times* newspaper, Papers of Jessie Margaret Strathdee or Johnston, Box 31, File 31, TD1800.

> We saw the Glasgow that St George's Tron members cared for—
> the Clyde, the suspension bridge, the coffee stalls, the neon-lit
> dance halls, cinemas, bars and model-lodging houses, the
> prostitutes.[167]

The height of this experience was during the Central Glasgow Church-es Campaign of 1958, the last of D. P. Thomson's major campaigns and the final mission endeavor to have an association with "Tell Scotland." St George's Tron was the fulcrum of activities in conjunction with other city center churches, providing many of the volunteers and opening its doors to those on the streets around them. As Thomson noted in his diary for 18 April 1958:

> The feature of the Campaign was coffee-stall work which went
> on night after night and brought in a strange miscellaneous
> crowd of thieves, pickpockets, prostitutes, drunkards etc-the
> most moving and thought provoking sight and experience of
> any Campaign I have ever been on . . . the way the young people
> of St George's Tron gave up their sleep to that work among
> thieves, prostitutes and social outcasts I will never forget.[168]

Given what he was experiencing around him, Allan became in-creasingly outspoken on social issues, particularly the appalling housing conditions in Glasgow's Victorian slums, and the link between poverty, en-vironment and crime.[169] However, as Allan expressed on television in 1961: "After five years, we are only just at the very beginning of things. We need something more to do this work than we can ever give through the ordinary life of any congregation. We need a place open seven nights a week, day and night, where folk . . . can be nurtured, cared for and guided and sustained by the love of God's people."[170]

If a concrete example was needed of Tom Allan's missiology in action, and of a concept of a church within which the laity were spurred into service of the disadvantaged by the fire of their faith, then it was the vision which led to the opening of the "Rehabilitation Centre" in Elmbank Street, Glasgow.

---

167. *News Review* of St George's Tron, June 1964, from Angus MacDonald "A Won-derful Partnership," Papers of Jessie Margaret Strathdee or Johnston, Box 31, File 31, TD1800.

168. "Diary of My Life," 18 April 1958, quoted in Bardgett, *Scotland's Evangelist*, 333.

169. e.g. AA6.11.7, *EC*, 31 December 1964 and AA6.5.7, Article 4.

170. *Meeting Point in a City Centre*, Editing Script at AA6.7.1, DVD of broadcast at AA6.7.14.

He explained to the *Glasgow Herald* of 15 November, 1957 that St George's Tron had plans to raise £20,000 (around £460,000 in 2017) for its 150th Anniversary in the following year. Half of the money would go to the renovation of the church building, and the other half for the social project. The original idea had been to open their own coffee stall beside the church, later developing into the possibility of constructing a refuge within the church building, to be formed by cutting down the size of the sanctuary and incorporating residential accommodation.

Allan set out his plans to the congregation, expressing an aim "to provide a Community Centre—a place where those in need can find help for body, mind and spirit and where they can be brought to newness of life through the power of Jesus Christ."[171]

But how and where was it to come about? Allan gave a speech at the Social Service night of the General Assembly of the Church of Scotland in 1960. In the speech he said: "How are we to communicate the Gospel . . . ? It is through our compassionate caring for men so that the Kingdom of God is made manifest in terms which men can understand, and in which the Word of the Gospel becomes relevant. It is as we exhibit the love of Christ in action that men see beyond our works to the One in Whose Name we are caring."[172]

Lewis Cameron, secretary and director of the Social Service Committee of the Church of Scotland, was in the audience and was inspired. Cameron began conversations with Allan about how the central church could unite with the congregation of St George's Tron in setting up a place of refuge and renewal for those lost on the streets of Glasgow. As Cameron later recalled, Allan approached the prospect with typical vigor and zeal: "One day after one of our discussions, he exclaimed, 'Lewis, something must be done to help these people now and the church must do it'!"[173]

Cameron arranged for the Church of Scotland to donate the use of premises at 23 Elmbank Street, Glasgow. Elmbank Street would come to house a drop-in advisory service, and also short-term residential accommodation for homeless women. A further property at West Princes Street would house on a longer-term basis younger girls who had been on the streets, in an attempt to bring them back into mainstream society. The centers were partly funded and staffed by the congregation of St George's Tron, and by some of Allan's old parishioners from North Kelvinside.

---

171. Allan, *1808–1958: One Hundred and Fifty Years of Worship and Witness*, 1.
172. AA6.2.18, Speech on Social Service Night, General Assembly, 25 May 1960.
173. Cameron, *Opportunity My Ally*, 237.

At the time of the opening on 8 June 1962, Allan was in no doubt about the theological foundation and justification for the Rehabilitation Centre, describing it as a place for those on the streets to be offered "friendship, a hand to help, a heart to believe in them."[174]

He responded to a letter to a newspaper which had described such people as "irredeemable" and condemned the waste of money from the Centre. Allan pulled no punches in reply: "If most churchgoers regard tramps, drifters and prostitutes as irredeemable then either they should give up going to church or start reading their Bibles and begin to believe what they profess to believe by their church membership . . . Success or failure has nothing to do with it. It is a question of obedience to Jesus Christ, who gave Himself—as He said—not for the righteous, but for those who are sinners, and know it."[175]

It was a practical social work within an overt Christian framework. The Centre was open for twenty-four hours per day, seven days per week, carrying out advisory work through two staff social workers and providing accommodation. The main problem encountered at the Centre was alcoholism, and also what were described as "character disorders." Many were noted to be unemployed, from broken homes, some younger men were drug addicts, some with marital problems. In 1969, it was re-named "The Tom Allan Centre" in his memory, and continues to flourish to this day in his name as a Counselling Centre.

The inspiration of the laity of the church by its minister had sparked encounters with the people in the streets and workplaces of the parish, with the Gospel as the crux. As Allan's friend and former colleague, David Orrock, reflected in 1964: "The people of St George's Tron have fully shared their minister's vision. The ever-open door of their church, their daily morning services, their witness in the open air, and their work among alcoholics and others in need of moral and spiritual help, all this has helped to make this truly a parish church and has forged a firm bond between minister and people."[176]

Allan's dream expressed in North Kelvinside, in *The Face of My Parish*, and in the early stages of the "Tell Scotland" Movement, had come to fruition.

174. AA6.5.7, Article 5.

175. AA6.11.7, *EC*, 16 June 1962.

176. David Orrock, "Tom Allan Talks to David Orrock," *Rally*, April 1964, 18–20, 20, AA6.11.15.

## Allan on the International Stage:
## Towards a Global Theology of Evangelism

The foundation of the Ecumenical Institute at Bossey and the formation of the World Council of Churches at the Amsterdam conference of 1948 was the beginning of a decade of dynamic cross-denominational international co-operation, in which Tom Allan was to play his part. Allan was inspired by the concept of ecumenical unity in the exercise of mission and worked prominently on the world stage to seek a broad-based theology of evangelism.

Allan's ecumenism found different expressions. He hinted that an organic, Eucharistic unity was what he sought: "I take it that unity means—whatever else—that we can sit down at the Lord's Table together."[177] He was sympathetic to the practices of other denominations. His visit to Rome included a "private audience" with Pope John XXIII,[178] and he denounced anti-Catholicism in Glasgow: "it will not serve the cause of Christ in our time either to deny our differences or to foment intolerance and bigotry—wrong and baleful things whoever holds them. There is a need for charity from us all, and a reaffirmation of our firm belief in freedom of conscience."[179]

He was considerably moved by Orthodox worship when in Russia, expressing: "the amazing atmosphere of reality and power in worship, [which] was worship with a significance far beyond the conventional church-going with which we are so familiar in the west."[180]

Ultimately, however, Allan's ecumenism was focused in the same way as the rest of his theology: in the context of mission. In a speech to the London Missionary Society in 1956, he expressed it thus: "The scandal of our divisions is assuredly blocking the channel of divine blessing . . . it is a matter for thanksgiving that the churches of the world, through the ecumenical movement, are being drawn together in the bonds of a common faith. Paradoxically, it is in the work of mission that essential unity is discovered. Unity of purpose is vastly more important than organic unity."[181]

The publication of the "Bishops Report" to the General Assembly of the Church of Scotland in 1957 recommending forms of episcopacy, described by Ian Henderson in his trenchant criticism of the ecumenism of

---

177. AA6.11.6, *EC*, 26 June 1963.

178. AA6.4.4.

179. AA6.5.10, *EC*, 09 June 1962.

180. AA6.5.2, "An Orthodox Bishop."

181. AA6.2.18.

the period as "a classic of diplomatic ineptitude,"[182] created a furore. The result was that "during the years 1957 to 1959, the Ecumenicals plunged Scotland into a controversy so acrimonious as to give satisfaction only to those opposed to Christianity."[183]

In its very expression, Henderson believed that "for two years the Bishops report controversy dragged on, distracting the attention of the Church of Scotland from the vastly more important tasks of evangelizing and adapting its approach to meet the situation created by the post-war industrial society."[184] This self-inflicted in-fighting came at an inopportune time for the church, as it was otherwise seeking to empower some form of outward mission in the fulfilment of "Tell Scotland" and struggling to react appropriately to the first stirrings of secularization.

In the wake of the storm and its effect on the potency of the church in mission, the expression of Allan's views became retrenched. It emphasized that for him that institutional, or indeed Eucharistic unity, was not fundamental, and so the focus should not be the union of denominations, but their collaboration in mission.

He cautioned in 1959 that "unity is not something which we ourselves achieve. It is the gift of God." Therefore, "in the coming together of the churches our main preoccupation should not be with outward forms— theological patterns or ecclesiastical organization, but with our obedience to Jesus Christ."[185]

In 1960, looking forward to the next fifty years of the Christianity in Scotland, Allan identified, in my view presciently and correctly, the two major issues which would face the church: "To my mind there are two special concerns which are going to occupy us during the next half-century . . . the first is unity, and the second is mission."

In the run up to the third WCC Assembly at New Delhi in 1961, to which he was invited but did not attend, Allan wrote "we have to be reminded constantly that the unity of the churches is never merely an end in itself, but a step towards a more effective fulfilment of our mission in the world."[186] His conclusion was that: "I am for unity in diversity . . . I am against uniformity," which would be a "stumbling block to be resisted."[187]

182. Henderson, *Power Without Glory*, 117.

183. Ibid., 119.

184. Ibid., 120.

185. AA6.2.18.

186. AA6.11.5, *EC*, 9 September 1961.

187. AA6.11.5, *EC*, 30 September 1961.

He was, nevertheless, highly critical of evangelicals who refused to engage with the World Council of Churches, declaring somewhat optimistically at the dawn of the sixties that it had "not shown itself to be anti-conservative."[188] It was, however, at that very stage, that the international ecumenical movement had its own concerns to the fore about the channeling of mission and evangelism through the church, much to the growing chagrin of the conservatives.

Allan's brand of ecumenism of the fifties was very much reflective of the international focus then, of unity for evangelism through the church seeking the Lordship of Christ over the whole world. Considering the global background of ecumenical mission and evangelism at the time of the formation of the World Council of Churches in 1948, and looking backwards to the Edinburgh 1910 conference, in the words of Dietrich Werner: "one cannot deny the fact that ecumenism as such owes its very existence to the evangelical concern."[189] The focus of the Western effort remained inter-denominational co-operation for evangelisation, as the message of Amsterdam in 1948 stated: "the evident demand of God in this situation is that the whole church should set itself the total task of winning the whole world for Christ."[190]

Therefore, at the time of the formation of Allan's missiology, and its development during the fifties, his focus was in tune with that of global ecumenism from the formation of the WCC, which had "affirmed the tradition from which it comes, namely, the inseparable connection between church unity and church mission or evangelisation."[191]

Allan did not merely reflect WCC missiology of the fifties, he played a significant role in forming it. Allan was a key figure in the WCC Working Committee on Evangelism from 1953 until 1961, seeking to find common ground on the world stage to identify a "theology of evangelism" (the word then being used almost interchangeably for "mission").

Allan reported his initial connection to the North Kelvinside Kirk Session on 7 April 1953. He had been invited to attend the World Council of Churches in Geneva "to prepare a paper on Evangelism to be read at the Conference in Illinois, USA."[192]

He duly attended the "Conference of the Evanston Commissions" as part of the "Commission on Evangelism" in Geneva in August 1953.

188. AA6.4.1.

189. Werner, "Evangelism," 184.

190. Ibid., 185.

191. Ibid., 186.

192. North Kelvinside Parish Church, Kirk Session Minutes.

Following the conference, the General Secretary of the WCC, W. A. Visser 't Hooft, invited Allan by letter of 28 August 1953 to Evanston as a "consultant" to work on the main theme." Allan noted the "great privilege," but declined by letter of 14 January 1954 due to "the pressure of work this winter in my new post as Evangelist to the Home Board."[193]

Allan was supportive of the second congress of the World Council of Churches in Evanston, Illinois, 1954, with its lay focus. Evanston had been heavily influenced by the Willingen conference of the International Missionary Council in 1952, with its conclusions centered on the church under a *missio Dei* concept. Passages of the report from Evanston could have been written from Allan's pen, such as: "Evangelisation is no specialized, separate or interim enterprise of the church. Instead, it is a fundamental dimension of all actions of the church. All that the church does has a fundamental evangelistic function. With all its dimensions the church participates in the sending of Christ."[194]

Allan was quick to draw a link, writing an article entitled "Evanston and 'Tell Scotland'" for *Life and Work* magazine,[195] and highlighting that the Movement in Scotland was reflective of a global transformation of the church and laity by the Spirit.

With his involvement in the World Council of Churches, Allan's theological horizons and outlook were broadened, influencing further his open-mindedness in engagement with all missiological forms and views. He retained a close friendship with J. P. Benoit, director of evangelism for the Reformed Church of France, and was praiseworthy of diverse figures that he had encountered in the world church.

Allan's work for the Department of Evangelism of the WCC continued throughout the decade. He was part of the first full global discussion of a theology of evangelism at a meeting of the Working Committee at Davos, Switzerland, in 1955. From this meeting further discussions developed, culminating particularly in two large-scale consultations at the Ecumenical Institute at Bossey, Switzerland, in 1958 and 1960 in which Allan was a key player. Their contrasting content and outcomes are an illumination of the shifting patterns of global missiology on the meaning and purpose of mission, and consequent rifts between ecumenicals and evangelicals, that have characterised and sometimes plagued global Christianity from the sixties to the present.

---

193. "Correspondence (Allan, 1953–54)," World Council of Churches Archives, Geneva, Switzerland, Box 42.003, File 1.

194. World Council of Churches, *Evanston Report*, sec. II, para. IIff.

195. Allan, "Evanston and 'Tell Scotland,'" 195–96.

The major consultation at Bossey from 19 to 25 March 1958 involved over fifty renowned theologians and active ministers from every continent. The discussions resulted in a first draft of "A Theology of Evangelism," which was further revised after another gathering to which Allan contributed in Spittal, Austria in 1959. Following final approval by the WCC Central Committee, the work was published in November 1959 as *A Theological Reflection on the Work of Evangelism*.

Dietrich Werner describes this publication as "the first fundamental WCC study and theological statement on evangelism." Whilst bearing early elements of what Werner terms a para-church "messianic theology of evangelism" that would become common currency in the sixties, the fundamental concepts to which Allan contributed chime with his missiology as expressed in *The Face of My Parish*, and would not have been out of place within it: "The document contains the affirmation of the Lordship of Christ over the world, the definition of an all-encompassing shalom as the final goal of mission/evangelisation, the affirmation of the evangelistic responsibilities of all members of the church, and the need for constant church reform in order for it to fulfil its missionary obligation."[196]

In the document, the language of "personal decision" in the light of the presentation of the Gospel is present, much heard also in Allan's work, in the definition offered of "evangelism": "it is the decisive confrontation of men with the Gospel in Jesus Christ to the end that they may believe in Him and believing find salvation in His service."[197]

The *Reflection* further recognized that mission is contextual and culturally attuned, but the challenge was reserved for the church to identify and employ the means of mission appropriately in that light, thus: "in its work of evangelism, the church is summoned anew today—to understand what God is doing in these times through all the changes that are taking place in the ways and circumstances of human life, to penetrate into the significance of the new forms of association in which persons find their social satisfaction, to ask how the Gospel may be related to men in their several needs as they seek to come to terms with life."[198]

Thus the church remained the sole instrument and end of all mission or evangelism: "Every form of legitimate evangelism must finally lead the evangelised into the church. Evangelism is the outreach of the church

196. This quote and preceding: Werner, "Evangelism," 188.
197. World Council of Churches, "A Theological Reflection," 7.
198. Ibid., 6.

in order that the evangelised may in their turn become the part of that outreach."[199]

The further Consultation on the future of mission and evangelism at Bossey from 6 to 11 July 1960 was the highpoint of Tom Allan's work with the WCC. It serves as a vivid illustration of a key turning point in global mission, and the upcoming schisms in the world church. The remit was entitled "The Relation of Revival within the Church and the Communication of the Gospel to the Outsider." In the event, major stumbling blocks on the Gospel and the nature of mission prevented any coherent conclusions.

Allan chaired the consultation and gave its closing address. The title of his speech, namely "Our Task Together," was to prove somewhat ironic. It was once more a diverse spread of around fifty of the world's leading theologians and practitioners. In attendance at Bossey in July 1960 were such world mission luminaries as Billy Graham, Bill Webber (co-founder and leader of the East Harlem Protestant Parish), Johannes Hoekendijk (chief missiologist of sixties radicalism), D. T. Niles (long-time ecumenical leader), and Ted Wickham (founder of the Sheffield Industrial Mission).

In the discussions, the cleft between Billy Graham and most of the other main protagonists was readily apparent. Graham argued to those at the consultation that they lived within an "age of revolt, of fear and uncertainty, of immorality . . . of secularism, of communism." This created a "crisis" which "calls for a verdict." He demanded that a theology of evangelism should be centered on confronting people with their "dependence on God's forgiveness" where "repentance is essential."[200]

In response, two key figures in industrial mission were most vocal, Horst Symanowski and Ted Wickham. The latter criticized Graham to his face, arguing that "A mere statement of the mighty works of God is utterly incomprehensible to men among whom I work unless you go on to speak of the 'secular relevance of the Gospel'. Great masses of industrial workers have rejected [the] Gospel. And [the] gospel they rejected was precisely the gospel [Billy Graham] preaches."

In preference, Symanowski talked of a "ministry of reconciliation. [The] church community must serve the world . . . and in the world."[201]

In "Unity in Evangelism, Report of a Notable Consultation" for the WCC, most probably written by Allan, the nature of the division was set out as "two contrasting concepts of evangelism itself," being:

---

199. Ibid., 44.

200. "Papers-Verbatums of Sessions," Summary of Discussions by Bill Webber. World Council of Churches Archives, Geneva, Box 26.19.10, File 13.

201. Ibid.

On the one side there was the tradition of mass evangelism. On the other, there was the idea of a long-term missionary penetration of the world outside the church, discussed among us particularly in reference to the world of the industrial worker. These two concepts can be symbolized by reference to the discussion in the consultation between Billy Graham, exponent of mass evangelism in the revivalistic tradition, and Bishop E. R. Wickham of Manchester and Horst Symanowski of the Rhein-Main industrial area, known for their work of awakening the church to enter deeply into the industrial world.

Allan argued that at their heart the contrasting concepts reflected "varying interpretations of the Gospel itself," or "preaching of two different 'words' of God." He concluded that "the basic ecumenical problem lies at this decisive point."[202]

In that "basic ecumenical problem," the conference of July 1960 marks a watershed period in world missiology, with many of the key figures present, representing the nuances of missiology with which they were associated, and also the tensions of the gradual departure from the focus of the fifties on church, laity and Christ's Lordship. It was a moment where the "Christocentric Universalism" to which Allan subscribed was just about to pass over supremacy after the WCC assembly of 1961 to the notion of the "world setting the agenda" beyond the church, characterizing much of the direction of missiology in the sixties. The spectrum of those present at the conference can be broadly summarized thus in terms of "contextualization":

- Right-wing: Graham—Gospel and mission as personal salvation, forgiveness and reconciliation, then church, with an "accommodation" of culture only, and little recognition of indigenous conditions.

- Centre-right: Allan—mission through the church laity, a contextualized message and church towards a "missionary parish," social action following conversion, but by now also influenced by the "All Scotland Crusade" of 1955, leaning towards both Graham and Webber.

- Centre-left: Webber—the contextualization of church and liturgy one step beyond Allan by the physical relocation of church to the urban street in the East Harlem Protestant Parish, laity and clergy united together.

- Left-wing: Hoekendijk, Symanowski, and Wickham—mission beyond the moribund institutional church and the role of laity within it,

202. "Unity in Evangelism, Report of a Notable Consultation," World Council of Churches Archives, Geneva, Box 26.19.10, File 13.

humanization of the Gospel to a secular world, social and political action, as in the later ethos of the Gorbals Group Ministry.

The church in mission has been hidebound in mission over the last half century over the continuing battle between the polar opposites of the positions set out at each extreme above of Graham or Hoekendijk. It is perhaps time for an imaginative retrieval of the center. The conclusion of this book will reflect that the "centrists" of Allan and Webber may now, once more, hold the key.

The 1960 consultation at Bossey was held in preparation for the Third Assembly of the World Council of Churches in New Delhi in 1961, which marked "the first and . . . only time in the history of the ecumenical movement attention was focused on the role and particular relevance of the local congregation for the evangelistic task of the churches."[203] It, in turn, led to the worldwide consultation from 1961 to 1967 on the "Missionary Structures of the Congregation," which affirmed the *missio Dei* as the starting point, and urged that "the basic task of the 'church for others' is to participate in the sending by God of shalom into society."[204]

As Werner notes, reflecting the demise globally for support for Allan's focus on mission in WCC circles from 1961 onwards: "never since then has the shape of the local congregation been top of the WCC agenda again, despite the constant affirmation that the primary places for missionary and evangelistic witness are the different forms of local Christian communities."[205]

The report of a WCC staffer on the consultation of July 1960 called for a "*consolatio fratrum*," so that there might be "reconciliation of all kinds of approaches to evangelism."[206] That was to prove sadly impossible during the next two decades, although initially Allan became entrusted with the task. For the next eighteen months after the conference, Allan played the role of mediator between the two sides. Graham became increasingly vocal in his criticism of the WCC following the consultation, and indicated that he intended to call a world evangelism conference of evangelicals. Allan sought to broker a peace meeting between Graham and the International Missionary Council in Manchester, London or Glasgow in 1961, which did not come to pass.[207]

203. Werner, "Evangelism," 188–89.

204. Ibid., 189.

205. Ibid.

206. "EVANGELISM CONFERENCE, Bossey, July 6–11, 1960," World Council of Churches Archives, Geneva, Box 26.19.10, File 13.

207. See ibid., File 11, "Billy Graham Correspondence 1958–1961."

Allan then agreed to chair a further consultation at Bossey, which was set for mid-1962. He hoped that Graham would once more attend, along with Wickham, Hoekendijk and others, to re-visit the areas of dispute and thus address "very frankly one or two major questions about evangelism . . . on which there is cleavage and division," for example the "objective of mission."[208] Very unfortunately, Allan's ill health from late 1961 led to such plans not coming to fruition.

In many of the precepts of his missiology and ecclesiology, which he had collated and expressed contextually in Scotland without broad consultation, Allan pre-empted the concept of *missio Dei*. Whilst ahead of his time in expressing a practical outpouring of the *missio Dei*, his missiology chimed with the dominant "traditional" strand of ecumenist mission which was prevalent in global terms until its highpoint at the New Delhi Assembly of the WCC in 1961. Allan's theological concentration on Christology, salvation and atonement would place his theology, missiology and brand of ecumenism in a line with a more prominent figure in the WCC of the era, Lesslie Newbigin.

At the highpoint for the focus on the local congregation of 1953 to 1961 in global terms, Tom Allan was at the very center, contributing significantly on that stage. But for his ill-health from 1961 onwards, Allan may have been able to play a key role on the world stage in continuing to act as an intermediary between the World Council of Churches and leading evangelicals such as Billy Graham. In turn, his presence may have assisted in mediating the rift which led to the birth of the Lausanne Movement in 1974, and the traumatic division of world Reformed Christianity.

## Final Years, 1961–1965

Allan worked throughout his ministry with an unflagging intensity and dedication to a seemingly overwhelming breadth of commitments. As early as 1950, he was given medical advice to take "complete rest" and his Kirk Session in North Kelvinside was encouraging him to take longer holidays to recuperate.[209] A heart attack in December 1961 led to a year's absence. He later recalled the source of the resulting passion in his work on his return in 1962 to 1963:

> Once the initial danger was over, I had a tremendous sense of being set aside for a period of renewal. It was a great spiritual experience. I had the time for prayer and Bible reading I have

208. Ibid., File 12, "Billy Graham Correspondence 1961," letter from Tom Allan to Hans Jochen Margull of the IMC, dated 28 September 1961.

209. North Kelvinside Kirk Session Minutes, 8 January 1950.

often longed to have while I was immersed in the demands of the active ministry. It was a time of great blessing to me and lead to a deepening of my spiritual understanding.[210]

Allan flew out in December 1963 to address a Billy Graham conference in Miami, but had a further severe heart attack on the first day of arrival, convalescing for several months in Florida before his return. He demitted as a result from St George's Tron on 31 March 1964, to be editorial director of *The Christian* newspaper, run by the Billy Graham Organisation. His last sermon was preached on Palm Sunday, 20 March 1964, his words being transmitted from a tape recorder in the pulpit. Allan was awarded the St Mungo Medal and Prize by the City of Glasgow in December 1964, for the citizen who had done most good for the city in the past three years.

This time, Allan spoke instead of a "Gethsemane experience," in that "I cannot bear the thought of leaving my dear people."[211] He wrote to his Session Clerk of "the profound sorrow that was in my heart when I had to write the Presbytery requesting to demit my charge."[212] Removed from his calling, his friend David Orrock reflected that "four years of semi-invalidism chafed his spirit." Without preaching, Allan felt "his usefulness was at an end."[213]

Tom Allan died of heart failure at Victoria Infirmary, Glasgow, on 8 September 1965, aged 49.

## Conclusions

Allan's missiology in theory and through action at local, national and international levels was evangelical yet compassionate; theologically astute and mature yet contextualized and comprehensible; structured upon the church yet dedicated to the people; and above all dynamic, active and engaged outwith formal structures, in an absolute self-giving to all. The focus was upon the primacy of the ministry of the lay people of the church congregation, to be inspired and empowered by their faith and recurring missionary action. The mission of the church was urgent, visible and credible.

Allan described his mark of a true church as "its inclusive character, its capacity to unite within itself men and women of every type and background."[214] By including the weak and the vulnerable as an essential part of his ministry and as a fundamental focus of the church, the realiza-

---

210. Orrock, "Tom Allan Talks to David Orrock," 18–19.

211. Ibid., 18.

212. Letter 18 February 1964 from Allan to John Strathdee—Papers of Jessie Strathdee or Johnston, Box 31, TD1800.

213. AA6.11.7, *The Christian*, 17/09/65, 8.

214. Allan, *The Face of My Parish*, 46.

tion of the full breadth of the Gospel and to whom it spoke was grasped by his congregations and broader society.

The implementation of his missiology was affected, however, by the challenges within its terms, the choices made by Allan, and its interaction with the inherent struggles developing in society and the church from the late fifties onwards.

The following chapter considers Allan's missiology in greater depth, by examining its sources and inspirations as well as national and international context, before identifying in chapter 4 the key tensions that impacted upon Allan's ideas in practice and the effect of secularization.

# 3

# The Mission of Tom Allan:
# Context and Sources

## Introduction

H OW DID ALLAN'S IDEAS on mission come about, and to what social and theological circumstances did he react? In this chapter, the context of Allan's work is examined in Scottish post-war church and society, and then the personal and theological sources and inspirations which helped to shape Allan's missiology: being the formative personal influences, and the powerful effect upon Allan of European missiological writing and the international prominence of a theology of the laity in the fifties.

## Context

### Post-war Scottish Church and Society

#### *Legacy of the Pre-War Church*

Allan's work was motivated to redress the distance of Christianity from the struggles of everyday life. He began his ministry in a post-war church in Scotland which needed radical re-alignment in that context, in the wake of its pre-war record, and the social, economic and spiritual fallout from the destruction of war.

As Allan began his ministry in 1946, memories were fresh of the Church of Scotland's efforts at mission in the inter-war years, particularly following the Union with the United Free Church of 1929 and during the "hunger of the Thirties." As Stewart J. Brown summarizes that period for the church: "During the decade between the Union of 1929 and the outbreak of the Second World War in 1939, the church committed itself to fulfilling the hopes raised by the Union for national religion in Scotland. The church's social policy was dominated by the attempt to achieve the ideal of a Christian society in the midst of the economic stagnation and social hardships resulting from the world depression."[1]

In relation to social issues, there were two distinctly unpleasant legacies of the thirties from which Allan in his dedication to ecumenism and to the working class would distance himself. Firstly, there was the unworthy, racist campaign in the fifteen years from 1923 against Irish immigration and the Roman Catholic Church, under the goal of establishing a covenanted Protestant Scotland. It flowed from the infamous report to the General Assembly of that year on "Irish Immigration and the Education Act 1918," which called for the church to lead the nation to "take whatever steps necessary" to rid the country of the Irish Catholic "menace."[2] Secondly, rancor remained at the Church of Scotland's failure to take any political stance which was critical of the government or state economic planning, instead concentrating on the moral failings of the working classes.

As a result, the church of the inter-war years in the industrial heartlands of central Scotland had grown further distant during the Depression from a working class mostly already lost, and increasingly drawn to left-wing politics, as Ralph Morton commented in 1953:

> In the depression of the 30s came the final disillusionment . . .
> the failure of the church over unemployment . . . It was not so
> much that the church did nothing. It was that the church did not
> care. When the unemployed sent a deputation to the General
> Assembly they were not received . . . It may be that the Assem-
> bly was right in refusing to pass a resolution that could have
> achieved nothing. But its effect on the men was disastrous. The
> church was not concerned with them.[3]

Allan had thus inherited an inter-war ethos on political issues in the Church of Scotland, which "withdrew from its earlier commitment to intervention and social criticism and increasingly adopted a policy of non-interference."[4] It was an inter-war period where, in the determination

---

1. Brown, "Social Ideal of the Church," 14.

2. See Brown, "Presbyterians and Catholics," 255–81.

3. Quoted in the "Scotland" section, most probably written by Ralph Morton, within World Council of Churches, *Factual Survey in Evangelism: The Mission of the Church to Those Outside Her Life: A Factual and Interpretative Survey of Developments since 1948, First Draft*, Assembly Studies, August 1953, 58–66 at 59–60, WCC Archives, Geneva, 32.001.

4. MacDonald, *Whaur Extremes Meet*, 278.

of John White to rebuild a "parish state," to be subsumed by ecclesiastical authority and marked by exclusive Presbyterian hegemony, as T. M. Devine puts it: "social criticism was abandoned and instead the nation's ills were blamed once again on individual failings which could be cured only by controlling laziness, intemperance, gambling and sexual licence."[5]

It was a national church then, in Will Storrar's words, "dangerously out of tune not only with many social realities within Scottish society but also with some of the grace notes in its own Reformed tradition."[6]

By the end of the decade, John White's vision of a "Godly Commonwealth" had failed to materialize. Brown concludes that, "After 1937, it was becoming increasingly clear that the ideal of the Christian commonwealth of small, closely-knit parish communities under the spiritual and moral direction of the national church had failed to capture the imagination of the nation."[7]

Therefore, "by the end of the 1930s, it was clear that there was a need for a new Christian vision, a new social ideal,"[8] where dynamic figures such as Tom Allan and George MacLeod were to play a key role.

As the life and ministry of Tom Allan emphasized, the thrust for mission and a renewed interaction of church with society in the immediate post-war period was still of the church, and in the parish system, but its new focus would be upon the centrality of the role of the laity as the whole people of God, with their witness often broken down to small units or cells, and dedicated to setting the message to the lives of those around them.

Nevertheless, the fundamental assumption remained, as one contemporary commentator set out in 1948, that the parish system was still "put forward as the best, and indeed the only, plan which can be devised whereby the community as a whole can be evangelised, brought under Christian influences, and enabled through a common fellowship to share consciously in a finer and fuller quality of community life. The age-long method of the church has been emphatically re-affirmed."[9] The default model for ecclesiology and mission in the immediate post-war period thus remained, "a defined area and community, with the church in the midst as the spiritual power-house of the communal life."[10]

5. Devine, *The Scottish Nation 1700–2000*, 383.

6. Storrar, "Liberating the Kirk," 60.

7. Brown, "Social Ideal of the Church," 25.

8. Ibid., 26.

9. P. D. Thomson, *Parish and Parish Church*, 286–87.

10. Ibid., 288.

However, even if there was no major departure from the dependence upon the church as both agent and object of mission, within the church the pre-war notion of what might constitute "mission" stood in contrast to that of the post-war period. The pre-war position was of an inward-looking church, based on the assumption verging on complacency that true "mission" remained a foreign territorial excursion. One need turn no further for evidence than the title of the immediate post-Union "Forward Movement" manifesto, *Call to Church*, to realise that the "movement" envisaged was for ordinary people to retrace their steps back towards an institution which had little intention of self-adaptation, and not in the other direction. Those conclusions are supported when it is considered that within the book's contents there are three pages devoted to what is quaintly termed "The Home Field" from two hundred and seventy pages overall, and passing mention as a novelty of "a form of evangelism which has been tried out in recent years," being "Campaigns" or "Intensive Missions," described in a similar form to the "Mission of Friendship" utilized by George MacLeod in Govan. By way of contrast, *Call to Church* has some one hundred and twenty-nine pages devoted to foreign "missions" to the Jews, India, West Africa and China.

As a result, the presentation of the Gospel in "mission at home" in the pre-war period in Scotland had been broadly taken to be the task of "evangelism" though calls for personal repentance, as opposed to its practical outpouring which would follow conversion of "Christian service." Furthermore, its expression was taken to be mono-cultural and mono-theological. In other words, it was thought capable of being expressed in unitary form in any part of the country, as the Evangelist to the Home Board, D. P. Thomson, demonstrated. This attitude reflected a broad assumption that the nation was already Christianized, and that the totems, symbols and rituals of the Reformed church had become part of the national DNA, of which every citizen would be aware from schooldays onwards. Therefore, the "mission" of the home church was essentially one of revivalism i.e. the enticement of those lapsed, baptized Christians lurking at the outer edges of Christian society back into the fold of the redeemed community.

In keeping, the oral message transmitted was "top-down" culturally and theologically. It was generated internally from a taught and "correct" doctrinal core, and passed from the central institution outwards. It thus placed much reliance on an educated and trained clergy, emanating from divinity colleges and elevated by ordained ministry. Insofar as the proclaimed Gospel was "inculturated" at all, it reflected much of the culture of power, and was presumed to remain unaffected in the transmission to the street and pulpit. This was the yawning gap which George MacLeod sought to narrow in the early intentions of the Iona Community by equipping ministers in training to work in industrialized, urban parishes, and which Allan departed from by applying new European missiology to his context.

Developments prior to 1945 in attitudes to the "contextualization" of the Gospel in mission to culture and the rhythm of the land and the people, were largely expressed in the "foreign mission field."

Assumptions in the missionary field abroad at the height of Empire in the late nineteenth century on the enlightening of those living in darkness through cultural Christian values, lingered too in the attitude within the Scottish nation to home mission, in particular towards the urban poor. Working-class culture was often seen as satanic, riddled with self-imposed immorality due to defects in character, intellect, racial ethnicity, education and moral fiber. The transmission of Christianity could be equated with the imposition of decency and respectability. Thus mission to the urban poor might involve a "cleaning-up" operation, whereby those in degradation would be saved by adopting another culture, and embracing human progress, without any general amelioration of social conditions.[11] State intervention at a universal level to relieve poverty and suffering without a prior moral "means test," or evidence of self-improvement and godliness, was to be disparaged as worthless. Thus, Thomas Chalmers stated: "The remedy against the extension of pauperism does not lie in the liberalities of the rich; it lies in the hearts and habits of the poor. There is no possible help for them if they will not help themselves. It is to a rise and reformation in the habits of our peasantry that we look for deliverance, not to the impotent crudities of a speculative legislation."[12]

As the political commentator Iain Macwhirter has recently written, Chalmers's attitudes "were deeply ingrained in Scottish public life. This is very much how middle-class Scots thought in the nineteenth, and most of the twentieth century—and they were the only group that counted politically."[13]

Allan's work was thus a strong reaction to what had gone before at home, and, indeed, a reflection of what was being implemented in some quarters abroad. For Scottish missionaries and teachers in the "foreign

11. There are, of course, exceptions. On the activity of the Christian Socialist Movement in the period, see, for example, Bryant, *Possible Dreams: A Personal History of the British Christian Socialists*. The 1908 book *Social Problems and the Church's Duty* by David Watson, a minister in Glasgow's East End, is a remarkably insightful sociological and theological analysis of the plight of the working class, calling on the Church to side with labor against capital.

12 Thomas Chalmers, *On Political Economy*, as quoted by Macwhirter, *The Road to Referendum*, 102.

13. Ibid.

mission field," a stark realization had occurred of the necessity of concepts which would now be referred to as "contextualization" and "cross-cultural translation."

The later Deputy Leader of the Iona Community, Ralph Morton, returned from missionary work in China in 1937. He later reflected that overseas there were three principles on which mission was based: "the necessity of learning the language of the people," in the sense of "coming to an understanding of their ways of life and thought"; "helping to build up a pattern of corporate Christian living which was not confined to what went on in church buildings"; and, "political involvement" as "inescapably part of the Gospel."[14]

This tradition within the Scottish missionary endeavour was reflected later in the building of the intentional cross-cultural community at Allipur, India by friends of those in the Gorbals Group Ministry, George and Dorothy More,[15] and more broadly in the work of David Lyon, both in India at Nagpur and Allipur and later as General Secretary of the Church of Scotland Overseas Council from 1972 onwards.[16]

By 1978, Lyon could write that "when we speak of entering another's world in mission, we are speaking of an approach to mission, which affects every aspect of our life. We have to speak the language of those among whom we live—and that not just in the narrowly linguistic sense; we have to live at their tempo; be moved by the images and symbols that move them; and we have to rethink . . . our basic understandings, in response to their needs and insights."[17]

This is precisely the understanding that had occurred to Allan in the late forties, and shaped also the work of the Gorbals Group Ministry and the lay ecumenism of Ian Fraser at Scottish Churches House considered below.

On his return from China in 1937, in relation to his "three principles" Ralph Morton was struck that: "The church at home did not seem to recognise these principles at all . . . It seemed to think that all it had to do was recall people to religion and to preach morality . . . It was very interested in its own language and in the language of the past . . . It was not interested in the language that people outside were using."[18]

Morton contended that the reason for the church speaking in a "secret, archaic language" was that "it was not really concerned with the life that its

14. Morton, *Iona Community*, 10–11.

15. See More and More, *This Is Our Life in Central India*.

16. See Lyon, *In Pursuit of a Vision*.

17. Lyon, *How Foreign Is Mission?*, 60.

18. Morton, *The Iona Community*, 11.

members were living in the world . . . The life of the church was limited to activities that went on in church buildings and sometimes in the houses of members. But such activities were mainly confined to the promotion of ecclesiastical interests and the discussion of private duty." He concluded that "to a returned missionary this sounded not only strange but blasphemous."[19]

There was, thus, an increasing comprehension filtering from abroad to the home church: that the cross-cultural experience of foreign mission, its relationship to everyday life, the building of community and the social and political consequences of the Gospel, highlighted comparative deficiencies in the Scottish churches.

We can begin to recognise, in the work of Allan and beyond, the dawning of the realization that such concerns were not confined only to foreign mission climes, but required also the "translation" of the Gospel in Scotland from the clergy to those on the streets, and the organic growth of "indigenous" church structures, particularly in urban, industrialized areas.

What does discussion of the realization of "cross-cultural translation" and "contextualization" teach us now in the task of applying such concepts to mission within Scotland?

Ian Fraser underlined the answer in his 1969 book, *Let's Get Moving*, in the process identifying the distinction between the "revivalism" of the pre-war period and the work of such as Billy Graham, as against the true expanse of post-war "mission," echoing views which Allan would have shared: "It is becoming clear that the action of the missionary overseas who has to leave known territory for unknown, learn another language which is the language of the people to whom he ministers, and get under the skin of a different culture—applies as much in Scotland as anywhere else."[20]

For Fraser, this required the distinctive nature of modern-day "mission" to be recognised, rather than a reversion to old-fashioned "revivalism":

> Revivalism has to do with taking committed people as they are, pressing them towards greater conviction and commitment, and drawing others in so that the community grows on the edges, absorbing newcomers into much the same ethos.
>
> Mission, on the other hand, has to do with leaving safe territory, grappling to understand alien thought-forms, learning a language which communicates. Mission is now being recognised as being no longer a basically territorial activity. Even in territorial aspects the need is to make contact with people . . . in places which are not on church premises or where religious

19. Ibid., 11–12.

20. Fraser, *Let's Get Moving*, 60–61.

meetings are held. The need is seen to learn a language which communicates to contemporaries and to wrestle with their thought-forms so that it is possible for mind to meet mind because person meets person.[21]

The pertinence of this discussion is that the danger that the church in Scotland might be sliding backwards over recent decades in its appreciation of the nature of mission from the time of Allan and Fraser, so that it now stands perilously close to falling foul of the very condemnations that Morton wrote of in relation to the church of 1937. In other words, it faces the danger of relying not on "mission" in its true sense as set out by Fraser, but the narrow "revivalism" that he also describes. It may be that only by becoming alert once more to those issues that a path can be found towards a more robust response.

## Post-war Society and the Reaction of the Churches

Allan's work was carried out in a post-war period where Scottish Christianity had the drive and resources to rise to the challenge of contextualizing the church through the laity, and Scottish society was ready to hear the message.

There was a positive remnant of the communal civilian experience in the Second World War, together with an ideological aftershock, which had differed from the First. As Duncan Forrester has commented: "Paradoxically, the sufferings of the civilian population in the blitz seemed to create a new and hospitable sense of community. And, in comparison with the Great War, the issues at stake seemed to almost everyone to be crucial and clearcut—an impression which was strengthened as details of the Holocaust and of Hitler's apocalyptic strategy became generally known."[22]

The effect of World War II and the Cold War "revived a flagging sense of national identity," giving national churches a role in "rebuilding moral and spiritual foundations after the horrors of Nazism" and in the face of the threat of Communism. This was aligned with a "desire to return to "normal" after all the disruption, encouraging a social conservatism.[23]

The war had thus set the ground for a receptive mood in the population for a Scottish Christianity which might provide a coherent social ideal with a vision of new, fairer society.

---

21. Ibid.
22. Forrester, *Theology in the Shadow of War*.
23. MacLeod, *The Religious Crisis of the 1960s*, 45.

The path was open for a faith which sought to humbly build that new society from the wreckage, but not in fulfillment of a utopian ideal that might be drawn from a liberal theology endorsing the inevitable march of Christian progress. As Tom Allan told his audience in a 1953 lecture in North Carolina, in times of such naïve idealism "civilization" had created monsters: "Instead of Utopia, we got Belsen. Instead of Land of Heart's Desire, we got Buchenwald and the gas-chambers of Auschwitz. The release of atomic energy which could revolutionise life is reserved for its destruction."[24]

Meanwhile, within society the platform remained in place in terms of the church's locus to speak in public life. Christianity was entitled as the natural assumption of most people to hold a central and rightful place in public discourse in a "Christian country," creating a "willing ear," as the social historian Hugh MacLeod reflects: "In the 1940s and 1950s, it was still possible to think of western Europe and North America as 'Christendom', in the sense that there were close links between religious and secular elites, that most children were socialized into membership of a Christian society, and that the church had a large presence in fields such as education and welfare, and a major influence on law and morality."[25]

There was therefore an alliance of social circumstances which set the ground for a revival of Christianity, particularly for mission centred on the realities of the everyday lives of ordinary people, as post-war hope allied with Cold War fear attuned to a new desire of social togetherness and communal safety. Frank Bardgett suggests of D. P. Thomson's work that "the success of North Kelvinside and the other estate and suburban campaigns may have had less to do with the techniques employed and more with the desire of their post-war populations for the stability of belonging: at any rate to social as well as spiritual factors."[26]

In the west of Scotland, these broad influences were further enhanced by a time of economic uncertainty, with the gradual decline of heavy industry and the shift of economic power towards the United States. As Christopher Harvie states: "It was no secret that the root cause of the

24. AA6.2.13—Ashlin White Bible Lectures 1953, Mooresville, North Carolina— *Christian Witness in the Secular World, 1. The Failure of Human Resources*, 7–8.

25. MacLeod, *The Religious Crisis of the 1960s*, 31.

26. Bardgett, *Scotland's Evangelist*, 51. The experience in Scotland was echoed in America, where the years between about 1945 and 1960 were a time of a "religious revival," with "a notable turn to religion." The three main influences towards the American revival identified by Hugh MacLeod apply to Scotland too: "the fear of nuclear annihilation . . . a resulting decline in faith in progress, and a corresponding vogue for the Neo-Orthodox theologians," and "the impact of popular preachers like the evangelist Billy Graham," Hugh MacLeod, *The Religious Crisis of the 1960s*, 34–35.

nation's problems lay in its economic structure," with its "overdependence on heavy industry," which was accurately felt to "have a limited shelf-life."[27] The United Kingdom was bankrupt following the war, with food rationing in place until July 1954. The military war demand and Empire markets were waning. The Scottish economy was in a state of flux.

By the early fifties, it was clear that urban poverty and class divisions had persisted, despite the implementation of the Welfare State. Nevertheless, the arrival of the Welfare State and the nationalization of heavy industry created a new sense of equality within society, which could potentially have been reflected within church life: that the church might not be the preserve of the managerial class any more, and the attendance of the working class not imply collusion.

The first steps towards the re-alignment of the church had been taken in Scotland during the war. Ground-breaking reports were presented to the General Assembly by the Commission for the Interpretation of God's Will in the Present Crisis (1940–45), known as the "Baillie Commission,"[28] after its chairman, the eminent theologian John Baillie. The Commission had castigated a church that was "complacently accepting the amenities, and availing ourselves of the privileges, of a social order which happened to offer these things to ourselves while denying them to others . . . There can be no doubt that it is to the failure of Christians to realise and act upon these social implications of the Gospel that the present weakness of the spiritual life of our land must in no small part be attributed."[29]

Will Storrar argues that "the Baillie Commission saved the Church of Scotland from itself and for the Gospel."[30] From the dark days of the late thirties, its "genius was to liberate the Kirk from that false vision and to bring it intellectually and theologically into its own time."[31]

The Church of Scotland report *Into All the World* of 1946[32] identified that an urgent regeneration of mission was required in the vastly altered social and economic context:

> There are . . . special periods of social change and crisis when
> it becomes necessary for the church to review and reconsider

27. Harvie, *No Gods*, 203.

28. Centered upon "The Report on the Will of God for our Time," a report to the General Assembly of 1945, edited by John Baillie, and published as *God's Will for Church and Nation*.

29. As quoted at Cheyne, *Transforming of the Kirk*, 192.

30. Storrar, "Liberating the Kirk," 60.

31. Ibid.

32. Church of Scotland Committee on Evangelism, *Into all The World*, Preamble.

the whole task and technique of the evangelistic enterprise. We are living at present through such a period of transition . . . The changes in the social environment, outlook and manner of life of the people in this country are so vast that some of the older methods of religious work have been inevitably outmoded, while others call for careful adaptation to new conditions. The eternal gospel remains itself unchanged, but it requires to be proclaimed in a new idiom, and presented in new ways and in fresh channels.[33]

The move towards a new form of community and parish structure, focusing on the role of the laity, was championed from diverse areas of Scottish church life. The Iona Community was at the forefront. From Ralph Morton's perspective within the Iona Community, "It is the duty of Christians today to make experiments in co-operative social living which will point the way to this new living society."[34]

As early as 1944, Ralph Morton had expressed that "we have to be prepared to scrap much that is dear and familiar in our life and worship for the sake of building up into a new and living fellowship for those who do not speak our language."[35] In his pamphlet of 1954 for the World Council of Churches entitled *Evangelism in Scotland*,[36] Morton declared Scotland no more to be a Christian country and advocated a fresh approach to home mission centred on the basics of the faith as related to modern, industrial life. In keeping with the Iona Community approach to mission, he commended that the connection with the lives of ordinary people must be made through the efforts of local congregation, not the clergy or special evangelist at a mass meeting. Rallies and campaigns were widely asserted to be of a departed era, as they failed to relate to the needs of the man in the street. As Morton had written in 1944: "the old evangelism is past . . . We know that already."[37]

Donald Baillie contributed an article to *The Coracle* in 1951, where he set out his view that the days of the visiting evangelist were over, to be replaced by the Iona model of "parish missions," by which: "The congregation itself should be the evangelising agent in its parish. That is what it is

---

33. *Into All the World: A Statement of Evangelism*, Foreword, 9. Falconer suggests that "in some ways, "Into All the World" provided a blueprint for the widespread efforts in evangelism which were to follow immediately on the cessation of World War II"—*Message, Media, Mission*, 84.

34. Morton, *Household of Faith*, 104.

35. Morton, *Missionary Principles*, 11.

36. Morton, *Evangelism in Scotland*.

37. Morton, *Missionary Principles*, 10.

there for-to be its own missioner . . . to be an active witness to Christ in its own bit of the world."[38]

Other notable figures drew similar conclusions to Allan, Morton and Baillie on the identity of those within the congregation who would be called. As one of four pamphlets under the grouping of *The New Evangelism*, Nevile Davidson wrote of *The Parish Church* in 1947 that "it is . . . valuable to have special 'cells' or groups of men and women within a congregation who feel themselves specially called to the work of evangelism."[39]

The sense of "winning" the remaining un-churched was palpable and the goal seemingly within grasp. Those leading the immediate post-war society, in both nation and church, had emerged from wartime service with a mentality which was attuned to organization, discipline, unflagging effort, and campaigns of large-scale endeavor. That mentality was to become allied to an ecclesiastical superstructure which was still of a scale that was capable of exuding power and confidence to significant effect.

There was reason for optimism that the result of evangelistic endeavour would be significant increases in Christian adherence, given the vast human and financial resources which the churches could call upon. Despite a drop in comparison with a pre-war peak of 1926, the figures for communicant membership in the largest denomination, the Church of Scotland, were still buoyant and rising, at 1.26 million in 1946.[40] In 1950 to 1951, the total communicant membership of the Scottish Christian churches was estimated at 2,016,400 (58 per cent of the population), and with the addition of regular attendees who were not members, the affiliation as estimated at 70 per cent of the whole country.[41] As Highet concluded in 1950, even with the doubts and worries, there remained a "church-minded nation."[42]

Set against a needy and receptive social backdrop, caught in the heady optimism of the times, and driven by inspirational figures such as Allan, Thomson and MacLeod, the churches responded on a dramatic scale, manifested in the audacious goals of "Tell Scotland." Highet could justifiably reflect in 1960: "The period since the end of the Second World War has seen evangelistic activities on a scale which in extent and variety must surely be unprecedented in the history of the Scottish churches. That very fact,

38. Baillie, "The Place of the Iona Community," 10.

39. Davidson, *The Parish Church*, 7.

40. The figures for the preceding decades in the Church of Scotland had indicated the following: 1901—1,163,594; 1911—1,219,587; 1921—1,277,634; 1926—1,298,355; 1931—1,280,620; 1941—1,268,839; 1945—1,259,927; 1946—1,261,646; Highet, *The Churches in Scotland Today*, 72.

41. Morton, World Council of Churches, *Factual Survey in Evangelism*, 58.

42. Highet, *The Churches in Scotland Today*, 79.

indeed, may well be thought to be the outstanding feature of Scottish church life in the mid-twentieth century."[43]

# Sources

## Personal Influences

What drove Allan towards the style of ministry and mission that he adopted in his early years in ministry in North Kelvinside?

Before Tom Allan entered parish ministry in 1946, there had been three formative influences upon his life and faith which would form a background to his later work—encounters and friendships with two individuals, and a life-changing "conversion" experience during the war. His evangelical, christologically-focused theology also increasingly mapped his direction.

### Upbringing in Pre-War Protestant Working Class Scotland and the Influence of William Fitch

Thomas Allan was born on 16 August 1916 into humble circumstances in the mill town of Newmilns, Ayrshire, as the youngest of eight children of the local butcher. He grew up in a location and within a working-class Presbyterian tradition which emphasized the centrality of family, community, personal faith, and biblical commitment and integrity: "we were brought up . . . to honour and cherish the . . . Christian faith from our earliest childhood."[44] Allan described his mother as "a saint . . . a great student of the Bible and a great woman of prayer," and his father, who like him died at a young age, as an "ordinary, conventional churchman with an extremely high sense of principle."[45]

There were three Reformed churches in Newmilns, his family attending the United Free Church on King Street, where his father was deacon, later to be named Loudon East after the reunion with the Church of Scotland in 1929.[46] Allan's interest in matters spiritual appears to have been patchy at an early age, later describing how he would count the panes of stained glass during the sermon![47] However, a crucial influence upon Allan's

---

43. Highet, *The Scottish Churches*, 70.

44. Allan, *Why I Believe*, 4.

45. Ibid.

46. See Girvan, "Religion in Newmilns," in *Historical Aspects of Newmilns*, 86–96.

47. Allan, *Why I Believe*, 4.

later ministry and theology was ordained and inducted there on 25 March 1936, whilst Allan was a Glasgow University student studying English, and intending a life in teaching: "A new minister arrived at Loudon East church in Newmilns—William Fitch, . . . Under his influence, Tom Allan got a vision of a new kind of adventurous Christian life–something unorthodox."[48]

The two men became lifelong friends and colleagues, Fitch later writing of the "indelible impression" that Allan had made at their first meeting at Fitch's ordination in March 1936: "His innate friendliness was tonic and uplifting . . . there was an instant rapport and on my part at least an assurance that God had given me a friend in my new congregation who would be a constant inspiration and source of strength."[49]

The parallels between Fitch and Allan are clear in their social background, upbringing and early church experience—it is plain why Allan was inspired by finding a similar young man of equal intellectual ability engaged in an energetic ministry. Bill Fitch was only around six years Allan's senior. He was one of six children within a poor working-class family from the Falkirk area, three of whom became Church of Scotland ministers.[50]

Fitch was a man of active personality, and an engaging communicator of no mean intellect. According to a family friend, Allan's later Professor at Trinity College Glasgow, Prof. J. G. Riddell, "told Bill's parents that he was the outstanding student of his time."[51] Fitch attained his PhD whilst at Newmilns, with a thesis on Søren Kierkegaard.

At his heart, Fitch "was a strong character of deep evangelical persuasion."[52] Fitch, like Allan, was thus a youthful, dynamic, driven, intellectually astute, working-class Protestant from a small Scottish industrial town, and from a background of a large family raised on discipline, determination and Godly dedication.

It was under Fitch that Allan was first to engage in mission, as Fitch later recalled: "he shared eagerly in the work of the seaside missions of the Church of Scotland. In 1938, he and I shared in the leadership of the mission at Millport—the first of a long series of evangelistic missions he was to lead in many different parts of the world."[53]

48. Leaflet for Allan's 1958 Calgary Mission, AA6.4.1

49. MacDonald, ed., *A Fraction of His Image*, 1.

50. The others comprised two doctors and one teacher (who married a minister!).

51. From a letter by Rev. Donald J. B. McAlister to David and Mary Stay, within personal papers relating to William Fitch held by Rev. Prof. A. T. B. MacGowan.

52. Ibid.

53. MacDonald, ed., *A Fraction of His Image*, 1–2.

Fitch's influence persuaded Allan away from a career as an English teacher and led him to apply for ministry in the Church of Scotland. Allan was admitted for training at Trinity College, Glasgow in 1938, following graduation with a First Class MA degree in English Language and Literature.

Fitch's theology throughout his ministry was a conservative evangelicalism of systematic biblical exposition, emphasizing personal decision, salvation and atonement.[54] He moved from Newmilns to Springburn Hill Parish Church, Glasgow on 27 January 1944, where his student assistants in the late forties included later prominent conservative evangelicals William Still, James Philip and George Philip. Fitch further inspired church member Eric Alexander into ministry. Alexander followed directly in Allan's footsteps as minister at Loudon East, Newmilns (1962 to 1977) and at St George's Tron, Glasgow (1977 to 1997).[55]

Fitch was heavily influenced by the preaching at his church on 6 April 1946 under the banner of "Youth for Christ" of a young American named Billy Graham. As Graham's song leader Stratton Shufelt recalled, Graham "gave an invitation, an unheard of thing in Scotland. In two or three minutes, sixty two people had come forward . . . Billy said the preacher (Fitch) came to him with tears in his eyes and threw his arms around him in a big hug. It was, he said, the best thing that had happened in his church in years."[56]

The influence of Fitch's support for Graham from that day forward was to have a pivotal effect on Allan's ministry, informing Allan's justification for the adaptation of his missiology in a seeming *volte face* in 1954 to 1955 to adhere once more to mass evangelism. In the wake of the "All Scotland Crusade" in 1955, when Allan sought to name those within the Church of Scotland who had, unlike himself, always remained convinced of such methods, he included Fitch amongst them.[57]

At the invitation of the "Tell Scotland" Committee, chaired by Allan, Fitch became the secretary of the Executive Committee for the Billy Graham "All Scotland Crusade" in 1955.[58] Before the Kirk Session at Springburn Hill on 19 September 1954, Fitch was in no doubt of the veracity of the decision

54. See, for example, the terms of one of Fitch's many books, *Enter into Life*.

55. See *Free Church Monthly Record*, "The Record Meets Eric Alexander," 6.

56. Wheaton College, Illinois, Billy Graham Crusades Collection 224: J Stratton Shufelt, 224.1.16.

57. Allan, ed.,*Crusade in Scotland*, 122.

58. Fitch's secretary during the Crusade was one of Allan's members from North Kelvinside, Betsy Shannon, who later married Allan's assistant minister at St George's Tron, Bill Shannon.

to invite Graham, stating it to his Kirk Session to be "obviously evangelism under the 'hand of God.'"[59]

After the Crusade, Fitch left Springburn for Knox Presbyterian Church in Toronto, where his ministry continued until 1972. Fitch died in Toronto in 1984, aged 73. Whilst in Canada, he wrote a successful series of popular books of evangelical theology and sponsored Allan's Canadian Crusades.

As of 1955, Fitch was in no doubt of the power and force of his theology and re-discovered zeal for conservative evangelicalism and biblical fundamentalism: "The witness of Springburn Hill is recognised all over Scotland as an Evangelical Witness. This is not by accident. I believe that we have been guided to this point at this time and that the testimony that has been raised is of God."[60]

In seeking explanations for Allan's reversion to mass evangelism with the invitation to Billy Graham, here is a partial answer—the influence of close friend and confidant, and his preaching of conservative theology which called for a "decision for Christ."

The formative influence of Fitch upon Allan was a key to Allan's theology, in Allan's developing enthusiasm for Billy Graham after early misgivings, in Allan's re-tuning of his views in 1954 to 1955 on mass evangelism, and in the continuing focus of Allan's parish ministry, all of which would in turn have a profound effect on national mission in Scotland in 1955 and beyond.

Fitch's final service at Springburn Hill before he left for Canada was held immediately before the Crusade on the evening of 20 March 1955. The service was a live radio broadcast, led by Fitch, where Tom Allan preached and Billy Graham was present, addressing the congregation after the broadcast. With their now similar theological outlook and shared belief in the power of the mass rally, the triumvirate that night within the small church in North Glasgow were about to re-direct the whole course of mission in Scotland from the following day.

### Allan's Conversion Experience at Reims

In the middle of ministry training at Trinity College, Glasgow, at the age of twenty-three in 1940, Allan volunteered for the RAF where he served

---

59. Notes of Kirk Session Minutes of Springburn Hill Parish Church, within the William Fitch papers.

60 All quotes from the *Springburn Hill Parish Supplement*, March 1955 (No 133), within the William Fitch papers.

until the war's conclusion.[61] From the disappointment of being refused pilot training due to his eyesight, within two years Allan rose to the rank of Flight Lieutenant working in Military Intelligence, latterly under General Eisenhower at the Supreme Headquarters Allied Expeditionary Force in France. During the war, Allan married Jean Dunn from his home town of Newmilns in 1941, and they went on to have three children: Maggie, Tom and Kenneth.

Whilst serving in France in the last months of the war, Allan was profoundly influenced in the future course of his life and ministry by events at a church service in Reims on Easter Day, 1945. Allan recalled that after departing from home and university, "within a few months" of entering the RAF, "there were certain pressures there in the Air Force which simply led me to a state of agnosticism . . . of moral breakdown, of unbelief, of disillusionment." The result was that "the kind of moral restraints, which I had been taught to honour all my life were gone." Allan began to believe that there was "nothing left to live for." He was taken, "much against my will," to the church service.[62]

Allan later wrote: "I owe my life and my Christian faith to . . . an unknown Negro G.I." When he sang 'Were You There When They Crucified My Lord,' Allan recalled that "God spoke to me, revealed the hollowness of my own life, in that moment of vision I understood what the death of Christ meant, knew that I <u>had</u> been there, that these hands had helped to nail him to the tree. Knew, too, that in spite of this his dying prayer, 'Father forgive . . .' was prayed for me: and that in the forgiveness of God alone can a man find rest for his soul." The experience "beyond any shadow of a doubt was the turning point of my life . . . this was my conversion."[63]

In this dramatic Damascene moment that he had experienced, can be seen too the seeds of his later willingness to accept and adopt "preaching for a decision" in his own ministry and missiology, and to endorse Graham's "altar call" as one to which he could relate, of itself being capable of bringing a person to a formative Christian experience.

## Trinity College

Allan was further influenced by his studies in theology and ministry at Trinity College, Glasgow from 1938 to 1940 and 1945 to 1946. When introducing an extract of the work of his Professor of Practical Theology, A. J. Gossip,

61. Allan served in the RAF from 15 August 1940 to 29 October 1945.
62. Allan, *Why I Believe*, 5–6.
63. Ibid.

to his congregation, Allan described him as "one of my most-loved teachers, and I could never say how much I owe to his teaching."[64]

He was further drawn by the lectures in Systematic Theology of Professor J. Gervase Riddell, who was to remain closely involved in Allan's ministry at North Kelvinside. Riddell's summary in 1937 of the doctrine of the Church of Scotland provides an insight as to how Allan would have been taught on matters of ecclesiology and missiology at Trinity, and in the role and prominence of the laity in mission: "The church is a missionary church . . . Mission work does not arise from any arrogance in the Christian church; mission is its cause and its life . . . The desire to win others for Christ—too often dormant in the 'average church member'—must be revived and given new opportunity. What we call the priesthood of all believers should be a living part of our faith . . . every Christian is to be an envoy for Christ."[65]

It was in his star pupil of 1946, the winner of the New Testament prize, that Riddell's aspirations for a missional church of all believers was attempted on a local and national scale. Already in his University work as a student, Allan's future thoughts on the interaction of church, ministry, laity and society were reaching crystallization. In his essay for Gossip's Practical Theology class of 1945 to 1946, Allan concluded:

> The purpose of God has been unmistakeably revealed—in the Community of the Redeemed in the goal of history. The mission of the church in the world then becomes clear. She is not only the goal of the historical process; she is the instrument by which history must be redeemed. She is the sole possessor of the absolute truth regarding the nature of man and alone holds the key to his full development as a child of God. She is the sole possessor of absolute truth regarding the nature of society and alone holds the key to its full redemption into the Kingdom of God.[66]

### Influence of D. P. Thomson

From 1934 until his retirement in 1966, David Patrick ("D. P.") Thomson worked as an Evangelist for the Church of Scotland in roles organizing Seaside Missions and latterly from 1949 onwards as Special Evangelist to the Home Board. He was an inspiring and dominating evangelical. From 1946

64. *The Congregational News Review*, North Kelvinside Parish Church, 1.12 (November 1950) 6.

65. Riddell, *What We Believe*, 23.

66. AA6.6, "The Importance of the Minister to the Community," 10.

to 1958, he pioneered the use of "visitation evangelism" in a series of high profile "campaigns" throughout Scotland, by utilizing teams from outwith the local area, often derived from student groups and "seaside missioners."

Allan had begun to develop his close relationship with D. P. Thomson whilst a student at Trinity College. He was one of the first to arrive at Thomson's student training course in evangelism in January 1946.[67] In March 1946, Allan was a member of the student team who undertook Thomson's initial post-war mission campaign in the Presbytery of Melrose.[68]

Allan was a leader of Thomson's summer Seaside Missions in 1946 to 1948 and ran the missions as a whole in 1949, as well as being involved in a mission to Bellshill, Lanarkshire in 1947 which attracted as Thomson's assistant a young Bill Shannon, later Allan's assistant minister. Allan further led the congregational aspects of Thomson's "Glasgow Commando Campaign" of 1950. As we have seen, Thomson was crucial to the initial decision to carry out a visitation survey in Allan's parish of North Kelvinside, setting Allan on the path he was to take.

Thomson shared with Allan a background in the United Free Church prior to the reunion with the established Kirk in 1929, being inducted as minister to Gillespie United Free Church, Dunfermline in February 1928. The United Free Church in the twenties had advocated a policy of "Active Evangelism," espousing area survey, visitation and open air meetings in conjunction with other churches, which would in turn renew the church's life.

Thomson confirmed in Allan the necessity of that outward-looking United Free Church missional focus which he knew from his childhood, just as both Allan and Thomson were to face throughout their ministries the reticence and opposition of those within the "Auld Kirk" to the idea of home mission.

Despite their differences, in particular during "Tell Scotland" and in Thomson's later opposition to Allan's support for mass evangelism, Allan retained a deep bond loyalty and respect, writing of Thomson in *The Face of My Parish*: "I do not know any man who has given himself so unsparingly to the work of the Kingdom . . . Hundreds of people throughout Scotland to-day owe their Christian faith to his ministry. Scores of ministers, like myself, have looked to him for guidance and inspiration."[69]

67. Bardgett, *Scotland's Evangelist*, 24.
68. See Doyle, "I Remember Tom Allan," 25.
69. Allan, *The Face of My Parish*, 17.

In Thomson and Fitch, Allan saw the zeal and missionary drive that was to mark his own ministry, with their "dedication, [which] caught my imagination . . . I felt that they were doing a work of tremendous importance."[70]

Thus we see key aspects of Allan's missiology emerging from his early formative influences: from Riddell and Gossip the centrality of the ordinary, lay person in mission, but the crucial role of the church, to be later developed by his encounter with the European missiology of the late forties; but also from Fitch, Thomson and Reims a belief in a dynamic, missional evangelicalism which would call for decision and commitment, and a willingness to endorse methods far beyond the local and ordinary. It was those apparent tensions, developed from his early formative influences, which would mark Allan's later ministry as he found it increasingly difficult to reconcile them.

## Allan's Underpinning Theology

Allan described himself as a "Calvinist and an evangelist."[71] His evangelical theology was christological. It emphasized the need for repentance. For Allan the desire to repent was the fundamental human approach to a God who required "the sacrifice of a broken heart and a contrite spirit." Before the cross, we make "the only cry which God is waiting to hear "God be merciful to me—a sinner."[72]

Substitutory atonement was the key to our understanding of Christ's purpose: "We have rebelled against the law. Christ dies in our stead and takes the curse of the law upon Himself . . . By our sins we are estranged from God . . . Christ, in dying, pays the penalty which man cannot pay."[73]

Justification was by faith alone: "No human righteousness; no amount of morality, however lofty and self-sacrificing, no works of service, however striking and impressive will bring a man into the Kingdom of God. The Reformed church believes . . . that we are saved by faith in Jesus Christ as God and Saviour."[74]

Allan's approach was essentially Barthian in its concentration of the penal nature of a Cross both "for us" and "against us." As in the work of P.T. Forsyth, whom he often quoted, Allan's theology was of the primacy

70. Allan, *Why I Believe*, 5.

71. AA6.5.6, Speech to Evangelism Conference, "The Structure of Church Life," 2.

72. AA6.2.3, Sermons on Matthew, Communion, 10 May 1959.

73. AA6.3.6, "The Atonement," Sermon, 07 February 1959.

74. AA6.2.3, Sermons on Matthew, 26 August 1956.

of the Cross as a restoration of righteousness out of the moral and spiritual degradation that he had witnessed and experienced in war.

From his church background, the influence of Thomson and Fitch, and his conversion experience of 1945, Allan's theology was thus resolutely evangelical. However, unusual for his time, it was set apart by, firstly, being united with a strong passion for social transformation and, secondly, a determination to bypass theological categorizations in the name of bringing the Gospel in word and deed to ordinary people in mission.

As much as such assessments are always broad generalizations, how can Allan's theology be categorized in its time?

David Bebbington identifies a "centrist school" of evangelicalism being the "prevailing stance in the Church of Scotland" in the immediate aftermath of World War II, a group identified by their efforts to minimize any cleft between liberal and conservatives in the name of Protestant unity and common mission.[75] Allan and Thomson are seen by Bebbington as being prime examples of such a school in Scotland, ignoring as they did theological divides in the cause of evangelism.

Alternatively, A. C. Cheyne would place Allan within a variant of that stable, being a "Liberal Evangelicalism," which in his view "probably continued to be the most important single strand in ecclesiastical life (and worship) right down into the nineteen-fifties."[76]

Particularly in his later ministry as a reaction to a developing youth counter-culture, secularization and a widening split in the church, Allan was to depart from that "liberal" or "centrist" inheritance more towards aligning himself with a "conservative" evangelicalism. Indeed, when considering a "new reluctance to sound the notes characteristic of Evangelicalism since Robertson Smith" in the mid-century, Cheyne concluded that "the most striking example of this was the increasingly conservative emphasis of Tom Allan's memorable ministries."[77]

By 1963, in reaction to the growing social upheaval around him, Allan had begun to speak of a "hunger for positive and authoritative bible teaching," and for the first time described himself as a "conservative evangelical," which he defined thus: "I stand by certain great fundamentals—the deity of Christ, the substitutory atonement, the physical resurrection of Christ, the personal return of our Lord . . . [the virgin birth] . . . and the authority of the Word of God."[78]

75. Bebbington, *Evangelicalism in Modern Britain*, 251.

76. Cheyne, *The Transforming of the* Kirk, 195.

77. Ibid., 198.

78. *The Observer*, 15 March 1962, magazine of United Church of Canada, interview

It is, however, difficult to restrict Allan to a particular categorization, when one considers his admirable dedication to social justice, and his considerable commitment to international ecumenism with the World Council of Churches. Like his mentor, D. P. Thomson, Allan distanced himself from cliques and theological camps. Just as he admired George MacLeod but would not have joined the Iona Community, he did not belong to the coterie of conservative evangelicals under William Still later to meet in 1970 as the "Crieff Fraternal." Ultimately, the labels were immaterial for Allan, as he refused to be pigeon-holed in a way that would inhibit the proclamation of the Gospel message: "He was determined to hold the middle ground . . . and turn neither to the right nor to the left in the direction of extreme positions. But without a doubt the focal point for him was primacy of evangelism."[79]

## European Influences on Allan's Missiology— Godin and *La France, Pays de Mission?*

Acutely aware of the need to communicate to those in his working-class parish from whom he felt distanced by his theological education, social standing and his very attire, Allan found a vital resource from international developments of contextual mission amongst the rank and file of society.

To his mix of personal and national influences, Allan added a broad reading of new European missiology that was mainly translated into English in the period from 1947 to 1949. The ideas Allan wrote of in 1953 in *The Face of My Parish* were not identified conveniently for publication. As Will Storrar comments, *The Face of My Parish* demonstrated that "Allan was deeply read in the kind of European theology which fostered such a trinitarian and yet also socially contextualized approach."[80]

In 1946 to 1953, Allan was swiftly applying his reading to the local context: "The North Kelvinside parish visitors that Allan trained went on to discover for themselves what Bonhoeffer and Ellul and Michonneau affirmed, that God was already at work in the lives of local people."[81]

During his ministry in North Kelvinside, Allan set out his interpretation of these influences in a speech to a "Retreat" entitled "The Congregational Group: Its Significance and Its Task,"[82] demonstrating in its course his broad knowledge and contextual grasp of contemporary developments in

---

by Kenneth Bagnell, 23, AA6.4.1

79. Shannon, *Tom Allan*, 30.

80. Storrar, "A Tale of Two Paradigms: Mission in Scotland from 1946," 63.

81. Ibid.

82. Speech given c.1950/51. His handwritten verbatim notes are at AA6.5.6.

mission and European theology. He had taken his admiration of the work of Emil Brunner from his mentor at Trinity College, Professor J.G. Riddell. In an exciting, vital exposition in the speech, he demonstrated that he had grasped also the impact for Scotland of Bonhoeffer, Ellul, Michonneau, Perrin, and Godin and Daniel.

Allan was acutely aware in the late forties of the air of crisis that was apparent throughout Europe, with a consequent urgency of the laity to express themselves in immediate mission and discipleship, distant from an overbearing reliance on the clergy.

In the "Retreat" speech, Allan identified strongly with the alienation of the pastor from the people by quoting Dillard's passage from *The Priest and the Proletariat*: "What was I to do, what was I to say to them? I felt that I was a stranger to them—that I belonged to another culture. My Latin, my liturgy, my theology, my prayers, my priestly duties—all cut me off form them and made me a being apart."[83]

Allan looked towards "two main pioneering experiments claiming the attention of the church today." Firstly, Allan set out in his "Retreat" speech how he was inspired by what he called "the greatest rediscovery in our church's life today—the apostolate of the laity,"[84] considered in greater depth later in this chapter. Allan recognised this resurgence in lay "vocational groups" that had sprung up since the war in different Christian denominations across Europe. He related that "the truth is being rediscovered in every country in the world, by both the Roman Catholic and the Protestant Communions. The Protestant Professional Associations in France, the Evangelical Academies in Germany, the Tor Movement in Greece—all are concerned with the Apostolate of the Laity, and what it involves in practice."

Inspiration was to be drawn, secondly, from "the courageous efforts which many priests and ministers of the church have been making—particularly in Europe and in the mission field—to get alongside the worker in his own environment and against his own background," which had led to a "new understanding of problems of the common life."[85]

Allan was referring in part to the "worker-priest movement" in Germany and France, whereby mission was embodied by clergy through working in factories and mines.[86] Flourishing until 1954 when it was suffocated by the Vatican, and led by the work of Cardinal Suhard and

---

83. Ibid.

84. Ibid.

85. Ibid.

86. See Perrin, *Priest-Workman in Germany*; and Harvey, *Bridging the Gap*, 86–91.

Henri Perrin, it fundamentally challenged the relevance and capability of the parish structure in the urban context.[87]

However, his main influence was the French priests Henri Godin and Yvan Daniel, with the former setting out their work in *La France, Pays de Mission?*,[88] supplemented by Georges Michonneau who did likewise in *Revolution in a City Parish*. Allan was also well versed in first translations of Dietrich Bonhoeffer's *Cost of Discipleship* and Jacques Ellul's *The Presence of the Kingdom*, the latter being referred to in depth within *The Face of My Parish*.[89]

Allan later described reading Godin's book as "one of the turning points of my ministry."[90] He wrote of reading *La France, Pays de Mission?* for the first time in the late forties:

> It came as a profound personal challenge to me to read of the absolute devotion and painful self-sacrifice which priests like Godin and Daniel were making to bring the message of their church to the unchurched masses of proletarian Paris. Many of the experiments in mission with which I have been associated since then owe a great deal to the insights and passion of these French priests who agonised over the lost millions of France.[91]

If we consider the terms of the book, the like foundation of Allan's missiology is clear. Indeed, although some of its language and cultural presumptions are of its age, the book reads in many ways as a precursor to much that is commonly recognised in a present-day consideration of missiology, in that Godin:

- Began with the assertion that "France is a Missionary Country."[92]

- Focused on the building of Christian community: "what must never be forgotten is that the missionary apostolate lies not in creating individual Christians . . . rather it consists in creating Christian communities:

87. Also embodied by the UK's first consciously oriented "worker-priest," Ian Fraser, in the Tullis Russell paper mill in Markinch, Fife, from 1942 to 1944—see chapter 5. For a fuller discussion of the worker-priest movement in Europe, e.g., Oscar L. Arnal, *Priests in Working-Class Blue* and, in the UK, Mantle, *Britain's First Worker-Priests*, 53–92.

88. Godin and Daniel (1943), English edition published in 1949 as Part II of *France Pagan? The Mission of Abbé Godin*.

89. Published in the UK in 1948 and 1951 respectively, with Michonneau published in 1948.

90. AA6.5.11 (vi), "Europe—A Mission Field?" for *The Christian*.

91. AA6.5.11.

92. Godin and Daniel, "France a Missionary Land?" 65.

every human community should be a Christian community, existent
or in the making."[93]

- Proceeded to identify the cross-cultural imperative and the need for an
  indigenous church: "A missionary must never Frenchify a Chinaman,
  he must not Europeanise him as a step towards converting him. He
  must build a Chinese church . . ."[94]

- Recognised that the place for mission is in all facets of the everyday
  life of the ordinary person, as "each individual belongs simultaneously
  to several milieux," as in "work, neighbourhood and leisure activities."
  He supported "winning over the real milieux that are to be met with
  naturally," rather than "a conquest by artificial means: taking Christians out of their natural environment to place them in another."[95]

- Identified that there was "a Christian community radically divided
  from the pagan community on which it should normally be acting."[96]
  Godin's answer, like Allan, was a form of congregational group,
  by which we must "seek out in the community Christians with a
  missionary vocation."[97] This group would form "fully native missions,"
  and seek to divest the message of the Gospel from the trappings of
  the culture from which they have come: "our religion must be religion
  pure and simple, stripped bare of all the human adjuncts, rich though
  these may be, which involve a different civilisation."[98]

- Insisted that the institutional church in present form was a hindrance:
  "Christ's doctrine does not frighten the poor . . . what puts them off
  and discourages them is our mass of little rules of human prudence,
  our cases of conscience elaborated in other epochs, suited to another
  age."[99] Thus, "the presentation of doctrine must be re-thought with
  the utmost care."[100]

- Echoed the *rayonnement* considered by Allan in *The Face of My
  Parish*, seeking the goal of "a Christian nucleus" in "all the existent

---

93. Ibid., 73.
94. Ibid., 74.
95. Ibid., 76–77.
96. Ibid., 89.
97. Ibid., 92.
98. Ibid., 128.
99. Ibid., 132.
100. Ibid., 146.

human communities," such that it "will itself become a light-bearing community."[101]

- Sought the meeting of Gospel and culture with "Christian action everywhere corresponding with life as it is being lived, moulded upon its shapes, built up with a missionary outlook, made to a missionary design."[102]

- Set out that the task of the clergy was to help the laity to meet the twofold task of the layman "to bring his share of good into the society" and "to contribute to the life of God in his brethren."[103]

- Identified social and political work as essential, as it is "temporal well-being which facilitates the spiritual development."[104]

- As Allan lived out in his life, believed it to be essential in order to seek to express Christianity with the poor in word and service that "all who undertake it must offer themselves in utter self-abandonment."[105]

The echoes of Godin in the practical ministry and missiology of Tom Allan are undoubted. Allan continued to write throughout his life of the importance of his influence. For example, in 1961, he wrote from Paris that:

> Men like Godin challenged all the churches around Europe to
> look seriously at the indifference and secularism around them,
> and inspired many pioneer experiments in evangelism all over
> the world.[106]

Beyond Godin, for the focus and goal of mission within the parish context, Allan drew also on the trinitarianism of Henri Perrin, who had written: "we had greater need than ever of the Christian Community. We knew ourselves that it was stronger than anything else, for it was modelled on the community of love in the Trinity."[107]

This quest for the formation of a true Christian community is much emphasized in *The Face of My Parish*, with Allan seeing the stress upon it given by Jacques Ellul as an "indispensable factor" in "bridging this wholly

101. Ibid., 178.
102. Ibid., 183.
103. Ibid., 187.
104. Ibid., 189.
105. Ibid., 133.
106. AA6.11.5, *EC*, 26 August 1961.
107  AA6.5.6, "Retreat" speech.

artificial gulf between personal faith and the demand for Christian social action."[108]

The goal from his "parochial evangelism" would be a "missionary parish" which could live out the words of Georges Michonneau: "If . . . we strip off the routine and turn boldly to new forms of the apostolate, the parish becomes a living cell, destined to propagate itself over an entire district."[109]

The foundation of Allan's missiology from *The Face of My Parish* was likewise based. The result was an exposition of the theology and missiological experience that Allan read, and the immediate contextualization of that theology, much of it newly translated, by Allan as a hard-working, young minster to his working-class parish in North Kelvinside.

## The International Prominence of the Laity

Allan's focus on the laity was part of an international re-discovery which he influenced in his work with the World Council of Churches, and which also inspired Allan in his early years and re-enforced his views as his ministry progressed.

If we were considering issues of mission and contextuality say fifty years ago, the present outlook in relation to the position of the laity in church and mission, and the sense of optimism for the direction in the future, would have been radically different. The immediate postwar period was a crucible in which a radical re-alignment of laity to church, clergy and world was begun internationally, if not finished.

As David Bosch describes the shift in the major institutions: "It dawned upon the churches, both Catholic and Protestant, that the traditional monolithic models of church office no longer matched realities. The theological *aggiornomento* in both main Western confessions discovered again that apostolicity was an attribute of the entire church and that the ordained ministry could be understood only as existing within the community of faith."[110]

There were two avenues in which the role of the church laity was considered in both Protestant and Roman Catholic traditions after World War II. The first was to emphasize the pivotal place of the laity in the engagement of the *missionary task of the church* within the world under the *missio Dei*. This was a particular emphasis in the ecumenical climate in the immediate post-war period in the early years of the World Council of Churches from

108. Allan, *The Face of My Parish*, 62.
109. Quoted in Allan, *The Face of My Parish*, 67.
110. Bosch, *Transforming Mission*, 471.

its formation in 1948, reaching its highpoint in the period from the second World Assembly at Evanston in 1954 until the years immediately following the third World Assembly at New Delhi in 1961. It was an emphasis, as we have seen, upon which Tom Allan centred during that period, and which was later emphasized by the Roman Catholic church following "Vatican II."

The second avenue was intertwined, in considering the *relationship of laity to clergy* and to internal institutional structures of the church, raising issues of power and authority, both in questions of scriptural interpretation and church governance. It thus envisaged the radical overhaul of the church, reflecting the second strand of Allan's missiology.

Writing in 1961, Hendrik Kraemer, the first director of the Ecumenical Institute of the World Council of Churches at Bossey and author of the influential *A Theology of the Laity*, said: "Never in church history, since its initial period, has the role and responsibility of the laity in the church and world been a matter of so basic, systematic, comprehensive and intensive discussion in the total *oikoumene* as today."[111]

At ground level in the two decades after World War II, the laity of the Western churches were energized into co-operative dialogue, inter-communication and action as never before. This awakening realization of the importance of the laity in the future of Christianity in the West was borne from the desperations of the Second World War, and the attitude that ordinary church people must play a key role in the direction of the future. The focus was to combat the extremes of totalitarianism and war, but also in recognition that the answers to the integration of Christianity to society could not lie solely within the domain of the ordained clergy, but must take as its starting point the everyday existence of those who formed the body. In a lesson appropriate for today, it was further a broadening of the provenance of Christ beyond the church into the detail of "secular" life. As the WCC General Secretary, W. A. Visser 't Hooft expressed to the Commissions in preparation for the Second WCC Assembly in Evanston in 1954:

> One reason why the churches have not helped the laity to see the Christian significance of their vocation in the world is that the churches had lost sight of the cosmic dimension of the Gospel. This could only lead to self-centred ecclesiasticism or pietism. When we realise again that Christ is the hope of the world, we see also that activity in the world is meaningful . . . At a time when—because of the collapse of the doctrine of progress—there is a great danger that all human effort is poisoned

---

111. Hendrik Kraemer, *Wending* (December 1961), 541, quoted in Weber, "The Rediscovery of the Laity in the Ecumenical Movement," 377.

by a sense of futility, the church has the great opportunity of re-creating a sense of the meaningfulness and worthwhileness of secular vocations.[112]

The confidence placed in this re-focus was absolute: that the emancipation of the laity would lead to purposeful and exciting directions in mission in the realities of life in the world; that it would re-cast ecclesial structures such that the face of the church would now reflect more confidently those within and outwith; that a re-shaping of the liturgy would occur towards the everyday concerns of the street; that the denominational barriers would be broken down in common mission enterprise if not confessionally too; and that an unfettered flow of faith and action for justice and peace would result between church and world through their virtual integration.

Writing in 1963 close to the decline of focus on the role of the laity, Hans-Ruedi Weber assigned the rediscovery to several factors.[113] The first was theological in the enlightening process of placing mission with the context of the *missio Dei* from Willingen onwards, as previously discussed. He summarized the remaining factors in this way, as indelibly linked to the future of the church and its position in post-war society:

> The rediscovery also stems partly our new world situation: the breakdown of the *corpus Christianum*; the processes of industrialization and secularization which tend to edge the church out of daily life into a religious ghetto; the fact that the church is becoming almost everywhere a minority which has great difficulty in communicating with the modern world. Wherever these new insights about the nature and the task of the church and these challenges of the modern world are taken seriously . . . the question of the role of the laity immediately becomes prominent.[114]

This reads also like a reflection of the present day, in times when the church laity are no longer triumphed so resoundingly.

Immediately after the war, there arose lay centers across Europe which sought to meet that challenge, some as gathering places and training centers, others as occupational organizations. The booklet drawn up for the Department of the Laity of the WCC in 1957 entitled *Signs of Renewal: The Life of the Lay Institute in Europe,* sets out the remarkable extent to

112. Visser 't Hooft, "Notes on the Relevance of the Main Theme for the Sections," 16 July 1954, World Council of Churches Archive, Geneva, Box 32.006, File 4.

113. Weber, "The Rediscovery of the Laity in the Ecumenical Movement."

114. Ibid., 378.

which such bodies had developed over the previous decade.[115] When its companion volume, *Centres of Renewal*, was published in 1964, the number of lay training centers and evangelical academies for the laity in Europe had risen from fifty to eighty-five (including the recently formed Scottish Churches House, Dunblane and St Ninian's Training Centre, Crieff), and a prime focus of the book was upon the fifty to sixty that had arisen in Asia, Africa, North America and Latin America.

The concern to reflect the resurgence in lay centrality was then reflected on the world stage, when the laity became one of the six key subjects at Evanston.

Section VI of the Evanston Report made the importance explicit in relation to the "battles of faith" in the ordinary places of the world: "Very often it is said that the church should "go into these spheres"; but the fact is, that the church *is* already in these spheres in the persons of its laity."[116]

Therefore, "It is the laity who draw together work and worship; it is they who bridge the gulf between the church and the world and it is they who manifest in word and action the Lordship of Christ . . . This, and not some new order or organization, is the ministry of the laity."[117]

As we have seen in Scotland, the excitement surrounding Evanston around the Western churches was considerable, and its impetus in relation to the laity had a direct impact on the work of the Scottish church in the years immediately following.

Furthermore, its development and enthusiasm amongst the young was intertwined in the United Kingdom with the heyday of the ecumenical Student Christian Movement. In this key period of its operation, the ideals of the SCM filtered back through its membership into church structures, invigorating them for change and unification, and influenced church leaders and politicians on the world stage in their attitudes towards the political landscape: "For those who experienced it, the decade of the 1950s represents the golden age of the SCM . . . Those were heady days."[118]

So what was the "theology of the laity" then expressed? Weber wrote in 1963 of the four central facets:

i. "the nature and task of the laity is no more defined by comparing them with a special group within the church—the ordained clergy, the theologian, the professional church worker—but by a new appreciation of the church in the world," thus the church as the whole people of God;

115. *Signs of Renewal: The Life of the Lay Institute in Europe*, 57.

116. "The Laity: The Christian in His Vocation," *Evanston Report*, 160–70.

117. Ibid.

118. Boyd, *The Witness of the Student Christian Movement*, 60.

ii. That "the laity shares in Christ's ministry to the world" not only in worship and church activities, but "when it is scattered abroad in every department of life";

iii. That each baptized person has received *charismata* from God, and thus "the task of ordained ministers can no more be to enlist the laity for preconceived and set church activities, but to help the charismatic laity to grow fully into its charismatic ministries" both in the church, at home and at work; and

iv. "to be a Christian in and for the world means self-offering . . . the aim of this mission is not to "churchify the world but to witness to Christ . . . True lay movements look beyond the world of the churches and draw them into the movement of God's love for the world."

He presciently finished his article by stating that the ecumenical movement "loses its true self, however, as soon as it no longer shows these four marks of a genuine lay movement."[119]

On the level of missiological theory, principal marking points of international consideration of the work of the laity, prior to the rapid development of the "humanization" agenda outwith the church in exercise of the *missio Dei*, were the work of the Roman Catholic theologian Yves Congar in his book published in English in 1957 as *Lay People in the Church: A Study for a Theology of the Laity*; and from a Protestant perspective, that of the first Director of the Ecumenical Institute at Bossey, Hendrik Kraemer, in *A Theology of the Laity* of 1958, taken from intended Gunning Lectures at New College, Edinburgh.

In the immediate wake of the Second Vatican Council and prior to the upheaval in Protestant mission theology caused at the fourth WCC Assembly in Uppsala in 1968, a late high point in the ecumenical and interactive theological consideration of the laity was the "Ecumenical Consultation" in September 1965 at Gazzada, Italy, jointly sponsored by the Permanent Committee for International Congresses of the Lay Apostolate of the Roman Catholic Church and the Department of the Laity of the World Council of Churches. Its co-chairman for the WCC was none other than one of our Scottish protagonists, Ian Fraser, then of Scottish Churches House. The proceedings were later published as *Laity Formation*, containing a Joint Statement and Resolution.

Before the demise of the focus on the role of the laity in mission in Protestant circles from the later sixties onwards, the Joint Statement serves as a concise exposition of the aims and elements of "laity formation," equally

119. Weber, "The Rediscovery of the Laity in the Ecumenical Movement," 391.

apposite to the present. Having noted the context of secularization, social upheaval, and the "crisis of belief," the Statement sets out:

> Laity Formation must equip a Christian to understand his faith and his worship as related to social, cultural and economic structures, and not just in terms of personal piety. Laity Formation aims not only at the training of the individual layman, but also at the development and radical renewal of the Christian community for its worship of God and its service to the world. The Christian must bring all his joys and sorrows, all his compromises and flatness and doubts into his liturgical life.[120]

Within the volume considering the work of the Gazzada consultation, one can appreciate the depth of application towards a theology of the role and work of the church laity that had been invested up to 1965. The spirit of that excitement is evident in Allan's work and those of his contemporaries, in Scotland and beyond.

And yet in ecumenical Protestant circles, speaking in 1993, the General Secretary of the World Council of Churches, Konrad Raiser, could then introduce his speech on a "Profile of the Laity in the Ecumenical Movement: Towards a New Definition" with the quizzical remarks:

> The 'laity' have almost disappeared from ecumenical discussion. This is all the more striking in that, only a generation ago, 'laity' was an ecumenical keyword. Since then the passionate enthusiasm of the early ecumenical movement—which, at least in some very important respects, saw itself as a lay movement— has somewhat declined . . . What became of the 'laity'? What caused the remarkable disappearance of this key ecumenical concept?[121]

---

120. World Council of Churches, *Laity Formation*, 10.
121. Raiser, "Profile of the Laity in the Ecumenical Movement," 12.

# 4

# Analysis of Tom Allan's Missiology: The Tensions of the "Modern" and "Postmodern"

## Introduction

THE RELEVANCE OF THE missiology of Allan and his contemporaries
to the present is that we continue to struggle with the same tensions
in "late modernity," against a cultural backdrop where the processes
of secularization may be more developed but remain incomplete. We,
therefore, continue to live, like them, in a time of uncertainty where what
has gone before in church and world is disappearing from view but has not
departed, requiring a reflective missiology which must recognise points of
conjunction and conflict with all that is developing.

What then were the key aspects of tension in Allan's missiological
model where Allan struggled to reconcile contrasts between "new" and "old"
which remain relevant to mission, and from which lessons can be learned?

Within this chapter, analysis is undertaken of Allan's place within
global missiological thinking, concentrating particularly on how his work
might reflect "a tale of two paradigms" by straddling the old and the new,
and on two central issues under that banner which served to undermine the
success of his model in practice: the centrality of the church in mission, and
the use of mass evangelism in contrast to local witness.

Thereafter, the chapter will seek to examine the effect upon the "apostolate of the laity" of rapid social secularization in the period from 1957 to
1963. The sharp decline that struck the buoyant institutional churches in the
late fifties and early sixties, and has continued ever since, is analysed in the
context of Allan's model and the effect of the "All Scotland Crusade" of 1955.
Did the Crusade contribute, or would it all have happened anyway? How
have the decisions taken by Allan and others affected church and mission

now? Does Allan's pre-1955 model survive the secularization process to retain some resonance in our present time?

Conclusions are then drawn at the end of the chapter as to the "success" or "failure" of Allan's model, and the key aspects that speak to us now, allowing Allan's work to be a springboard for moving forward in mission.

## "A Tale of Two Paradigms"—Allan and Bosch

Tom Allan viewed his work as part of a worldwide movement of God to empower the laity. As we have seen, he was positioned at the centre of a dynamic arc or bridge of missiological ideas and action that spanned from Europe to the USA, via Scotland. He drew from European missiology, and lectured and led rallies in North America. He wholeheartedly endorsed the nation's most famous religious export, Billy Graham, from 1954 onwards. Allan's name was known internationally through *The Face of My Parish* being a bestseller, the influence of the book on those who followed him, and by his contributions to the World Council of Churches.

Allan was thus at the forefront of developments in world mission, both through *The Face of My Parish* and given his profile, but also when considering his missiology in global context. As expressed in *The Face of My Parish*, the founding documents of "Tell Scotland," and his contributions to WCC theologies of mission and evangelism, Allan's missional perspective was in keeping with the emerging realisation on the world stage that the church's mission existed not as a human function but as a product of the Triune God. As Will Storrar comments, "though he did not use the language of the *missio Dei*, Allan clearly understood mission theologically in these terms."[1] For example, in relation to the importance of mission to the church, Allan wrote: "Evangelism is . . . not an additional activity. It is not a secondary function. It is not a prerogative of the professional evangelist. All of us in the churches, whatever our denomination may be, need to recognize that evangelism, as the seedbed of life, is central to the existence of the church itself. It is part of the basis and being of the church."[2]

Further, in a Canadian speech in 1963, the connection is again obvious: "we're being called to participate . . . in Christ's mission to the world because He is already at work in the world."[3]

---

1. Storrar, "A Tale of Two Paradigms," 63.

2. "The Seedbed of Life," *Decision*, February 1964, 4, AA6.11.15.

3. Allan, *The National Conference of United Churchmen: The Company of the Committed*, Recording of Speech, June 1963.

How do we place Allan within the world missiological landscape prevalent in the fifties and *missio Dei* theology?

Within the loose conglomeration of *missio Dei* theology, there is a firmer delineation of two central approaches in Allan's time with which we might isolate Allan's strand a little further. In one corner stands a "redemptive historical-ecclesiological approach," associated with the initiators in the fifties of the *missio Dei* concept such as Karl Barth and Lesslie Newbigin; and in the other an "historical-eschatological interpretation" which came to prominence in the sixties with such as Hoekendijk and Aring.[4]

Expressed otherwise, the first aspect is the "classical" approach which saw mission as christological: centred on the meaning of the Cross, of the need for atonement and redemption in God's world, with a primary role for the church in doing so and the ultimate goal of the evangelisation of the world, under the banner "Jesus is Lord."

Allan was resolutely "classical" in his appreciation. His missiology was representative of the predominant worldview in the fifties of "Christocentric Universalism," as described by Konrad Raiser: "the Christocentric orientation, concentration on the church, a universal perspective and history as the central category of thought."[5]

The concentration emphasised "the universal significance of the Christ event, in which the idea of the "lordship of Christ over the world and the church" played a decisive role."[6] Transformational Christology and lay evangelism through the church was thus central to the world missiology of the fifties. Allan not only contributed to the prominence of such missiology within *The Face of My Parish* and his work at the World Council of Churches, but importantly worked it out in practice. Newbigin's declaration in 1953 that "an unchurchly mission is as much a monstrosity as an unmissionary church,"[7] thereafter began to lose credence.

In the sixties, the "classical approach" which had been at the heart of the formation of the ecumenical movement in its link of mission to world evangelisation through the churches, was set in increasing opposition to a "conciliar" approach. This viewed the world and the political arena, not the church, as the initiator and true field of mission, with the primary goal of Christian mission no longer being to establish Christ's Lordship over all nations. Instead, it was to implement God's Kingdom of justice and peace,

---

4. See Thomas Kramm, quoted by Flett, *The Witness of God*, 54 n57.

5. Raiser, *Ecumenism in Transition*, 41.

6. Ibid., 91.

7. Newbigin, *The Household of God*, 148.

under a banner of "shalom," accepting all secular means which tended to do so, and rejecting all those institutional structures which did not.

The chief theologian of the re-aligned missionary era of the sixties with its diminished focus on the roe of the church was Allan's friend and colleague from the 1958 and 1960 Bossey consultations, Johannes Hoek-endijk, who had written as early as 1950: "I believe in the church which is a function of the Apostolate, that is, an instrument of God's redemptive action in this world . . . The church is nothing more (but also nothing less!) than a means in God's hands to establish *shalom* in this world."[8]

However, delimiting Allan's missiology simply to historical interest as a "classical" expression of *missio Dei* theology is insufficient, because Allan's openness to engage with a broad range of influences within mission practice means that his missiology also pre-empted traits that might recognised as central in the present "late modern" era. In this way, by his missiology in some aspects being ahead of its time, it retains a freshness and impor-tance for consideration now. Looked at broadly, indeed, the very attempt to embrace elements of both the "old" and the "new" is reflective of our own times; secularization and the progress towards a "postmodern" society being incomplete.

David Bosch in his seminal work *Transforming Mission* identified since World War II the beginnings of a "paradigm shift" in mission, if such sociological tags are ever sufficient to adequately describe the ever-evolving present. Bosch focused upon a movement from Küng's "modern, Enlight-enment paradigm" towards the identification of "elements of an emerging ecumenical paradigm," elsewhere described by Bosch as "postmodern."[9]

With the benefit of hindsight, and with reservations in the use of "paradigms" as coherent descriptive terms, where in such a shift would Al-lan's missiology lie?

In Allan's time as now, in Bosch's words, "the new paradigm is . . . still emerging and it is, as yet, not clear which shape it will eventually adopt. For the most part we are, at the moment, thinking and working in terms of two paradigms."[10] Allan's missiology engaged with tensions which per-sist in present "late modernity" in that overlap, and succeeded in placing within a cohesive whole both definitive "modern" and "emerging" elements, in Bosch's terminology. Therein partly lies the appeal of his work for the

8. Hoekendijk, "The Call to Evangelism," 162–75.

9. The latter being "an awkward term" which he later replaces with "ecumeni-cal"–at 531, fn1.

10. Bosch, *Transforming Mission*, 349.

present, where that friction persists. For, as Bosch comments, "a time of paradigm shift is a time of deep uncertainty."[11]

Even if the use of the concept of "paradigm shifts" were set aside, there is little doubt that Allan was working on the cusp of an extraordinary social transformation of Western society in the sixties, with inevitable effect on church and mission, whose ramifications continue. At that point, Allan was engaging in multi-faceted methods; some very much of the past, but also in others which might survive the transition.

The traditional notion of Protestant mission in the early fifties under the "modern paradigm" concentrated on Christianity as the supreme meta-narrative, and the linking of all human history and experience directly to an authoritative and unassailable infinite, to be located in the authority of scripture. It was a top-down revelation, centred on the ultimate Enlighten-ment symbols: the writing, distribution and exhortation of words.[12] It thus attempted to challenge secular modernity's separation of facts and values by proclaiming the ultimate "facts" of Christ.[13] This strand is identifiable in much of Allan's concept of parish and national mission. Therefore, on the one hand, in his focus on the church, the primacy of biblical edu-cation and training in theological literacy, the role of Billy Graham, the "All Scotland Crusade" and Allan's "conversion" post-1954 to the place of preaching and mass evangelism in his missiology, Allan's practice would undoubtedly, as Storrar notes, "conform to the pattern of Bosch's modern paradigm of mission."[14]

However, of significant importance for the landscape of mission in Scotland, then and now, is the realisation that such one-dimensional "modern" expressions are "certainly not the whole picture with Tom Allan himself."[15] As we have seen, Allan was marked by his willingness to engage with any form of theological expression, in a resolute attempt to bring the Gospel by whatever means.

Therefore, in Storrar's words, "we may describe Allan's ministry in both North Kelvinside and the 'All Scotland Crusade' as "a tale of two paradigms."[16] Storrar identifies the overlap in post-war Scotland and in Al-lan's life and work:

11. Ibid.
12. Ibid., 358.
13. Ibid., 58.
14. Storrar, "A Tale of Two Paradigms," 62.
15. Ibid.
16. Ibid.

The picture of mission that we find in the ten years from the end
of the Second World War is an ambiguous one, in the terms of
Bosch's missiological analysis. On the one hand, we can find so
many of the traits of modern mission in the impressive initiatives
in evangelism which are such a marked feature of Scottish
church life from 1946–55. On the other hand, there are clear
features of what Bosch would wish to call postmodern mission
theology and practice present in that same postwar movement.
No one typifies this creative tension between overlapping
mission paradigms better than Tom Allan . . ."[17]

Therefore, running in conjunction with the ingrained streak of the
"modern" oral exhortation of the Word, is Allan's "brilliant anticipation of
key elements of later, postmodern missiology," within *The Face of My Parish*
and in his practice throughout his life, in its starkest form in parish ministry. For Storrar, these features are "central to the postmodern understanding and practice of mission, discerned by Allan and his post-war French
mentors forty years before the publication of Bosch's seminal study of the
trend."[18] They are as follows:

- "central to his mission was the local congregation";

- "the role of the ordained ministry was to equip and enable the members to engage in that missionary encounter . . . especially in the small
  group";

- The adoption of a "trinitarian and yet also socially contextualized approach" from being "deeply read in . . . European theology and studies
  of ministry and mission"; and

- The recognition in the face of "the resistance of some of his own church
  members," of the necessary "restructuring of internal church life . . .
  required by Christ's call to be a missionary congregation."

In Allan's implementation of those principles, Storrar finds clear parallels to be drawn to the present, in the focus on the laity, the concentration
on the formation of community as true *koinonia*, and the importance of the
local and the everyday (my emphasis):

we can also discern a recurring and growing appreciation of Allan's insight that mission is to be affirmed as God's many-sided
but inclusive mission in the wider world, into which the local
congregation and its ordinary members are called to participate

17. Ibid., 60–61.

18. This quote and those below at ibid., 63–64.

> in fellowship, witness and service . . . [Mission in late moder-
> nity] *departs from the rational and apologetic in favour of the
> experimental, experiential, and the formation of community
> without pre-determined authoritative structures. This focus on
> the contextual and the communal . . . is essential both to Bosch's
> understanding of the emerging paradigm and Allan's concept of
> mission sixty years ago.*

Not only might we thus identify Allan's model as a precursor of much that has concerned missiology in the Northern hemisphere in the last half-century, as it has strived to cope with the transition at the end of a Christendom model which Bosch would label "a paradigm shift," we can also see in Allan a bold attempt in practice to "ride two horses" in an effort to relate to Scotland in both "rational and apologetic" (modern) and "contextual and communal" (postmodern) terms, an outpouring of his "both/and" missiology.

The constituent parts may have been partially derivative or adapted from elsewhere, but the originality is in their mixture and application.[19] It is not fanciful to name Allan as one of Bosch's "group of pioneers" who were at the cusp of the translation towards the postmodern, embracing the potential of elasticity and experiment dependent on the context.

At its heart, as Storrar affirms, was an embrace from Allan's theological sources of the transcendence of God, but in conjunction with His imminent presence in the glory and tragedy of the passing days. It was God present within the very ordinariness and mundanity of life in all its facets, such that the church could not claim to speak as an exalted guardian of an immutable truth without context, but had to recognise that its very existence in theology and community owed a principal debt to the people around and within it: "The North Kelvinside parish visitors that Allan trained went on to discover for themselves what Bonhoeffer and Ellul and Michonneau affirmed, that God was already at work in the lives of local people."[20]

With that background, there were two principal tensions in Allan's work between the "rational and apologetic" and the "contextual and communal," or indeed between the "two paradigms," connected and derived from the centrality of church and laity in mission. Their friction was to influence the practical outcome of Allan's missiology, and informs our own appreciation of a relevant "theology of the laity" for the present.

---

19. Bardgett, however, believes that "Storrar over-emphasises Allan's originality as a missionary thinker"; *Scotland's Evangelist,* chapter 11n9, a view with which it is perhaps evident that I would respectfully disagree.

20. Storrar, *A Tale of Two Paradigms,* 63.

## Tension 1: Revolutionizing the
## Church versus Opposition to Change

Frank Bardgett asks in relation to the dissipation and demise of "Tell Scotland":

> What was the chief obstacle in developing missionary congregations? Was it the persistence of a traditional evangelicalism in speaking a worn-out language or the persistence of a traditional ecclesiology of the one-man band? Was it the essential theological ignorance of so many church members? Faced with many layered institutional inertia, forced by events to handle both gains and losses from its association with the All Scotland Crusade, Tell Scotland's ideals achieved less currency than its name.[21]

Under Allan's missional model, the institutional church was set a high goal of purging and regeneration as a predication of its success, as well as being the focal point of an inspired departure and welcoming return. This defining emphasis on the parochial community as agent and object of mission, to be reformed and purified, remained a central tenet of Allan's missiology from 1946 onwards; in direct conflict with the "many layered institutional inertia" which it encountered.

The lifelong goal for Allan in evangelism was thus captured in his definition of the term (my emphasis): "Evangelism is that activity, of whatever kind, which brings persons into a saving knowledge of God in Christ, and *leads them into the church, which is the sphere of Christ's continuing work in a fallen world.*"[22]

The church was therefore for Allan "a fellowship of chosen people . . . not a human institution, but a divine creation."[23] The church as divinely appointed sole agent and object of God's mission to the world and conduit of God's eschatological promise was developed in a 1956 broadcast (my emphasis):

> How does the Christ prepare the world for his coming again? . . .
> [He is] preparing the world for his Second Coming *through the church* . . . The church is part of the divine strategy. It is called into existence by the Word of God . . . [The church] *is both the*

---

21. Bardgett, "The 'Tell Scotland' Movement: Failure and Success," 149.

22. AA6.7.6, Broadcast on the Scottish Home Service, 21 June 1956.

23. AA6.2.13, "Nature and Function of the Church," Ashlin White Bible Lectures, Mooresville, North Carolina.

*visible manifestation and the divinely appointed agent of the king-dom of God.*[24]

Along with his later reliance on mass evangelism, the concentration on the church in this regard was the other element of Allan's missiology which Bosch would determine as resolutely "modern." However, there were two aspects of Allan's view of the church that can be marked out as "new," "innovative" or, in Bosch's terms, "emerging" or "postmodern."

Firstly, he recognised that the very *raison d'être* of the church is mission, without which it is a shadow of its purported self. Allan's approach to the "Nature and Function of the Church" is clear from a 1953 lecture of that name: "the church is a fellowship of missionary people," which means that "a church which is not a missionary church is, in no sense of the word, a church at all."[25]

Secondly, Allan had identified from the beginning that "today in Scotland the church has become largely irrelevant to the life and needs of the vast majority of the people."[26] In order to address "the problem of communicating our gospel to the masses outside the church," this would entail an "imperative need to re-examine the pattern of our church's life." Allan's theology meant that the two requirements would be held "inextricably bound together, inter-related and inseparable."[27]

Allan was inevitably undertaking a battle with the forces of reaction within the existing institution. He recognised early on in *The Face of My Parish* that "the most crushing and bewildering opposition to the work of mission in Scotland today does not come from the pagan masses outside the church, but from those people inside it, for whom the church is not the instrument of God's redemptive purpose, but an exclusive spiritual club for the selected few."[28]

Allan nevertheless predicated the success of his mission plan on the church being sufficiently purged so as to be redirected towards a vibrant parochial community, dependent on the existing church being capable of three central processes: (a) of producing the lay individuals who might begin the mission in the parish; (b) of receiving and nourishing those who became part of the community as a result; and (c) of consequently being willingly changed and adapted in its life and liturgy. He knew that the strength in numbers and influence of those reactionary forces had the

24. AA6.7.4, "Why Did Jesus Come?" 8–11, Broadcast, 16 December 1956.

25. AA6.2.13, Ashlin White Bible Lectures, Mooresville, North Carolina, 1953.

26. Ibid., "5. The Witness of the Layman," 5.

27. Both at Allan, *The Face of My Parish*, 49.

28. AA6.2.13, Ashlin White Bible Lectures 1953, "5. The Witness of the Layman," 5.

potential to scupper his whole missiological focus by inhibiting any or all of those three essential requirements. He wrote of the potentially destructive effect of institutional conservatism in a further scathing passage within *The Face of My Parish*, referring to: "those for whom religion is a matter of comfortable and respectable conformity . . . an attitude of mind which is implacably opposed to any change in the routine of conventional religion, and which sets itself against any effort to confront a congregation with its missionary responsibility."[29]

Recounting his experiences in North Kelvinside, Allan asserted in 1953 that: "There are vast sections of the membership of the church who are blind to their responsibilities as Christians and actively opposed to any movement to reclaim the masses for Christ and his Kingdom."[30]

Echoes of the departure of people of faith from the institutional church in Scotland due to its failure to support and equip an adequate missionary ethos can be found in the present day. In the recent ethnographic research of church leavers carried out by Steve Aisthorpe, he reached the worrying conclusion that "for some, their concern to be effective in mission was instrumental in deciding to move out, or remain out, of congregational life."[31]

As a large-scale example, what impact the negative opposing forces have in Scotland to Allan's model of mission at a national level in "Tell Scotland"? At the conclusion of the All Scotland Crusade, Billy Graham warned that the mantle was passed over to the churches to consolidate the gains made through the laity, emphasising that any failure to do so was the churches'' responsibility.[32] However, in the coming months, the reality was that often the church was often unable or unwilling to respond: "on the one hand, the ministry persisted in performing as disparate one-man bands; on the other too, many of the laity were spiritually illiterate. Missionary stasis resulted."[33]

Furthermore, if a congregation baulked at the depth of commitment and engagement required by the "Tell Scotland" principles, the Crusade gave them the perfect exit strategy. It created the impression that "Tell Scotland," or indeed Christian mission as a whole, was defined by Crusade evangelism, and thus allowed them "to breathe sighs of relief and say: "Leave it all to Graham."[34]

---

29. Allan, *The Face of My Parish*, 31–32.

30. AA6.2.13, Ashlin White Bible Lectures 1953, "5. The Witness of the Layman," 7.

31. Aisthorpe, *The Invisible Church*, 167.

32. Burnham, *Billy Graham*, 74.

33. Bardgett, "D. P. Thomson and the Orkney Expedition—a Tell Scotland"Case Study, 21.

34. Falconer, *Kilt*, 82.

There appeared further to have been a widespread inability to provide an appropriate fellowship to newcomers. As early as April 1956, an article in *Life and Work* entitled "What Has Happened to the Enquirers?" commented: "Some churches report that only a minority of those who were welcomed into the congregations at the end of the Crusade are still with them . . . were the churches not ready to receive them?"[35]

Allan's solution to counter the forces of internal reaction of apathy and opposition was, in itself, prone to difficulty. Allan was effectively promoting ecclesiastical upheaval by ignoring the existence of "the rump" altogether, for an initial mission outwith the normal ordinances of religion. How was this deliberate separation of the engaged laity from the worshipping faithful to be balanced and reconciled within a later unified church community?

The concept of the "congregational group" amalgamated all those who had been inspired by the implementation or by the fruits of parish mission into a tight nucleus of faith, living out Allan's realization that the only way to prepare a church for mission was to do mission itself. However, in concerns that may be reflective of the eventual failure of the idea in practice, Allan was "not at all certain" as to "how far this approach is likely to succeed against the conventional background of church life" for four reasons:

a. "the group can so easily become separatist, exclusive and Pharasaical"

b. "the mixed character of its membership" as it "inevitably attracts the crank"

c. "the danger of subjectivism and introspection" on spiritual matters; and

d. "tremendous differences . . . in spiritual capacity and awareness"[36]

The creation of the "congregational group" brought with it serious risks to the fulfilment of an overall "apostolate of the laity," by its very nature dividing the congregation, and creating a sect that might confront any newcomer. It ran the danger of the elevation of a separate class of "super-Christian," somehow anointed at a higher level.

These were risks which Allan had, indeed, previously commented upon in *The Face of My Parish*. He there identified "as the most serious problem," that the formation of the group would "drive the members of it into an inevitable "holier-than-thou" attitude." Not only that, it also "introduces an element of conflict and unease in the minds of those outside the group,"

35. As quoted in Falconer, *Kilt*, 92.

36. Allan, *The Face of My Parish*, 80–81.

by which "it may vitiate the group's work in its first evangelistic responsibility—within its own congregation."[37]

To this list, Allan could have added with the benefit of his experience in "Tell Scotland" that the main detriment for the groups to be formed and maintained was that they required a significant degree of commitment to mission, and a zeal borne of a depth of faith, in order to persist in their task. It was patient, long-term local commitment that was required, and not a "quick-fix" burst of excitement which Graham's Crusade could so easily encourage. Such dedicated zeal was abundant in his own life, but often insufficient within individual Christians and in congregations throughout Scotland. As Highet concluded from his research in 1960 in the wake of Billy Graham and in the end days of "Tell Scotland," the hope for a rolling programme of mission and service in the parish was often reduced to a one-off event-based engagement, perhaps influenced by Graham's style, noting that: "Fewer congregations are currently engaged on [mission] than one would have expected from the enthusiasm engendered a few years ago, and that a good many who expressed their resolve not to do just a once-for-all mission but to follow it up have allowed a longer period to elapse than was their original intention."[38]

The bottom line is that the gargantuan efforts of Allan, Thomson and Graham failed to shift to a sufficient extent the almost immoveable mass that formed the bulk of the church membership in the fifties, leading Highet to conclude in referring directly to the passages above from *The Face of My Parish*: "In the thirteen years since [North Kelvinside], this opposition has been overcome to greater or lesser degree in different areas and in different congregations, but it is difficult not to feel that the laity in general has not responded to the call to evangelism to the extent hoped for in the late 1940s and early 1950s."[39]

In the late fifties and early sixties, Allan came to appreciate, from personal experience in the church and Highet's work, that when the moment had presented itself nationally, his goal had not been accomplished. How then did he assess the relative failure of his efforts to permeate society with Christianity and evangelize Scotland? Looking back, he wrote: "It was a time of unparalleled outreach to those masses of people outwith the membership of the churches. And yet in spite of this extraordinary missionary

37. All at Allan, *The Face of My Parish*, 80.

38. Highet, *The Scottish Churches*, 85.

39. Ibid., 77.

endeavour I think it's true to say that, by and large, the non-churchgoing masses remained curiously unimpressed."[40]

Allan blamed not the method from North Kelvinside, or the incongruity of mass evangelism, but the complacency of the churches in their response. Writing in 1960 of Highet's *The Scottish Churches*, Allan described the book as "ruthlessly realistic in assessing the results of our missions." However, Allan could not accept that the responses of ministers within the book indicated that the missiology was misguided, but instead that the church's resistance had stymied the fruition of the missiology:

> I utterly deny and refute from my own personal experience the findings of so many of my colleagues about these campaigns. D. P. Thomson came to my first parish in 1947 with a campaign of visitation evangelism, and completely transformed my own work as a minister and the whole life of the congregation.
>
> Is it not, rather, a reason for examining ourselves? Is it not a possibility that the failure of evangelism is directly related to some equal failure in the church? That there is something about us that fails to hold those who have been contacted and won?

Highet's "brilliant book" therefore, should be a "text-book for study in our congregations . . . for its shattering attack on our complacency."[41]

Bardgett would agree with Allan: "at its outset, the leaders of "Tell Scotland" intended to challenge complacency and clericalism in the Kirk: a failure to rise to that challenge . . . goes some way to explaining the fading of the Movement."[42] Ultimately, the writer is drawn further to agree with Bardgett, in turn, that "the failure of the 1950s was the widespread inability to understand how profound was the challenge to the call of mission to the existing culture, power-structures and institutions of the kirks."[43] The same challenges persist in the present day.

Despite his incisive diagnosis in his early years of ministry of the absolute failure of the parish system to deliver effective mission, Allan undertook to resuscitate the aged relation back to rude health, and predicated his entire missiology upon it. In doing so, the sharp conflict created in the implementation of the theoretical elements of his missiology, much of which can be defined as "emerging" or "post-modern" within Bosch's classifications, both underlined and yet undermined the bravery of the missiology itself.

40. AA6.5.11, "Attitude to the Gospel," for *The Christian*, 4.

41. AA6.5.8, "My Week—The Scottish Churches," 1960.

42. Bardgett, "D. P. Thomson and the Orkney Expedition—a "Tell Scotland" Case Study," 21.

43. Bardgett, "The "Tell Scotland" Movement: Failure and Success," 150.

It was the clash, on the one hand, of Allan's upbringing, his Presbyterian ecclesiology and evangelical theology with, on the other, his startling recognition of a new social order and the requirement for a "new evangelism," and his discovery of a radical, ecumenical, ecclesiologically-neutral missiology from Europe. Allan attempted to fit one into the other, with potentially dramatic but ultimately inconclusive results. The fuller application to his context of his European influences was thus, arguably, incomplete.

Allan's high ecclesiology, very much reflective of pre-war Scotland but also of his times, was soon to be strongly challenged in the sixties in the bypassing of the church under a conciliar ecumenist outlook on mission. Was Allan's ecclesiology the real encumbrance to the implementation of his radical pre-1955 missiology? What if Allan had proceeded with his pre-1955 model, but not insisted that the purpose of mission was to bring the whole parish into the ecclesiastical fold, and had thus avoided the stumbling block of the assimilation of new converts to church culture? Would this in turn have created a new and dynamic church in parallel—a "Fresh Expression" even?

Martin Johnstone's angle on the centrality of the church in the mission of Allan and his predecessors is as follows:

> Although important and genuine attempts to engage with those living in poverty in Glasgow, the strategies of [Thomas] Chalmers, [George] MacLeod and [Tom] Allan were all based upon the presupposition that the institutional church is the redeemed community and that once those in poverty realise this, they will wish to become part of it . . .
>
> Their strategies were also based on an implicit acceptance of what Margull identified as a form of 'structural fundamentalism" prevalent within the church . . . , which understands the prevailing models of organisation, at both national but even more critically at local levels, as foundational and predetermined.[44]

John Harvey similarly argues that the weakness was that "[Allan] remained convinced that these souls would eventually come into the church . . . as a result of the faithful and corporate activity of the renewed Christian congregation.[45]

What if, Harvey asks of the church, it is the "very manner, style and internal context of its being there"[46] that was preventative to the success of

---

44. Johnstone, *Towards a Practical Ecclesiology for Urban Scotland*, 214–15.

45. Harvey, *Bridging the Gap*, 72.

46. Ibid.

Allan's model? Harvey thus proposes that mission should begin not within the church, but "out there in the world."[47]

In *The Face of My Parish*, Allan recognised the drastic state of the institutional church around Europe in the immediate post-war period: "the church has long since ceased to be anything but a pale reflection of the true Christian community . . . I believe that on the church's attitude to this problem depends, not only to its future effectiveness, but its future existence as an institution."[48]

He further acknowledged the "distrust of the traditional parish system" within emerging post-war European lay groupings based "not on the place of residence, but on a common ground of interest."[49]

Allan, therefore, was aware, and addressed as early as 1953, the argument that was to gain particular currency a decade later in world missiology: that the institution should be temporarily abandoned as a starting point of mission and that "church" could as validly be formed in the world.

The lay movements across Europe in Allan's time, recognitions that God was already at work and alive in mission beyond and without the church, were practical reflections of the emergence of *missio Dei* theology in the mid-fifties, and indeed of the incarnational ministries of the sixties and the "emerging church" movement of the present. They were of considerable importance to Allan and a key influence upon him. The important distinction, however, is to recognise that they did not inspire Allan as a destructive force ecclesiologically, in other words to abandon the traditional church, but rather as an illumination of the church's failings which consequently brought a determination to purge and cleanse its very soul.

Therefore, whilst Godin's thinking was central to Tom Allan's *missiology*, it lost in a contest over against his *ecclesiology*. Allan was aware of the issue that the rejection of the church by Godin and alternative lay communities raised, but whilst drawing inspiration from their recognition of the need within the church laity and in society for a supra-church community, he ultimately rejected the idea that their departure from the structure was the solution, or indeed that they could even inherently be called Christian organisations.

Allan raised the question in *The Face of My Parish*, "can they provide any real alternative to the traditional pattern of the church's life out of the ineffectiveness of which they were born?" In response, Allan made two points,

---

47. Ibid., 73.
48. Allan, *The Face of My Parish*, 42–43.
49. Ibid.

which could be applied not only to sixties radicalism but to the emerging church of today.

Firstly, he argued that the underlying problem might, in time, be the same, and it was only by addressing them that any progress could be made. Thus, such communities might be an "escape from facing up to a more radical issue, and an admission of defeat," in that "the same problems which paralyse the institutional church [might] in time make their appearance there."[50]

Secondly, "These functional groups cells cannot by their very nature be called "Christian communities" in the deepest sense.," given that they "must of necessity be exclusive fellowships." Therefore, he concluded:

> It seems to me that there is in all this a dangerous tendency to idealise the secular community—the workers" world, for example—and almost to regard it being in itself "Christian," simply because there is evidence of some kind of sense of community to be found there . . . to go the length of saying that God has fact ceased to speak through his church, and that his Word is being heard to-day in the so-called pagan world. Such an attitude proceeds out of a double misunderstanding. It betrays a curious blindness to the true meaning of the Christian community; and it also betrays a profound misunderstanding of the nature and function of the church . . . There are those who believe the answer has to be found within the church itself, and who realize all that this involves in conflict and heartbreak for those who seek such an answer.[51]

This conclusion also later tempered Allan's attitude to experiments in incarnational ministry and mission in Scotland. He wrote positively of the efforts of Scottish worker-priests and industrial chaplains to relate the Gospel to the work environment of ordinary people, as: "a serious attempt to be identified with their people in the most real possible way, and so to demonstrate the relevance of Christianity on the spot. It may not be the whole answer, but it is an honest effort to bridge what can be a wide and terrible gulf."[52]

Allan was receptive to the Gorbals Group Ministry nearby in the city of Glasgow, and to their inspiration from the East Harlem Protestant Parish: "All honour to the men in East Harlem for the work they are doing and the way they are doing it. There are people right here in Glasgow engaged in

50. Allan, *The Face of My Parish*, 45–46.

51. Ibid., 46–47.

52. AA6.5.10, *EC*, "Automation and the Dignity of Work."

the same kind of challenging work, and many others dealing with the same kind of situation."[53]

Ultimately, however, it was "one view" as part of the overall picture, and a valid one at that, but not his own. If there was a purpose of such a theology of "identification" within Allan's missiology, it did not mean validity *per se*, but for Allan was a return to what he had always advocated—it may be advantageous for gaining a true understanding of the ordinary working person in the parish in order to contextualise mission, which ultimately would end in the church.

Such groups or cells could not, therefore, replace the role of the traditional church structure in mission. For Allan, they did not highlight its fundamental inadequacy, as Harvey might suggest, but their existence served merely to spotlight the flaws. The "structural fundamentalism" of Margull was seen by Allan as a likely strength and not a weakness or encumbrance. Allan saw little alternative but to embrace the "conflict and heartbreak" of which he wrote.

However, the Scottish churches in 1945 to 1960 were not purged. The essential pre-condition remained unfulfilled. The consequent effect of the "church-centrism," that Allan shared with nearly all contemporaries as being foundational to a mission plan, was in practice to stifle the flow of adequate communication through the church laity with ordinary people in the parish which he sought, and to diminish the contact which had been obtained from visitation evangelism in its infancy. It was the "structural fundamentalism" which partly defeated an otherwise dynamic missiology and, with the advance of secularism in the sixties, tainted Christianity and the very notion of a "parish mission" with the life of a conservative institutional church, viewed with increasing scepticism if not disdain by the younger generation. That Christianity *was* the Kirk in its then form became an impediment to mission rather than a beneficial status. There thus emerged a direct conflict of youth with a pre-war organisation which Allan's generation had inherited and failed to fully turn around.

Had Allan persisted at a national level with his pre-1955 lay missiology, it may not have initiated a rapid groundswell nationwide of Christian adherence, but it may at the least have set the church on a course towards a fuller contextualization of the Gospel; a closer interaction with culture; a movement towards the breaking down of the clergy/laity divide; and placed the church as institution at a more integrated level within society. In doing so, this may have more readily permitted the assimilation of those who wished to become part of the church from mission, and geared the church

53. AA6.11.6, *EC*, 22 June 1963.

more strongly to ride the wave of growing secularization from the late fifties onwards, lessening the rapidity of decline.

If mission is now to be re-formed as centred upon the life and witness of ordinary people, the public perception of the church, and of Christianity itself, remains a significant obstacle. Whilst Christian laity may once more become the vanguard of mission, it cannot again be under a determined pretext that the institutional church is the ultimate destination of their mission, or that their task *per se* is church regeneration. The church laity in mission must be unfettered in their paths and goals, allowing new forms of community to arise as a result of their encounters where appropriate.

## Tension 2: Local Witness versus Mass Evangelism

Did mass evangelism also contribute to a failure in the "apostolate of the laity"?

It was the seeming inability of the church to form and retain vibrant "congregational groups" in "Tell Scotland" which led Allan to introduce a further "modern/postmodern" tension within the model: the apparent paradox of trying to create local witness by mass evangelism.

Allan had been firmly against mass evangelism as a tool of mission. In his early years in ministry, he had thus expressed his opposition to "that pietistic evangelicalism, which has its roots in the revival movements of the last century, and which expresses itself in a concern for what it calls a "personal salvation," to the exclusion of any interest in, let alone concern for, the world in which the soul lives."[54]

Allan had further warned in *The Face of My Parish*: "I am convinced that [evangelicalism's] inevitable "personalism" has to be guarded against. Too often the concern for individual salvation meant a retreat from the actual world in which men earn their bread."[55]

Not only had he lived out that opposition in practice in North Kelvinside and committed himself instead to the world before him, he had concentrated on local action and the formation of community in *The Face of My Parish*. That ethos then informed the founding principles of "Tell Scotland."

Allan had first encountered Billy Graham by attending a "Youth for Christ rally" in a Glasgow church in 1946, where he later recalled: "being impressed by the strangely compelling sincerity of the preacher, but thinking also that—whatever the approach to evangelism might be—this was

54. AA6.5.6, Speech to "Retreat," c.1950/1.
55. Allan, *The Face of My Parish*, 62.

not it," decrying the flashiness of the "exaggerated draped suits of striking shades, exotically brilliant ties . . . gold trombones."[56]

As if to turn full circle, only a few months after *The Face of My Parish* was published in early 1954, the "old evangelism" was back. Allan wrote in June 1955 following the Crusade that mass evangelism had been "unjustifiably neglected."[57] Even the later *de facto* leader of the conservative evangelical wing of the Church of Scotland, William Still, had come to believe that mass evangelism was "obsolete . . . evangelistic entertainment."[58] So why the *volte face*?

As indicated in chapter 2, Allan's forthright validation of Graham was based on the hope of unblocking the inertia. As he explained in late 1954, "Dr Graham has reminded us of the place of evangelistic preaching in the recruitment of the laity."[59] Allan envisaged Graham as the spark for the creation of "congregational groups," just as he recalled them emerging from his own preaching in the parish.

In inviting Graham, it is clear that Allan's primary expectation was not of a revival outside of the church. Allan was pinning his hopes on the success of Graham in fulfilling the Phase II recruitment of the laity. Since national mission under Phase III was dependant on Phase II, Allan was predicating the creation of the "missionary parish" on Billy Graham's ability to deliver the churchgoers to "Tell Scotland."[60]

The casualty was his prior missiology. Whilst maintaining his insistence on an overall holistic approach to mission, Allan was now ready to endorse the widespread public proclamation of what he readily recognised was only "half a message." In the defensive pamphlet on Graham that he wrote for "Tell Scotland" in 1954, Allan explained that: "The evangelist is called by God to lead men into the community of the redeemed . . . And it is for this limited task that Dr Graham knows himself to be called. [There is a] false dilemma between the so-called "individual salvation" and the so-called 'social gospelism.' *It is not either/or. It is both/and.* Dr Graham as an evangelist is concerned with the first."[61]

---

56. AA6.5.6, *Rally*, September 1956, 4.

57. Allan, ed., *Crusade in Scotland,* 122.

58. Still, *Dying to Live,* 117–18.

59. Allan, *The Agent of Mission,* 22–23.

60. "The more I reflect on this intensely practical question of the recruitment of the laity, the more I regard it as the crux of the "Tell Scotland" movement. And it is certain that the second phase (Sept 54 to Summer 55) will wholly determine whether or not the third phase is to take place." Ibid., 22.

61. AA6.5.6, *The "Tell Scotland" Movement and Billy Graham,* 2 (my emphasis).

Allan wholeheartedly lived out a "both/and" missiology in *his* life and work. However, the danger from inviting Graham's acknowledged concentration only on "individual salvation" without "social gospelism" was to pre-suppose that the two can be separated chronologically, which was the main basis of MacLeod's opposition. In that cleft, Allan remained in 1960 "keenly aware of the limitations of Billy Graham's kind of evangelism."[62] He was nonetheless willing to utilise it to seek the formation of a "new" or "postmodern" gathering of "congregational groups," not now from the local, organic growth as he envisaged in *The Face of My Parish*, but from one of the most starkly "old" or "modern" methods imaginable.

Allan never wavered in his view that the Crusade was a success, and its method justified. He repeatedly used his weekly newspaper column to defend Graham against persistent opposition.[63] Allan and Graham remained close personal friends. Allan was part of Graham's team for his New York Crusade of 1957, addressing a thousand ministers in New York on "parochial evangelism."[64] Graham further invited Allan to be "associate evangelist" in his Australasian Crusade of 1959.[65] Allan was the key player in the return of Graham to Scotland for a one-off rally at Ibrox Park on 24 June 1961, and supported the proposal for his London Crusade of 1965.

Prior to the 1961 Ibrox Rally, both Graham and Allan were asked to comment upon the results of the surveys within Highet's 1960 book on the apparently minimal effect of the 1955 Crusade, which had cast a shadow on any claim that in the longer term either many outside the churches had been evangelized as a result, or that Graham's Crusade had galvanized the laity of the churches towards mission. Graham responded that "I would have considered my visit to Scotland worthwhile if only one person had been truly converted to Christ." Allan replied: "Remember that when people came forward at the Kelvin Hall, they were never claimed as converts by Graham: they were inquirers. Some of them already were church members, but went forward as an act of commitment. They are better churchmen and churchwomen now as a result."[66]

Allan faced significant personal criticism over his support for Crusade-style mass evangelism and for Billy Graham himself. The renowned "Iona" minister in the new housing area of Pollok in Glasgow, James Currie,

62. AA6.11.2, *EC*, 24 September 1960.

63. Allan wrote ten articles supporting Graham from 4 October 1958 to 16 November 1963, at AA6.11.1 to AA6.11.7.

64. AA6.5.6, *Rally*, August 1957.

65. AA6.11.1, *EC*, 4 October 1958.

66. AA6.11.8, Duncan McNicol, "Billy Graham's Moment of Truth," *Daily Express*, 18 May 1961.

was a vocal critic in the public forum. In response to Allan's repeated justifications of Graham, Currie wrote to the *Evening Citizen* newspaper, seeking to remind Allan of his pre-1954 position: "Mr Allan knows well enough that effective evangelism lies not in the mass meeting but in the local situation, where a congregation is eager to witness and to serve in its own parish . . . to the conscientious parish minister, the Kelvin Hall was and remains a horrible nightmare. I can only hope and pray that never again will the true work of the church be distorted by the mass hysteria and ballyhoo of those days."[67]

Allan firmly believed, however, that Graham was just as much part of the same evangelistic movement of the Spirit since the war as Godin, Michonneau or Bonhoeffer. Allan's speech at the welcome service for Graham at Glasgow Cathedral in 1955 reflected that belief: "Today in every country in the world, the church in all its branches is fired with a new sense of its missionary responsibility, and is humbly seeking to discharge its commission to make disciples of all nations. The Crusade which begins tomorrow is part of a world-wide movement of the Spirit of God."[68]

By 1960, Allan was indicating also that he had become convinced of the efficacy of mass evangelism by two forces: the responsibility as Field Director of "Tell Scotland" for the evangelisation of the nation, and the experience of the "All Scotland Crusade," which in turn re-emphasised for him the need for a revivalist "personal decision," in which we can see shadows of his own experience at Reims:

> I am fully persuaded that there is a place for mass evangelism within the totality of Christian mission . . . I did not always believe this. In my little book *The Face of My Parish* . . . I put it on record when I wrote that book eight years ago that, as far as I am concerned mass evangelism has no longer any positive contribution to make in the particular cultural setting in which our work is placed today. I said that eight years ago and I profoundly believed it. The events of these eight years have caused me, under God, to change my mind.

The reason for Allan's change of mind was that: "I have been compelled to do the work of an evangelist in a way that I never did before. I have come to the point of realising that whatever method we use in the field of men there comes a point at which man is confronted by the eternal claims of the living Christ."

He concluded that: "I do not believe for one single moment that it is adequate to bear the strains and pressures of our contemporary world, but I

67. AA6.11.1, Letter to *EC*, 11 October 1958.

68. AA6.2.18.

believe that within the wholeness of the mission of the church there must be a place for mass evangelism."[69]

The consequence of this was a re-direction of the force of his missiology away from congregational growth and towards a re-discovery of the importance of preaching for an instant decision.

Allan continued his evangelistic rallies on Saturday nights once per month at St George's Tron. An extract from his speech at the rally on 5 January 1957 is illustrative of the more confrontational form that they now took, post-Graham:

> Tonight you are standing at the crossroads, which way are you going to take? The broad road that leads to destruction: or the narrow difficult road that leads to life: ONLY YOU CAN DECIDE . . .
>
>     Will you change direction tonight: repent of your sin, believe in Christ, trust him now? You were born for this. Will you tonight turn over your life to God?[70]

In Allan's Canadian Campaigns of 1958 to 1961, he would make a call for decision at the end of the service in Graham's style: a report from Winnipeg in 1958 stated his "sincere brand of revivalism led 30 people down the aisle to declare for Christ."[71] In 1962, he made such a call in the context of a Communion Service at St George's Tron, writing that "I'm becoming more convinced that this kind of appeal should be made more often in our churches and not be left to evangelistic mission."[72]

D. P. Thomson despaired in February 1955 at the direction Allan had taken, noting in his diary following an "All Scotland Crusade" meeting: "He and I are far apart now in our thinking on many points . . . Tom Allan has gone over to the "raise your hand" school of evangelism. A big step down and back to my very great sorrow."[73]

Beyond a respective comparison of likely long-term benefit, how was Allan's pre-1954 missiological thought compromised as a result of Graham?

Rallies were nothing new for Allan and, indeed, were an inherent part of mission in both of his parishes. Allan had opened a "Week of Witness" at North Kelvinside Parish church in 1948 with an evangelistic youth rally and

---

69. AA6.2.19, *Rally* Magazine, from an address in Birmingham, England on Mass Evangelism c.1960, 3, 4, 16 and 17.

70. AA6.2.3, "Sermons on Matthew."

71. AA6.4.1, Cutting of "Winnipeg 1958."

72. AA6.11.5, *Evening Citizen*, 8 September 1962.

73. "The Diary of My Life," 16 May 1953, quoted by Bardgett, *Scotland's Evangelist*, 317.

had carried them out ever since. As has been considered, he continued to do so to great popular success every month at St George's Tron in the late fifties. On Saturday nights in North Kelvinside, he would take the youth group to testify outside the pubs on Maryhill Road. At St George's Tron, he repeated the practice, culminating in a 10pm prayer meeting in the church. Drinkers in the streets of Glasgow were confronted with the nationally known media figure, the friend of the European theological élite, preaching on a wooden platform known as the "Witness Box."

Street preaching and youth rallies were therefore an inherent part of Allan's mission in the parish. He was continuing the inheritance of the Reformed church in Scotland, as was Graham.

In open air preaching, Allan was following a Scottish tradition that Stuart Blythe describes, "of Celtic missionaries such as Ninian, Mungo and Columba, the preaching of the Reformers such as George Wishart, the open-air preaching at outdoor Communion services associated with Scottish and Irish revivalism, and the field preaching of the Covenanters."[74] Preaching to large public audiences had been central to Scottish "revivals" in the recent past, such as Cambuslang in 1742. They remained a cultural phenomenon in the early Twentieth century, and were experienced contemporaneously in Lewis in 1949 to 1953 and North Uist in 1957 to 1958.[75]

When located in the parish context, the "mass rally" was also part of the Scottish religious psyche. The connection of Allan's "local rallies" with the Scottish tradition of "Holy Fairs" is marked. As Leigh Eric Schmidt argues, the Scottish communion seasons in the eighteenth and nineteenth centuries "were envisioned as the bulwarks of Christian community, as the nodal events in a religion that was staged outdoors in wide-open public spaces for all to see and experience."[76] Therefore, the misfit for Scotland was not necessarily mission by public preaching to large crowds and calls for decision, particularly in the parish context for the purpose of centring the church at the heart of the community. Indeed, it could be argued that Allan's partial rejection prior to 1954 of those methods in favour of a lay, personalized witness was more obviously misaligned.

In my view, therefore, arguing that Allan's pre-1954 model was scuppered simply by the employment of evangelistic rallies is insufficient. The true difficulty for Allan's pre-1954 missiology arose, instead, from its clash with the *type* of mass evangelism, in the one-off theatrical "Crusade" style, that was initiated by Graham and replicated by Allan in Canada. It was

74. Stuart Blythe, "Open-Air Preaching," 253.

75. See Lennie, *Glory in the Glen*, and Ferguson, ed., *When God Came Down*.

76. Schmidt, *Holy Fairs*, 217.

in this more limited sense that, in my opinion, Ronald Falconer's caustic remark on Billy Graham holds true: "his message would have been more appropriate to 1855 than 1955."[77]

Central to Allan's missiology was the "problem of a cultural gap between the congregation and the parish, the church and the world"[78] and the identification of the means by which it might be bridged. Allan's incisive writing and practice at North Kelvinside and in the early years of "Tell Scotland" were focused on re-establishing the church and the Gospel locally, as the glue that welded society together from its lowest social levels, in order to recover the parochial system.

In the local parish, as Allan wrote of preaching outdoors in Glasgow in 1961, "to stand in Renfield Street is to be forced to ask ourselves what, in fact, is the message we have for men, and how it is related to their present and pressing needs."[79] The type of evangelistic youth rally and open air preaching that Allan exercised in his parishes was compatible with his pre-1955 missiology. It was based on a direct linkage between the preacher and those in the audience, just like the "Holy Fair," formed by their common social and geographical locus—same place, same class, same problems, same challenges, same God. Its purpose was to demonstrate a passion for the local people and a visible face of a church which they had previously ignored or rejected, *in conjunction with* the other aspects of a "missionary parish" of witness and service.

This is the nub of the validation of the type of evangelistic youth rally and open air preaching that Allan exercised in his parishes, and the reason why the rally evangelism of the visiting preacher in the larger arena was largely incompatible—losing the local, emphasising the internal rather than incorporating the external. The former was based on a geographical locus as the parish minister, and made Allan visibly known for the passion of his faith to all the people of the parish, particularly those who would never have approached a church. It provided the opportunity for gathering, fellowship and the inspiration of the parish youth. Furthermore, its demonstration of dedication to the people of the parish, as the outward face of the church, presented an ethos which could then be replicated in other ways within a constant mission of service by an ardent congregational group. In essence, rallies and open air preaching by the parish minister, or indeed members of the local congregation, could be seen as compatible with the overall

77. Falconer, *Kilt*, 81.

78. Whyte, Preface, iii.

79. AA6.11.4, *EC*, 6 May 1961.

missiology of establishing contact and demonstrating compassion for ordinary people in their context.

As Bill Shannon therefore asserts in relation to Allan's St George's Tron rallies, "it is wrong to describe it as 'following Graham's ways' . . . this was effective evangelism, not sporadic or short term but sustained, accountable, tested and appreciated. Many congregations and individuals used these rallies as an added dimension of their own work."[80]

The "Crusade-style" mass evangelism of Billy Graham in the Kelvin Hall, or indeed of Allan in Canada, was cut of a different cloth: a visiting preacher with no knowledge or connection to the local context, of social issues or concerns of faith which affected his audience. The fundamental questions of the common people which Allan would bravely respond to on that platform in Renfield Street, could not be voiced before a mass robed choir in an auditorium in a foreign land.

The difficulty in Scotland of translating and merging cultural experience with the Gospel which Allan was trying to solve was instead heightened by the effect of Billy Graham and the "All Scotland Crusade." Allan's missiology emphasised the necessity of making the Gospel "real" to the lives of ordinary people—church *with* the world. The purpose of communication was to weave Christ into every byway of life domestically and in the public realm. Graham had nothing to say about that connection, of "bridging the gap" between church *and* world—his message was church *over* the world.

This broader point was cogently addressed in 1955 by Ronald Gregor Smith in lectures given in Australasia, published the following year as *The New Man*. He wrote that:

> The church cannot stand over the world with a whip; nor can it get behind it with a load of dynamite. The whip and the dynamite, where available, would be better used on itself. The world is not, I think, "hungry for God" in the sense of popular conservatising evangelists, who really mean by that a hunger to hear their own words in the old accepted terminology . . . The world . . . has had long experience of the unbridled ambitions of the church over against the world. What the world would really see gladly is an honest and complete recognition, without any ulterior motives . . . of the existence of the world with all its own principles of movement, hopes and possibilities.[81]

This is the heart of the conflict between Allan's pre-1955 missiology and the work of Graham. Graham's method of "Crusade evangelism" with

80. Shannon, *Tom Allan*, 15.
81. Gregor Smith, *The New Man*, 68–69.

the "whip and the dynamite," in contrast to Allan's prior missiology, served instead to widen the "cultural gap." The underpinning of the Gospel in the local context was far distant from the context of a Crusade rally, and so by endorsing that form of mass evangelism Allan was effectively undermining the foundations that he had laid.

Beyond its consequences on Allan's model, did the reversion to Crusade-style mass evangelism with the "All Scotland Crusade" of 1955 have a more significant long-term effect on notions of mission in Scotland?

The longer-term difficulty of mass evangelism of the type propagated by Graham, and later emulated by Allan in Canada, was more fundamentally deep-rooted in what it did for the impression of organised Christianity within broader society, which has persisted into the present, and for the view it gave of mission within the church. In that context, the contrast with Allan's pre-1954 missiology became stark in juxtaposition, and one is then tempted to lionise his pre-1954 position, regret the decision to invite Graham, and imagine "what may have been" otherwise.

Beyond the short-term, the Crusade had little positive missional impact outwith the pre-existing church. That, after all, had not been the purpose of the Crusade at all, as Allan had repeatedly stated. In that sense, as James Whyte reflected, "Graham had not been an evangelist, but an old fashioned revivalist. His impact on those outwith the church was minimal; his main influence had been on Christian believers."[82]

The implication of that realisation is twofold. His impact on those outwith the church may have been "minimal" in terms of conversion or integration into ecclesiastical structure, but Graham's impact was profound in the breadth of its communication through the mass media.

The message of Graham that permeated beyond the church said little of Allan's concentration on the integration of faith and everyday life at the local level. This criticism was voiced most vociferously from the proposal of Graham's invitation onwards by George MacLeod and Ralph Morton of the Iona Community. The attack was essentially that the involvement of Graham was undermining the very principles of "Tell Scotland" which Allan had for the most part drafted and established.

However, more markedly in the social turmoil of the sixties, the presentation of the Crusade rallies of 1955 and their media exposure created lasting images which have been imprinted upon the consciousness of the Scottish public; that this was "Christianity" and this was "Christian mission," of a bygone age and now a stick with which organised Protestantism could be beaten.

---

82. Whyte, Preface, vi.

The second lasting effect was upon those within the church itself, also setting a norm for a definition of what "doing mission" might be, which to an extent persists to this day. Graham and mass evangelism "broadened the gap" and created unfortunate stereotypes of mission and evangelism not only for the wider public, but also for the very church members who were due to advance in missionary zeal into the parish.

Graham and mass evangelism removed the necessity for the local individual or congregational group to properly think out the meaning of the Gospel in their locality and contextualize the form of mission accordingly. As Whyte reflected: "the process of thinking stopped before it began in the face of the simplistic certainties of Graham's preaching."[83]

Graham enabled a hibernation of local mission and "congregational groups" in apathy, thus, "the majority sat back in happy passivity, assured that the task of evangelism would be accomplished by the "magic helper" from across the ocean."[84]

The reversion to Crusade-style mass evangelism was in the end, as George MacLeod had argued in its wake within the Report of the Iona Community to the General Assembly of 1956, ". . . a confusing factor in the more drawn out and costly witness of a congregation." It had harboured "a growing impression that the "Tell Scotland" *pattern* stems from the Kelvin Hall and can best be fostered by constant recurrence to mass evangelism." As MacLeod asserted, the focus had been lost along the way, with unfortunate consequences for the grand plan: "Mass Mission was not the instigator of the parish approach and never has been. Mass Mission implies withdrawal of congregational forces to mass centres of experience and renders cold in experience the less exciting fellowships of the ongoing local church."[85]

MacLeod re-asserted that, as a result of Graham, the Iona Community were "more deeply convinced that the congregation, as it is with all its praise and blame is yet . . . the sole starting point of mission."[86]

In conclusion, it is not fully in his reversion to mass evangelism *per se* that we identify the tension and contradiction of Allan's missiology from 1955 onwards, it is in his promotion through Graham and in his own ministry of a form of those evangelistic means which was entirely divorced from the local and the lay, and from service as part of the building of the Christian community. In Allan's reversion to Crusade-style mass evangelism, not

83. Whyte, Preface, vi.

84. Ibid.

85. All at Report of the Iona Community to the General Assembly of the Church of Scotland, RGA 1956, 740.

86. Ibid.

only did "the "Tell Scotland"Movement never recover from this colossal diversion,"[87] the "All Scotland Crusade" had a broader effect: firstly, in sociological terms in the longer-term public projection of Christ, church, and Christian mission; and, secondly, internally within the church in undermining the emerging local development and further accentuating the very apathy of the institutional church which Allan had identified as fatal to mission.

The Crusade thus unwittingly mixed a cocktail of a re-enforcement of institutional inadequacies in the church at local level, a theological division in the church at national level, and fostered a skewed vision of the church in broader society, which in turn left the church vulnerable and weak to withstand the onrush of secularization from 1958 to 1963.

## The "Apostolate of the Laity" versus Secularization

> Evaluation of Billy Graham's ministry in Scotland still arouses controversy . . . It will remain a matter of debate as to how far the Crusade contributed to, or was simply a casualty of, the tide of social change which was by the mid-1950s adversely affecting all the churches.[88]

—Peter Bisset, 1993

We will approach the rapid process of religious decline in Scotland in the fifties and sixties from several angles. What was the cause of the sharp decline in adherence to institutional religion in Scotland so soon after its buoyancy in the post-war decade, beginning in 1958 and continuing unremittingly since then? What was its effect on the models of mission that this book has considered? Did "Tell Scotland" and Billy Graham play a part in its occurrence, or was it all inevitable anyway? Did the failure of Allan's model to hold back the tide mean it is now indelibly tarnished? Do the radically altered social and ecclesial circumstances of the present day render the models of mission of the fifties and sixties redundant, or do their central beliefs and aims remain as relevant today as they did then?

The four Scottish models considered in the present book had the unknowing historical misfortune to be pitching their message to a population whose social demographic was in the early stages of a dramatic flux. Viewed back through the lens of the sixties, the seismic effect of social secularization on church adherence in Scotland leads the historian Tom Gallagher to conclude that "Tell Scotland" and the Billy Graham Crusade did no more

---

87. Whyte, Preface, vi.

88. Bisset, "William Franklin Graham," 376.

than "conveyed the impression of surface vigour and continuing popular appeal for Protestantism,"[89] whereas reality was about to bite.

The burgeoning growth of dynamic forms of Christianity in the period examined in this book in the decade following 1945 proves that the development of industrialization from the mid-nineteenth century did not cause the departure from organised religion in Scotland. A century-high peak in membership of the Church of Scotland was reached of around 1.32 million in 1956, and remained at 1.315 million in 1958. Instead, the decline in organised religion in Scotland began with the social revolution that then occurred in the United Kingdom, and elsewhere in the West.

As if without warning, as the historian Callum Brown has written: "In the late 50s and especially the 1960s, social forces were unleashed (especially amongst the young) which were to propel the Scottish Protestant churches into one of the most severe slides of church adherence yet experienced in the western world."[90]

Within a few short years from the all-time peak in the strength of the Christian churches in Scotland in society, and seemingly at the height of the radical movements in mission that this book has described, there was a sudden collapse. By 1963, the level of church connection was the lowest in the century, suggesting a drastic drop in the space of seven years. The following years of 1963 to 1965 then witnessed a plunge in the numbers of new communicants, baptisms and Sunday School attendance.[91]

For Peter Bisset, "the year 1958 was a watershed,"[92] given that the membership of the Church of Scotland "peaked in 1956, faltered, and by 1958 had plunged into a gradient of decline which has continued with little remission ever since." The identification by Bisset of the year 1958 as a turning point in Scotland is supported in broader perspective in the work of the social historians Hugh Macleod and Arthur Marwick. MacLeod adopts Marwick's concept of the "long 1960s" from 1958 to 1974 as "marking a rupture as profound as that brought about by the Reformation."[93] Referring to this quote, according to Macwhirter the fall in Scotland was of greater depth and intensity, given its prior global position as a bastion of Presbyterianism: "Since Scotland was one of the countries that led the Reformation in the 16th Century, this rupture was all the more dramatic here. Scotland has had

---

89. Gallagher, "Protestantism and Politics," 100.

90. C. G. Brown, "Each Take Off Their Several Way?" 81.

91. C. G. Brown, *Religion and Society in Scotland since 1707*, 159.

92. Bisset, "Training for Evangelism," 115, and graph on membership from 1948 to 1984 on the same page.

93. MacLeod, *The Religious Crisis of the 1960s*, 1, from Marwick, *The Sixties*, 7.

a history of militant Christianity from the Covenanters to the Disruption, and an education system largely shaped by the Kirk. It is hard to believe that all this could disappear, in historical terms, overnight. And yet it did."[94]

In the "long 1960s" from 1958 to 1974, the net loss of membership in the Church of Scotland was over a quarter of a million people down to 1,061,706. It has continued to fall at roughly the same rate since 1974, of around 150,000 to 165,000 people per decade, to a level in 2016 of 351,934.

Crucial to the decline of institutional Christianity within this period are the years of 1958 to 1963, during which Allan was still very much at the forefront of Scottish public life, and was recognising the gathering storm and reacting demonstratively against it. Those years are described by Hugh MacLeod as "a period of cautious questioning, of still tentative beginnings, in which some of the movements and trends that were to be characteristic of the years following began to be heard and seen."[95]

The gradual winding-down of the public prominence of Allan's missional model in those "bridge years" thus reflects not its essential utility but primarily the mood of its object, being ordinary people in wider society, summarised in this way by Hugh MacLeod: "The post-war church boom had come to an end . . . The power and prestige which the churches had often enjoyed in the years after the war and the associated atmosphere of moral conservatism were increasingly resented and were coming under attack—often in indirect ways."[96]

Macwhirter identifies three particular social forces which served to undermine the Kirk in these years:

- A change in the cultural dynamic—"the rise of youth culture, consumerism, the contraceptive pill and the spread of television";

- A change in the social dynamic—"Urban renewal and the growth of new towns . . . broke up the family networks and the connections between communities and local ministries"; and

- A change in the political dynamic—"religious dogmatism was challenged by the spread of progressive ideas . . . people had seen what government could achieve, and social progress undermined the community of faith.[97]

94. Macwhirter, *The Road to Referendum*, 147.

95. MacLeod, *The Religious Crisis of the 1960s*, 60.

96. Ibid., 82.

97. Macwhirter, *The Road to Referendum*, 147–48.

The underlying social fabric of the United Kingdom was experiencing rapid shifts in economic terms too. In contrast to the continued austerity in the decade following the Second World War, the period thereafter in the fifties and sixties "were decades of rising living standards and an expanding economy."[98] This manifested itself in a boom in consumerism for household and luxury goods, seen in a dramatic increase in the extent of home, car and television ownership, supermarkets and foreign holidays. The relative affluence was partly funded by the expansion of employment for women, particularly in part-time jobs, bringing them increasing independence and social mobility. The church failed to adapt to the changing culture, or positively engage with it in its liturgy, ecclesiology and public pronouncements.

With Christianity rapidly becoming side-lined from the mainstream in the late fifties and early sixties, that lay missiology which relied upon the church got lost in a national scale was partly a sign of the times, another casualty of the old order. Allan, MacLeod and the church as it then stood were in some ways powerless to counteract the alienation. The complacency of the church to which Allan often referred was, in part, inevitable. It was borne of the movement of society away from the institution, caused by the church's internal obduracy but also by social forces beyond its control.

Did the post-war church boom in some way contribute to the sharpness of the decline? Callum Brown argues that the evangelical discourse, of which Allan and Graham were an obvious continuance, was subject to a sudden discontinuation due to the very nature of its appeal in the postwar years. There is a connection between the strength of the church in the midfifties and the identity of the groups who departed in the decline which is difficult to overlook. Young people formed a large proportion of the missioners for "Tell Scotland" and D. P. Thomson's campaigns. The figures presented by Allan for the demographic of enquirers at the Crusade in 1955 indicate a predominance of young people.[99] These factors were in keeping with the times, as Callum Brown indicates: "The evidence suggests that the strong interest in organised religion [during 1946 to 1956] was amongst young people, perhaps especially those born just before and during the war years. It was this generation that experienced the last major exposure to the 'home mission.'"[100]

It was the departure of youth from the church which heralded the decline. The generation born in the period from 1930 to 1945 was the last which maintained, as a matter of generality, a close connection to

98. Pugh, *State and Society*, 279.

99. Allan, ed.*Crusade in Scotland*, 108.

100. C. G. Brown, *Religion and Society in Scotland since 1707*, 162–63.

organised religion. Once they had emerged from their formative experiences in the midfifties, they become integrated into the institutional church. Their successors in the late fifties and early sixties did not automatically follow. Those born postwar, "the Baby Boomers," were swept along in the social revolution of sixties Britain, with its significant "role of prosperity-induced cultural change in reducing the social significance of religion in people's lives."[101]

Allan recognised in 1962 that the moment may have now passed as the nation's youth began to confront the institution with their apathy or even antagonism:

> I think that in the years following the war the church . . . had the ball at its feet. Evangelism was easier then than it is today. More doors were open. There was a readiness to listen, to debate, to discuss—I'm thinking particularly of young people—which I don't believe is present to the same extent today.
>
> I don't doubt that the church itself is partly to blame for this. We failed to grasp our opportunities. It may have been a failure in understanding of the young people themselves, or a failure in courage to proclaim the total demands of the Christian faith to a generation which was prepared for commitment.[102]

The dramatic sea-change in the attitude of the nation's youth in the years between 1956 and 1963 is reflected in Allan's own writing. In mid-1956, Allan was preparing to lead a rally at the Kelvin Hall, Glasgow for 3,500 people, with another 2,000 people attending the adjoining arena for the rally to be transmitted by CCTV. Around three-quarters were to be young people between the ages of eighteen and twenty-five. Allan concluded that "young people today are more deeply concerned about religion than any generation in the past hundred years."[103]

However, by mid-1962, he commented on the departure of teenagers from the church because of: "The climate of the times and the failure on the part of the kirk. We're not capturing the imagination of young folk and their eagerness to the cause."[104]

Allan also presciently identified in that year that "our young people's rejection of the image of the church is part of a much more significant social and cultural change." Noting "new prophets" such as John Osborne, Jack

---

101. Ibid., 166.

102. AA6.11.5, *EC*, "The Young Ones, The Kirk Must Face the Challenge," 26 May 1962.

103. AA6.11.8, *Evening Times*, 11 May 1956.

104. AA.6.11.15, *The Sunday Post*, 8 July 1962.

Kerouac and Arnold Wesker, he correctly detected "an attitude of revolt and despair, of rejection and bitterness."[105]

By late 1963, he now recognised that where there might have been prior indifference, this was now replaced by "openly-expressed and articulate hostility [which] finds its main expression in the growing revolt against traditionally accepted Christian standards of moral behaviour: and its means of expression are virtually unlimited."[106]

Like many of his church contemporaries, Allan's response was not engagement, but in adopting a reactionary stance in a swing to the right. He concluded that the church would not win the youth back by "brighter services or jazzing up its liturgy. The issue is an ideological one."[107] Whilst socially and politically he remained firmly left-wing, on personal morality his writing became increasingly conservative. Inspired anew by meeting John Stott, the leading evangelical of the younger generation,[108] Allan wrote that: "The deepest social problem in Scotland today is the "couldn't care less" attitude of so many people who seem to spend all their energies in the immediate gratification of their material desires . . . Scotland needs a new moral dynamic, a new set of values, a new will to achievement, a new sense of direction . . . [to be found] . . . only from God himself . . . For me there is no answer to our problems apart from a revival of true religion."[109]

Likewise in the fifties, "the theatricality of the revivalist preacher" appealed to young women in an era which still placed strong religious connotations upon femininity, piety and the traditional social roles of women.[110] Women became the backbone of church life in subordinate, gender-specific positions. A key cultural change was the corrosion of those assumptions, as Callum Brown has notably concluded being: "the product of a 'de-pietisation of femininity,' combined with a 'de-feminisation of piety.' From the 1960s . . . being religious could no longer be founded on 'old' female virtues, and being feminine could no longer be founded on religious ones."[111]

The alienation of youth, particularly female, due to the change in cultural, social and political dynamics outlined above, thus contributed to the movement away from the church as institution. Because the vibrant lay

---

105. AA6.11.5, *EC*, "The Young Ones, The Kirk Must Face the Challenge," 26 May 1962.

106. AA6.11.12, *The Christian*, 18 October 1963.

107. Ibid.

108. AA6.11.1, *EC*, 24 November 1959.

109. AA6.5.9, TV Broadcast, "It's My Belief," c.1960.

110. C. G. Brown, *Religion and Society in Scotland since 1707*, 198.

111. Ibid., 204.

missiology had remained indelibly linked to the church, it too was a target. The sixties would thus indeed see the beginning of the transformation of the Kirk, but not in the manner Allan had envisaged. Instead of a shelter for regeneration for all, especially the lost and downtrodden, as Allan had desired, the Kirk became increasingly dependent upon affluent suburbia, re-enforcing a public image of standing and respectability. In the sixties and seventies, as Harvie comments: "Among professions with a strong sense of local position—such as law or banking—church membership remained strong, but its grip on the lower middle and working classes, which had survived the 1950s largely due to church extension programmes, could not cope with the social changes and population movement of the 1960s."[112]

The political outlook of the core of the church re-enforced the public perception of an increasing divergence. Its often conservative stance reflected not only its primarily upper-middle class composition, but also a history of working and "artisan" class Protestantism and Unionism of a previous generation, often linked to Freemasonry, the Orange Order and opposition to Irish Catholic immigration. A survey of Commissioners to the General Assembly of the Church of Scotland in 1964 found that 74 per cent voted Conservative, 13 per cent Liberal and 13 per cent Labour.[113] As the country, and its youth in particular, swung politically to the left, upon the "secularization of society" was super-imposed a "secularization of social prophecy" which had been growing from the foundation of the Labour movement in the 1890s, thus in political terms "sweeping aside the relevance of church connection."[114]

The need to identify with Protestantism for employment and personal advancement also began to diminish, as Roman Catholic emancipation became increasingly marked in social and legal frameworks. Protestantism as a way of life, dictating loyalty to a set of political allegiances, monarchism, and concepts of national identity, was drawing its final breaths.

The Church of Scotland's apparent links to a particular class, political affiliation, the professions and the establishment did not serve it well in the face of decline. Moreover, having failed to act on the outward-focused mission initiatives of the fifties, "a routine focused inwardly on the ordinances of religion, on recruitment by nurture, proved incapable of resisting secular trends."[115]

---

112. Harvie, *No Gods*, 155.

113. D.R. Robertson, "The Relationship between Church and Social Class in Scotland." PhD diss., University of Edinburgh, 1966, quoted in Callum G. Brown, "Each Take Off Their Several Way?" 82.

114. Callum G. Brown, "Each Take Off Their Several Way?" 81.

115. Bardgett, *Scotland's Evangelist*, 337.

In short, in complete anathema to Allan's driving ethos, in the words of Callum Brown, the Protestant churches "became estranged from the fulcrum of community identity."[116]

In the midst of such turmoil, or some would say as partly the cause of it, in the sixties a younger generation of clergy sought to change the direction of the institution towards a dedication to the poor and an engagement with the developing culture, influenced by liberation theology and international ecumenism, the theology of Dietrich Bonhoeffer,[117] the "demythologising" project of Rudolf Bultmann, and the "Honest to God" debate initiated by Bishop John Robinson. Many encountered such radicalism under the teaching of Ronald Gregor Smith and Ian Henderson at Trinity College, Glasgow. The historian Christopher Harvie writes of the sixties in the Church of Scotland:

> The church remained a paradox. Middle-class in recruitment and leadership, and on the whole evangelical in theology, it nevertheless adopted, largely at the behest of the clergy, a range of liberal policies on race, the arts, sexual morality, and home rule. Until the 1960s it was, effectively, the last redoubt of old-fashioned Scottish liberalism. But its appeal to the progressive young was dangerously limited, and in due course a generation of intellectuals who could sympathise with the church's radicals, such as [George] MacLeod or Kenneth McKenzie, personally and on political issues, simply faded away from formal belief.[118]

For a period at least, liberal, progressive Christianity could retain a public, intellectual voice in the social sciences, and as an alternative youth sub-culture in the "hippie" era. However, the attempt by some within the ministerial ranks of the Church of Scotland to meet the challenges of the sixties emphasised foreboding division internally. On an evangelical/ecumenical axis, centred on the Iona Community and the Crieff Fraternal, it created precisely the kind of factionalism which Allan was at pains to avoid throughout his life and ministry. It further produced a gulf with many of the older generations within the Kirk who were at the heart of the resistance to change which Allan had experienced in the previous decade. Their grounds of opposition now were to a radicalism which was in many ways more

116. Callum G. Brown, "Each Take Off Their Several Way?" 81.

117. In particular, the influence of Dietrich Bonhoeffer, *The Cost of Discipleship* and *Letters and Papers from Prison*.

118. Harvie, *No Gods*, 83–84. Kenneth McKenzie (1920–71) was a progressive Church of Scotland minister in central Africa, serving in present day Malawi and Zambia as they moved towards independence, and on his return to Scotland was a founder of the anti-apartheid movement.

extreme than the emancipated social theology of Allan. In comparison, Allan's missiological drive in the fifties to purge and re-invent the church as a socially-compassionate agent and object of mission must have by then seemed mild and benign to the church's bedrock parishioners.

Some would argue that the departure from a core evangelical message hastened the decline, or even was contributory to its creation. Many of the leading figures in traditional Scottish church life of the fifties, who had been supportive of Allan and Graham, viewed any attempt to engage or align with the cultural shifts as doomed and destructive.

Whichever direction Allan may have taken had he lived longer, with his missiological insight and concentration on the integration of Gospel and culture, he would have been amongst the first to recognise the present dilemma of contextualization that, in Will Storrar's words, "the churches must acknowledge that cultural change from modern to postmodern Scotland and re-think not only their patterns of church life and mission but their understanding and practice of the Gospel itself."[119]

Whilst the radically altered social context will mean that those "re-thought patterns" cannot simply mimic the past, and that some of Allan's methods such as "visitation evangelism," public preaching or mass evangelism are likely obsolete, the essence of Allan's work which pre-figured and in part directed mission in "late modern" times, needs to be retrieved and re-focused as a guide to the present and future, such as the primacy of the lives and witness of ordinary people.

Looking back, if there was ever a "window" in which a model relying on the laity of a re-invigorated institutional church as both agent and object of mission could have borne lasting fruit on a national scale in Scotland, it was in the decade from 1946 onwards. Church affiliation was high, a dedicated band of young people had enthusiastically engaged with the institution, the church retained a strong body of gifted and inspirational leaders, and the forces of secularization had not yet imposed a strident narrative in the alternative. It was within sight of making a lasting impact, certainly prior to 1955. The period, however, transpired to be "the last hurrah" of large-scale home mission.

As can be seen in the "Tell Scotland" reports at Wiston Lodge in 1958, if the church could not be turned around, the ministry themselves with their dominant position within the Kirk must shoulder some of the blame, for as the journalist Harry Reid comments:

> The 1950s in particular were a fat and good period for the Kirk,
> but the alarming decline that has set in since then may well be

119. Storrar, "A Tale of Two Paradigms," 69.

rooted in a lack of far-sightedness at that time and in a failure to respond adequately and imaginatively to the fresh challenges that were beginning to emerge . . . Maybe . . . the ministers of fifty years ago did not do a sufficiently rigorous and forward-looking job at a time when the current was, for the most part, with them.[120]

The bottom line is that the missionary focus on the laity of 1945 to 1960 was lost or abandoned, along with much of the church's social standing. With the enthusiasm for mission and ecumenism waning amongst church leaders and ministers, by reflection an ignored laity lost interest. It is difficult not to agree with Frank Bardgett when he concludes that "the "new evangelism" of the post-war era had run into the sands" and with his comments of the church at a general level that "a historic opportunity to prepare the Kirk for the post-modern era had been lost." Thus, in the absence of any vision taking hold to transform the church, "conventional, minister-centred life and reticent laity proved enduringly resistant to all challenges to change."[121]

In conclusion, as the late fifties and early sixties unfolded, the church became increasingly incapable of establishing the "missionary parish" because of the growing progress of secularization, and its direct impact upon youth and women in the church, the mainstays of the model. Allan's model centred upon the church. Secularization militates now against the church as the sole *object* of mission, albeit it does not, in the writer's view, of itself rule out the focus of Allan on the church laity as the potential *agent* of mission.

## Conclusions on the Missiology of Tom Allan

Despite the frictions inherent within the "tale of two paradigms" and their adverse consequences in the "tensions" identified, practical and theological highpoints of Allan's missiology can be identified. These demonstrate that his missiology should not be viewed primarily in terms of practical "failure" viewed from the present vantage point, but in many ways as a success and source of inspiration.

Firstly, at the local level as a parish minister, the achievements of Tom Allan at North Kelvinside and St George's Tron were substantial. He brought about the transformation and regeneration of two dormant congregations within Scotland's largest industrial city. Churches that had been introspective, self-satisfied, formalised, decaying and near-empty

120. Reid, *Outside Verdict*, 55.
121. Bardgett, *Scotland's Evangelist*, 336.

when he arrived, were left energised, outward-looking and multiplied. The sheer dynamism of Allan's personality, his obvious commitment and integrity, his empathy for and care towards that man and woman on the street, and his gifts as a preacher and pastor were integral. As his friend Ian Doyle described him, Allan "was a man with a genius for friendship, a wonderful gift of leadership and radiant and winsome personality that made him the centre of any gathering."[122] Through his public persona and oratorical gifts in the pulpit and national media, united with a deep faith, Allan fulfilled the criteria to meet one of the key building blocks of mission that he had identified, that of effective communication of the Gospel.

In his preaching, public speaking and broadcasts, Allan illuminated and radiated the Gospel, such that he became the embodiment of the depth of communication of faith described by his colleague James S. Stewart in *A Faith to Proclaim*: "Christian preaching begins only when faith in the message has reached a pitch that the man or the community proclaiming it becomes part of the message proclaimed . . . therefore, the problem of communication resolves itself into a question of faith: faith in the message, the kind of faith which, being *fiducia* and not mere *assensus*, is an act uniting the messenger to the Christ of whom his message tells."[123]

Through his public proclamations and action, Allan became identified by his congregations and those with whom he interacted nationally and internationally as being not only a messenger of the Christian narrative, but in himself as part of the message. The extraordinary renovation that he achieved of redundant parish congregations relates partly to the abilities of the man in his words and deeds to engage with ordinary people and draw them towards an encounter with Christ and His church.

It was a mission and ministry of action. As he neared the end of his ministry at St George's Tron, one of full engagement and self-offering to all around him, Tom Allan wrote: "Jesus orders us out into the highways and byways, into the streets and lanes of the city, to meet with people wherever they are, and whether they recognise their need for God or not."[124]

In those encounters in the streets and lanes of the city, at the core of his ministry Allan's demonstration was of compassion to all as an outpouring of God's love, seeking expression of the Gospel in word and deed, towards common understanding and growth of community. It was reflective of the nature of God, revealed through Christ as familial and interdependent.

122. AA6.11.15, Ian Doyle, "My Friend Tom," newspaper cutting late 1965.
123. Stewart, *A Faith to Proclaim*, 45.
124. AA6.5.2 and AA6.11.7, *EC*, "My Friend the Criminal," 10 August 1963.

Secondly, on a national stage, despite its failings, what was achieved through Allan's missiology still stands well above much that has come before or since. Allan was at the forefront of an extraordinary recovery of the church and mission in the period from 1946 to 1958, as he described: "if I were asked to sum up in a word what is the most significant development in the church in the post-war world, I should answer without any hesitation—the rediscovery of the church's missionary task."[125]

This was evident in the immediate post-war years as a matter of generality, as D. P. Thomson reflected in May 1950: "The last 4 1/2 years have seen an influence on the church beyond anything I achieved in the previous 25—not so vital an influence on individuals but rather the whole policy and outlook of the church in evangelism."[126]

Furthermore, the additional effect of Allan's missiology on church and nation in the period immediately following was profound, as Bardgett reflects: "For a time, the missionary banner of the multi-faceted "Tell Scotland" Movement brought multitudes of ordinary church members both into the streets and to new conceptions of their vocation. Even that level of success was remarkable."[127]

Despite the rupture of the sixties and the decline to the present, there also remains within the continuing life of the church, both in pulpit and pew, an older generation who were deeply influenced by Allan and Graham. Bisset commented in 1987 that, "there are many who still remember these days with warm thankfulness."[128]

Those heady days may not be repeated. The departure of liberal Christianity towards a "conciliar," worldly reading of the *missio Dei* in the early sixties led to the beginnings of an evangelical/ecumenical split that has thereafter dogged Scottish Christianity and world ecumenism. As the divergence became deeply rooted in theology, the centrality of the humble witness of the lay member also became increasingly marginalised, as it "re-emphasised the role of the theologically trained, the ministers of Word and Sacrament."[129]

The local effect was that, as Bebbington notes, "confidence in evangelistic campaigns . . . waned among the less conservative in the 1960s. In Britain as a whole, as the distance between the poles of theological opinion

125. AA6.2.13, "The Witness of the Layman," Ashlin White Bible Lectures, USA, 1953.

126. *The Diary of My Life*, 3 May 1950, quoted in Frank Bardgett, *Scotland's Evangelist*, 189.

127. Bardgett, "The 'Tell Scotland' Movement: Failure and Success," 150.

128. Bisset, "Training for Evangelism," 116.

129. Bardgett, *Scotland's Evangelist*, 337.

widened, the scope for centrist enterprise declined."[130] The days of large-scale, ecumenically based missionary endeavor had passed.

Secularization has further rendered the nation to be of a markedly different hue. From a present-day perspective, the method of house-to-house visitation now seems counter-productive in a different social climate, whilst the institutional church is numerically and publically weak in comparison.

It is therefore unlikely that such a large-scale movement as "Tell Scotland" will be replicated in the near future.

If Allan's choices had been different, could his model have worked? On one view, as already expressed, a church that had been held closer to Allan's pre-1955 model of local church growth might have withstood secularization in the sixties with greater rigor, as it may have been rooted more closely in the lives of ordinary people and distanced further from the hierarchy. Then again, maybe the whole model, Graham included, did fulfil the extent of its potential in the circumstances of church and nation, as Highet suggested in 1960: "Perhaps churchmen will feel that the best that can be said is that post-war evangelism has worked as a holding operation and that . . . things would have been much worse without it."[131]

Social context may then account in part for both the post-war boom in religion in Scotland from 1946 to 1958 in which Allan played a significant part, as well as the start of the decline in the "watershed" period of 1958 to 1963.

Sociological explanations are not, however, sufficient of themselves for the heady optimism of the former period. It took the presence and intervention of gifted men in Christian mission on the national and international stage as the catalyst, amongst whom Tom Allan is entitled to a particular prominence. However, as Allan wrote, "The work of evangelism doesn't depend on the gifts or genius of any outstanding man, but on the existence of a community of dedicated people who are prepared to work at their faith and translate it into action."[132] It is that focus which forms the basis of a re-application to the present. Despite the clear decline in the presence and influence of Scottish Christianity after the moment in the sun from 1946 to 1958, the lasting power of the work during that period retains a purpose in being positively retrieved.

What might then be recovered for the present from the life and work of Tom Allan?

---

130. Bebbington, *Evangelicalism in Modern Britain*, 253.
131. Highet, *The Scottish Churches*, 121.
132. AA6.11.8, *EC*, 23 October 1959.

No matter the roots of its success or failure of the model in its time, as James Whyte comments of *The Face of My Parish* "we may need to sit down with the seriousness, honesty and charity which Tom Allan demonstrated ... and learn with him the lessons of the 1950s."[133]

If but one legacy remains, it is the certainty that Allan held that the laity of the church should prevail, and that only the ordinary people who populated the church's pews would prove themselves capable of expressing Christian faith in word and deed to the prevailing culture.

For organised Christianity, Allan's missiology invites us not to give up. Despite the possible "conflict and heartbreak" involved, it re-affirms the potential strength of an embattled institution: that it might yet be a radical, prophetic community, a revitalised "Church Without Walls."[134]

Allan recognised the temptation of deliberately distancing the focus of the building of Christian *koinonia* and *ekklesia* from the pre-existing church structure, and of asserting that unsullied individual witness might present a purer picture of Christ without the baggage of institution. Allan, however, dissented from that view, despite his castigation of the church's failings, retaining faith in the church's capacity to ultimately fulfil its God-given purpose.

Allan's views on the remaining capacity of the institutional church are reminiscent of some critics in the present day. In their attack on the theology in the Church of England of the 2004 Report *Mission Shaped Church*, and its practical application that is "Fresh Expressions," Andrew Davison and Alison Millbank stringently re-assert the value for Christian mission of the church, and thus of a missional emphasis based on structure, stability and the parochial system.

Davison and Milbank speak of the parish as satisfying the need for local, sacred place, the open inclusivity of worship, the priority of public sacraments, and as a "springboard for mission and for engagement with the needs of our contemporary culture."[135] The Christian parish community is capable of meeting those ends as it exists as a perfect "devolved and mediating structure." Furthermore, the parish is "not just important in nurturing a sense of belonging but for configuring a vision of humanity that embraces a sense of the local and the universal together."[136] Their solution to the national institutional church crisis is "rebuilding a Christian imaginary in the

133. Whyte, Preface, vi.

134. The analogy between the missiology of the 2001 Church of Scotland report of that name and *The Face of My Parish* is drawn by Bardgett, "Missions and Missionaries: Home," 508.

135. Davison and Milbank, *For the Parish*, 169.

136. Ibid.

parish."[137] They envisage a revitalised church more capable of responding to a secularized world, not a wholesale abandonment of the institution and all those held within it.

Allan's missiology survives later theological trends because defied narrow categorization, particularly prior to 1955, and was willing to consider the employment of *any* means of mission possible. His missiology would not have dismissed the relevance of "emerging church," as do Davison and Millbank, but would have embraced it as an overall strategy which also involved the church.

That openness is brought to light in correspondence with Bruce Kenrick, a long-term friend who appears in Allan's address book as early as 1948.[138]

When Kenrick's book on the East Harlem Protestant Parish, *Come Out the Wilderness*, was published in the UK in 1962, it was lauded by those pursuing an incarnational approach to mission and social justice. Reviews in Scotland suggested that mass evangelism was now finished. Allan responded in his newspaper column, praising the EHPP, but concluding: "It's not a question of this kind of evangelism or another. It's a question of *using every God-given method* to reach men, wherever they are, with the Gospel."[139]

Kenrick wrote to Allan in support, praising him as a minister "who puts both sides of the Gospel first in his own church in central Glasgow . . . with the clear proclamation from the pulpit of the Word that became flesh . . . and the clear demonstration from the rescue work in the streets of the Word that is becoming flesh."[140]

Late in his life, Allan described his ministry and model of mission as "walking a tightrope" between the extremes of a salvationist, conservative evangelicalism that was set in opposition to a growing incarnational, liberal ecumenism.[141] Distanced from both camps, Allan defied typecast and balanced on the tension of the separating wire, in a distinctive attempt to employ or support all means at hand, whether preaching, rallies, small groups, incarnational living or direct social and political action, in order to communicate the Christian Gospel in word and deed.

In "walking the tightrope," the diverse nature of much of Allan's missiological approach and its openness to influence from any angle, proved on

137. Ibid., 170.

138. AA6.9.

139. AA6.11.6, *EC*, 22 February 1963, (my emphasis).

140. AA6.11.6, letter from Bruce Kenrick to Tom Allan, dated 28 February 1963.

141. From conversations with Bill and Betsy Shannon, Pitlochry, 22 November 2010. Bill Shannon was Allan's student assistant in North Kelvinside, assistant minister at St George's Tron, and close friend.

the national stage to present a risk to its consistency and direction, but is also a mark of its depth of character, adaptability and maturity.

Allan's missiology offers a welcome transcendence beyond the evangelical/incarnational polarization which has inhibited mission in the United Kingdom for the past half-century. The future of mission lies with the same fusion of the personal and corporate transformative experience of the Gospel with its social responsibility.

It is Allan's ability to formulate a dynamic mission plan that was theologically rich and contextually appropriate by utilising contemporary thought, combined with his willingness to cross any divides in the name of Christ, that establishes a locus for his missiology to be heard in the present. The same "both/and" missiology to act in speech and action across the theological divides is required.

Allan's work was at the "beginning of the end" for Bosch's "modern, Enlightenment paradigm" of church and mission, whose endgame we may be approaching. Allan's missiology thus encompassed varying strands, with inevitable friction and no little contradiction. On the one hand, it adhered to a "top down" loyalty to the institutional church, on the other to a "bottom up" dedication to the empowerment of the individual. It dismissed the immediate inheritance of the inter-war years of social quietism, sectarianism and occasional bursts of parish mission, but yet saw fit to reclaim an age-old evangelism of preaching for a decision.

In Allan's attempted mixture of both "modern" and "postmodern" elements, he speaks to us of a struggle that continues for present day Christianity in Scotland. He faced the challenge of how to live missiologically in recognising that one social milieu might be drifting towards oblivion but with stubborn resistance, whilst seeking to implement elements that potentially might establish new ground under stolid opposition. The conundrum for him, as now, was which aspects of each might be compatible with the state of society in order to form an effective whole, to which we shall later turn.

At its core, if there is to be a transplantation to the present of a model of mission based on the "apostolate of the laity," given those tensions, the institutional church must no longer be relied upon solely as the object and end of mission, to allow space for the development of "emergent" forms that might in turn illuminate the church's path but not be dependent upon it. Likewise, the bludgeon of mass evangelism is far distant from the social, ecclesial and cultural landscape, and hence should be confined to discussion and analysis, rather than implementation.

What is needed instead of division between those who exercise experimental forms of ministry and the church as institution, is, like Allan, a desire to embrace all possible methods as informing and complementing the others, and thus an incorporation of the theological nuances of "Fresh Expressions" *within* the outlook of the church and its laity to guide the direction of mission: the church learning from, but not seeking to take over, such forms.[142]

The church must therefore be confident that it may retain a potential role in nourishing and equipping appropriate forms of contextual mission to build Christian communities, but in recognition that it may not be the institutional community that is built up as a result.

Through his absolute personal commitment to Christ and to the people, when married to his missiological theory, Tom Allan made a profound impact for over a decade upon the Scottish church and nation, which continues to resonate. Allan wrote in 1960, on the 400th anniversary of the Scottish Reformation: "No great figure has emerged since the war who might lead the Kirk into the next phase of its expanding life."[143]

From the vantage point of a further half century, the identity of a "great figure" who did so, and may have continued to do so in compelling ways had he survived beyond another five short years, is not challenging to locate.

Allan's life's purpose, both in a spiritual and practical sense, followed the title of a 1959 series for the *Evening Citizen*: to "Rescue the Fallen."[144] In doing so, Allan fulfilled his own criteria for discipleship which he spoke of in his final sermon: "it is for this that we are called as Christians . . . that the world should look beyond us to Christ, seeing perhaps in us a fraction of his image."[145]

142. The Mission and Discipleship Report to the General Assembly of the Church of Scotland 2014 indicates a partnership as from 1 October 2013 between the Mission and Discipleship Council, the Ministries Council and the Church of England "Fresh Expressions" Movement, which may provide a channel for such insight–RGA 2014, Mission and Discipleship Report, 3.1.

143. AA6.5.8, "The Church of Scotland Today."

144. AA6.5.7.

145. MacDonald, ed., *A Fraction of His Image*, 35.

# 5

# Concurrent Scottish and American Streams

The fact of the Incarnation, lived out in the lives of Christians and in the lifestyle of the church, is, and always will be, the clearest statement on the Christian Social Vision in this and any society, in this and any age.[1]

—John Harvey, 1993

## Introduction

HOW DID THE WORK of Allan's contemporaries serve to complement and enhance his own in developing the contextualization of the Gospel to the ordinary and the everyday, or indeed contrast in its focus?

Allan's pre-1955 model suffered significantly from the concentration on the church as the sole agent and object of mission, and the reversion to mass evangelism. Other models consciously rejected both of those concentrations, whilst also like Allan seeking to re-focus the Gospel upon life on the street. This chapter will consider their content, theology and impact. Do they provide a more coherent direction that could be adapted to the present, either in appreciating their "successes" or by recognising the terms of their "failures"?

Their thread of mission development led beyond the prior one-dimensional transmission of an immutable Gospel, and the jolt of initial contextualization from the work of Tom Allan, towards the further development of a language and mode that might more fully integrate the work of the church and the message of the Gospel with the lives of the people.

---

1. Harvey, "What There Is to See," 75.

If we contrast the apparent failure of the "Forward Movement" to gal-
vanize the parish church with the advances in Scotland of the immediate
post-war period, the difference may lie partly in the social climate and the
role of inspirational figures such as Allan. However, to a significant extent it
reflected a change of ethos: the deeper concentration on the laity in church
and mission; and in the church embracing an outward vision, seeking a
Christianity rooted in the daily experience and looking to correlate it with
the Gospel. Rather than a "come to church" movement which sought to impose an unchanging, ecclesiastically enshrined strain of Protestantism *upon*
the parish, mission became an "encounter the Gospel" movement seeking to
align the ecclesiology of Protestantism *with* the parish.

Disappearing, at least amongst the more forward-thinking clergy,
was a notion of supremacy through the power and domination which the
church had asserted in Scottish society over the centuries—of a desire to
create a Protestant "parish-state" bent on eradicating theological difference.
The direction was towards a church and parish built from a greater humility,
seeking dialogue, understanding and relationship.

Approaching the same underlying issues of relevance and authenticity
from a different angle, the questions then asked were: did the processes of
the new mainstream model go far enough? Was the re-vitalisation from
within of the existing church as agent and object of mission actually a
necessary pre-requisite, given the impediments to mission that it produced?
Could other methods withstand the growing secularization of society in
a more robust form, or even embrace it as the work of God? Could the
Gospel not be contextualized instead by avoiding the pre-existing church,
by being expressed anew, and with ordinary people thus granted the space
for spiritual formation without the baggage of the past?

The following streams of missional exploration believed that this
might occur through (a) the development of a connected bond of the life
of the church with that of the industrial worker at home and in the factory
(The Iona Community); (b) the literal re-location of the church's buildings
and clergy to the street front (the East Harlem Protestant Parish); (c) the
deliberate shunning of the old institution in favour of a life on the streets
from which God might grow a new form of church community (the Gorbals
Group Ministry); and (d) allowing the laity of all church denominations
to meet on neutral ground to develop common strands that would
revolutionize and unite their institutions (the ecumenism of Robert Mackie,
Ian Fraser, and Scottish Churches House).

In the two decades following World War II, these were separate exten-
sions in such directions, also stretching beyond "evangelism" by oral proclamation alone, towards a more holistic vision of the presence of the whole

people of God in the world. They offer further illumination of what Allan was seeking, and contribute to the development of derivations and principles based on what the historical picture of that period may mean for us now.

## The Church in the Parish, Factory and Home of the Worker—The Iona Community

### Parish Mission—the "Mission of Friendship"

There were echoes of Tom Allan's mode of mission in the recent life of the church in Scotland. He believed that he was following what Thomas Chalmers had begun in his campaign of "aggressive visitation" in Glasgow from 1819, writing that "he carried out a mission to his parish which was an absolutely new departure in missionary strategy, and anticipated by more than a century the very things for which "Tell Scotland" stands today. Parish Mission began with Thomas Chalmers in St John's."[2]

He recognised also the debt to the words and work of John White whilst in the parish of Shettleston in 1901. White wrote to his people in surprisingly similar terms to Allan: "There is a need of an organised effort being made to bridge the gulf between the church and the lapsed masses in our large towns and cities; the one question is how? We do not disparage the old method and policy of the church . . . we require to readjust our methods . . . We must supplement the regular army of the ministry with the volunteer efforts of the laity."[3]

White formed a lay group from the congregation named the "Septuagint," being seventy men who carried out "visitation evangelism" two-by-two. It had the goal of "the evangelisation of the whole parish."[4] As White's biographer suggests, "the motto on its banner might have been "Tell Shettleston" as it was an early prototype of the "Tell Scotland" movement."[5]

Writing in 1960, Allan referred to the "Septuagint" practising "visitation evangelism" in Shettleston and acknowledged that White "was conducting Parish missions fifty years in advance of their time."[6]

On the method of implementation of his model which he had championed with D. P. Thomson, Allan further acknowledged, "there is nothing new

2. AA6.5.8, "Thomas Chalmers and the Disruption."

3. Papers of John White, Box 95, New College Library, University of Edinburgh, *Shettleston Parish Magazine*, April 1901, vol. 11, no. 4, "The City and the Church."

4. Ibid., May 1901.

5. Muir, *John White*, 42.

6. AA6.5.8, "Landmarks of the Kirk, 4. John White—Reunion and Extension," 10.

in the technique of house-to-house visitation in parochial evangelism."[7] Not only had White employed the method, Allan knew that it had "in America . . . been worked out in the past thirty years with devastating thoroughness."[8]

Most significantly, the parallels in theory and method with the parish mission of the Iona Community are clear. For twenty years, Tom Allan enjoyed a fractious but always respectful relationship with the founder of the Iona Community, George MacLeod. On the 21st anniversary of the founding of the Iona Community, Allan wrote in the *Evening Citizen*:

> For my own part, I have never been, am not now and—so far as I can see—never will be a member of the Iona Community. Yet I thank God for George MacLeod.
>
> Like every revolutionary in the church's history, he inspires among his colleagues either devotion or opposition. But never apathy or indifference.
>
> You may disagree with him, but you can never ignore him. And his insistent emphasis during the past twenty years on the integration of faith and ordinary life, his brilliant insights into so much that is hypocritical or bogus in conventional religion, his pleading for the underprivileged—all these have compelled us to re-examine our faith against the background of life, and have driven some of us back for the first time to a real study of the Word of God.[9]

In turn, MacLeod liked Allan, but became distant from him over the change of direction in "Tell Scotland" through the invitation to Billy Graham in 1954 to 1955, as MacLeod's biographer Ron Ferguson reflects: "There is no doubt that George MacLeod was disappointed in what he saw as the individualistic direction taken by Tom Allan, whose zeal for Christ he admired."[10] Underlying MacLeod's admiration was a frustration at Allan's refusal to be held down by one wing of Christianity, but to endorse both salvationism and social justice in equal measure as essential components of Christian mission. As Allan's close friend Andy Moyes recalled, "George MacLeod was to say of him, 'Tom Allan has a pain in the groin through having a foot in both camps!'"[11]

7. Allan, *The Face of My Parish*, 20.

8. For its use in the USA in the 1920s, see Kernahan, *Visitation Evangelism* and *Adventures in Visitation Evangelism*.

9. AA6.11.2, *EC*, 4 July 1959.

10. Ferguson, *George MacLeod*, 271–272.

11. Moyes, "The Face of My (Missionary) Parish," 16.

They were, however, closely linked in their passion for the Christian faith and social justice: "Few have proclaimed the power of the Gospel to transform lives as Tom Allan and George MacLeod. Few also have had such passionate concern for the social implications of the Gospel . . . Tom's concern was as much with discipleship and service, as with rebirth."[12]

Moreover, their mutual focus on parish mission and the centrality of the church is readily identifiable. George MacLeod was "a fanatic for the church," wanting to purge it to its "life—and world—changing potential."[13] He was Moderator of the General Assembly of the Church of Scotland in 1957, and for many years from 1958 the Chairman of the Church Extension Committee of the Home Board during its height, planting traditional models of church in the rapidly expanding peripheral housing developments in Scotland's cities.

Ralph Morton wrote in 1956, in words that now seem incongruous, "The Iona Community exists to further the Mission of the church."[14] From 1938 until the rebuilding of Iona Abbey was completed in 1965, the very essence of the Iona Community was parish mission. This was a reflection for Morton of "the Iona Community as George MacLeod saw it at the beginning—a practical scheme for the training of young ministers. And this is how he continued to see it . . . There is no question that it was for this purpose that the Iona Community was originally founded."[15]

Parish mission was inherent both in the purpose of a brotherhood of ministry candidates being made fit for urban parishes through their summer work with the tradesmen in the rebuilding of Iona Abbey, and in the parish "Missions of Friendship." Therefore, as Ralph Morton recalled: "When at the beginning . . . George MacLeod expounded the aims of the new community, he did so in terms of the renewal of the parish. In the fifties this was still the dominant idea. When members talked about experiments it was to experiments in the parish that they usually referred."[16]

MacLeod's mission plan was therefore concerned with the renovation of church life, re-iterated as a starting point in his manifesto of the Community in 1946, *We Shall Rebuild*: "in the world as it is there appears a primary demand . . . It is that the church must be turned around."[17] The church and its surrounding society would begin to merge, the church to act as a beacon

12. Simpson, "Faith and Works," 19.

13. Bardgett, *Scotland's Evangelist*, 170.

14. Morton, "The House Church: The Next Step? Or a First Step?," 5.

15. Morton, *The Iona Community*, 110.

16. Ibid., 91.

17. MacLeod, *We Shall Rebuild*, 11.

of Christian community, and thus be the means by which the wider public would be evangelized. It was, like Allan, rolling exponential growth which he anticipated.

MacLeod wrote in *We Shall Rebuild*, that "if the church is to leaven the Lump of the world,"[18] it would do so by a "Message of Friendship" which "will be quite unlike the sudden coming of a complete stranger . . . to pour forth in a concentrated week a series of rather astonishing sentences in which the word Salvation appears a remarkable number of times."[19]

Instead, he advocated the following successive steps in a parish mission:

- Visitation by the congregation

- A census

- Mission to the households in the parish with no church connection, imparting Christian literature and invitations to social gatherings; and

- "It is then—but only then—possible to envisage a week of meetings in the church, with an outside missioner."[20]

MacLeod's thinking in 1946 was related to his practice in the "Mission of Friendship," as lived out in his Govan ministry from 1933 to 1934 onwards, and thereafter transposed by the Iona Community in the post-war period to other urban parishes. It bears a remarkable resemblance to Tom Allan's early missiology, with its emphasis on lay action and visitation. Ferguson's view is that Allan's missiology at North Kelvinside was "influenced by the Iona mission of friendship model,"[21] an opinion which is reinforced by repeated references to that model and to *We Shall Rebuild* within *The Face of My Parish.*[22]

Therefore, as regards the concentration on the possibilities of saving the church by developing new forms of socially-aware community, and in utilising visitation by the congregation as a method of establishing contact with those in the parish, Allan was in tune with the missionary aims of the Iona Community, which in Allan's time had gained a mark of security by its integration within the auspices of the national church.[23] So where was the point of departure between Allan and Macleod?

18. As quoted by Ferguson, *George MacLeod*, 99.

19. Ibid., 107.

20. Ibid., 108–9.

21. Ferguson, *George MacLeod*, 270.

22. For example, reference to both appears at 98.

23. The Iona Community was integrated within the structures of the Church of

Despite their common ground on the goal of a transformed community, and on some of the methods of mission, there remained an underlying difference in emphasis on how to attain that goal. Both men accepted the need for a personal conversion and commitment to faith, and also for social witness. Allan, though, would come to require the first as a prerequisite of the second. Conversely, MacLeod warned against "an extractionist salvation,"[24] which would draw the convert out of the world, as if being removed from a swamp. From his perspective, the involvement of the individual with social and political reality was part of the formative conversion experience, not attainable solely by an alteration of the spiritual state. The formation of the new community would run concurrently with conversion and commitment, not the latter in separation from the former as a mass evangelist would propose.

In the "Report of Committee Anent Iona Community" to the General Assembly of May 1955, some six weeks after the "All Scotland Crusade," MacLeod resumed the attack upon it, stating that it is "very dangerous to demand a precisely dated conversion or to prescribe a single type of experience ... the responsibility of the church is not merely to men as individuals, but to men in their total life—in their occupations, in their social groupings, in their political life."[25]

The 1956 General Assembly report of the Iona Community under MacLeod's convenorship confronted the direction in which "Tell Scotland" was headed: "The problem can be focused in the question—which is nearest scripture as the *fons et origo* of mission: the converted individual or the divine society that is the Body of our Lord."[26]

This split in emphasis between MacLeod and Allan was well known to them both, and had been apparent from an early meeting at Community House, as mutual friend John Sim recalled:

> I knew that Tom ... had fire in his belly about peace and justice, and I knew, too, that many had been converted under George. I felt deeply that the two had more in common than most people thought. So I sat back and watched and prayed as the two joined battle. Both agreed on the implications of the faith, and Tom was as left-wing as George having come from a poor working class home. But Tom insisted that in order to work out the political implications of the faith, one must first be a

Scotland by the General Assembly of 1951.

24. Ferguson, *George MacLeod*, 272.

25. RGA 1955, 739.

26. RGA 1956, 740–741.

Christian. To spell out the implications to the unconverted was a waste of time. George insisted that unless one took the "one way" he had outlined, one could not become a real Christian. So the two parted.[27]

Allan was firmly a man of the people, committed to social welfare as an intimate relation to an embodied faith in Christ. However, in words which reflected the dispute between Allan and MacLeod, Allan asserted in the aftermath of the Graham Crusade that individuals would have "no prophetic word to speak to the age, and no relevant social witness to make, unless . . . they are converted men."[28]

For Allan, the church's primary task was therefore *not* to confront unjust social structures, but instead to bring the Gospel to those outwith the church, to evangelize first in the sense of winning souls by a personal salvation. Allan did value social action *per se*, but saw its main utility, like much else, as "an absolute pre-condition for effective evangelism."[29] This was "cause and effect" missiology as it relates to social justice, salvation first and social action as a result, which was common in evangelical circles at least until the Lausanne gathering in 1974.

Whilst that distinction was trivial at their early meeting described by Sim, when the power balance reflected Allan as a parish minister and MacLeod as an esteemed church leader, it would become central to the very future of the church when Allan assumed control and direction beyond even that of MacLeod.

## House Church Movement

In seeking to re-align the expression of the Gospel with the life of the urban worker, the parish church focus of the Iona Community would thus call "Iona Men" to widely implement "Missions of Friendship" in their city parishes in the forties and fifties, particularly in the new housing areas created by slum clearance. It would also call them to express a desire to witness through innovative forms of re-connection with the home and the factory, in the House Church Movement, and in industrial mission.

As for the latter, the Community was at the forefront of the first experiment in industrial chaplaincy with the employment of Ian Fraser at the Tullis Russell paper mill in Markinch in the early 1940s; of the first appointment

27. Ferguson, *George MacLeod*, 271.

28. Allan, ed., *Crusade in Scotland*, 111 (my emphasis).

29. AA6.2.18, Speech on Social Service Night, General Assembly, 25 May 1960.

of a full-time industrial chaplain in 1962, being Cameron Wallace to the shipyards of Greenock and Port Glasgow; and through George Wilkie of the creation of workers' groups such as the Scottish Christian Workers League, and the forum of the Scottish Churches Industrial Council. The presence within industry became marked: there were over one hundred industrial chaplains in post via the Church of Scotland by 1965.[30]

In relation to the former, The House Church Movement connected more directly with the regeneration of the traditional model of parish church and mission. If Ralph Morton could assert that the "old evangelism" was past, and if George MacLeod was adamant that Allan's invitation to Graham was an error in missiological theory, what could be the alternatives within the parish if the congregation was truly to become the agent of mission? The first was the "congregational group" which Allan sought to implement, particularly in his pre-1954 missiology. The opposite extreme was the radical implantation of a cell from outside within a community, to live and work alongside the community, as was implemented by the Gorbals Group Ministry. The middle ground would be the House Church Movement, instigated within the United Kingdom by the Church of England in the late forties, and expressed and publicised in particular by the Iona Community as "the first step" for the laity in the mid-fifties, especially in the wake of Evanston.

In other words, the "House Church" was to be the means by which ordinary people would be introduced to Christianity and be nurtured in the faith amongst their fellows, before any reference was made to the institution. It would not simply be a staging post towards a fuller church membership, but rather a means and an end in itself, in microcosm of the larger church—a surprisingly similar concept in its infancy to the "basic Christian communities" lionised by liberation theologians in the seventies, the "emerging church" groups of today in the West, and the present House Churches throughout Asia, in particular in China.

Writing in 1950, John Robinson, later famous as the Bishop of Woolwich and author of *Honest to God*, described the potential of House Churches as "not simply bits of the church; they are the Body of Christ in its totality, as it exists in this cell. Each cell is a microcosm, on its own scale perfectly formed."[31]

---

30. On industrial chaplaincy in the sixties, see Johnston and McFarland, "Out in the Open in a Threatening World," 1–27. The Iona Community was influenced in this direction by the Sheffield Industrial Mission of Ted Wickham, at the forefront also of Allan's 1958 and 1960 WCC consultations on evangelism at Bossey.

31. Robinson, "The House Church and the Parish Church," 283.

As we cast an eye towards Allan's ideas for the "congregational group," Robinson warned against any appreciation of the House Church "as purely a temporary expedient . . . until the parish church can be constituted," or as 'simply an evangelistic weapon . . . a halfway house for the semi-converted."[32] The House Church was not "an *ad hoc* expedient," but rather was reflective of the "cellular structure of each parish . . . essentially of the same mixture as the lump, except that the area of natural community is smaller (e.g. a street-group) and may, in these days when communities are often not geographical at all, be outside the parish altogether (for instance, in an office or factory)."[33]

The House Church was thus "itself the church, the church in the basement, at the molecular level,"[34] by which "the cell-church is what feeds new life into the parish church, as the innumerable tap-roots nourish the stock of the vine."[35]

In the Church of England, the individual who became synonymous as a pioneer in the House Church movement in the decade after the war was Ernest W. Southcott, vicar in the working class area of Halton, Leeds, who brought together his experiences in the book *The Parish Comes Alive* in 1956.[36]

For Southcott, the House Church meant the re-discovery of worship, prayer, and in particular the Eucharist, in the local setting, to re-unite Christianity with the everyday and with life in the home and workplace. It arose from Southcott's conviction that "no amount of special services, special conventions and missions, visual aids and so on will bring home to the bulk of our people the meaning and challenge of the church; but in the domestic situation in the surroundings of the home, the church can be built up, the church can be renewed, the church may become real to the lapsed communicant."[37]

There was thus for Southcott through the House Church "a new sense of belonging" that would arise amongst ordinary people, whereby "baptism

32. Ibid.

33. Ibid., 284.

34. Ibid., 289.

35. Ibid., 285.

36. Southcott, *The Parish Comes Alive*. It is clear that the influences for the House Church Movement were similar to Allan–Robinson referring to Godin's *France Pagan*, and Southcott quoting from Michonneau's *Revolution in a City Parish* on the first page of *The Parish Comes Alive*, as well as from the Iona Community and the great international lay movements of the day.

37. Southcott, *The Parish Comes* Alive, 79–80.

is being rescued from superstition and individualism" through the realisation of its import for the baptised and their families.[38]

In Scotland, the chief promoter of the value of the House Church was Ralph Morton. Morton described the House Church as the "most conspicuous of these experiments" in parish mission for the Iona Community.[39]

In an article in *The Coracle* of March 1956, Morton described the work of several "Iona" ministers in forming House Church, indicating that "they all arise from the conviction that the impersonal way of life of the conventional congregation is not adequate to the demands of Christian living today."[40]

Reflecting on the Billy Graham "All Scotland Crusade" of the previous year, Morton suggested that as "the mass meeting has come into its own again," those involved were seeking "a next stage" whereby those who had been "converted" in such a Crusade could be integrated into the life of the church, and saw the House Churches as a possible avenue. He asked, however, "are they the next step in an evangelistic strategy which sees the first step as 'visitation' or 'mass evangelism.' Or are they our first step in a new direction?"[41]

In answering for the latter, Morton relied on "three quite simple but ... revolutionary convictions":

1. "that the church is not a building but a people," therefore it must be "found where its people are in their homes and in their work";

2. "the content of the church's life is the actual life of its members," as "it is here that the real obedience of men in their daily lives will be worked out, very slowly. Here Bible Study will become relevant. And here their personal and domestic concerns will be seen to have a wider significance and the total demands of the faith will be seen as personal"; and

3. "it is only by this means that we shall find the way to action: because action will arise naturally out of the life of the people."[42]

It was in the appreciation of the potential role for such as the House Church that Morton saw an expression of the "new divide" in mission and the interpretation of the Gospel between social action and conversion in the wake of Graham; a "divide" that has plagued the church in Scotland since

38. Ibid., 81.
39. Morton, *The Iona Community*, 151.
40. Morton, "The House Church," 1.
41. Ibid., 4.
42. Ibid., 4–5.

then. Morton wrote that there were those like himself, and in his opinion those within House Churches, who "certainly didn't see the Gospel as . . . something apart from them, over against the world . . . They seemed to think of the Gospel as a way of life . . . Certainly they did not talk about technique. They were concerned about first steps, not about the next step."[43]

How then was the House Church integrated into the structure of the parish by "Iona" ministers in urban areas?

Prominent in advocating the role of the House Church was the "Iona" minister, Bill Cattanach in Larkfield, Greenock. Cattanach had begun weekly meetings led by an elder of members in all districts, which were regarded as local meetings of the church. Their programme involved prayer, Bible study, and a discussion of topics in parish and the welfare of people to serve needs around them, reporting back to the minister every Sunday.[44]

David Orr was an "Iona" minister in the Church of Scotland, initially in Burntisland, Fife and thereafter for several decades as George MacLeod's successor at Govan Old in Glasgow. In an Iona publication entitled *The House Church*, Orr asserted that it was the proper reflection of the ideals of the "Tell Scotland" Movement. If the founding principles of "Tell Scotland" were that mission was not sporadic but an "on-going, normal feature of church life," and that "the agent of mission is the whole congregation," then "The House Church provides the means whereby these principles can be embodied in the life of the congregation."[45]

Orr set out what he viewed as the essential components of the House Church in the parish. It would be set up as per the districts of elders, but could also comprise "vocational or interest groups." Gatherings of twelve to fifteen people would meet, usually monthly, "in any kind of house from mansions to pre-fabs to single ends."[46]

The House Church for Orr was not "an elaborate gimmick to pep up our flagging congregations," or "a religious service," or "a temporary device to get people to "come to church," or a "particular technique or method of organisation."[47] Instead, it would meet for specific purposes and goals. The meeting would cover a discussion of questions regarding faith and church, personal problems of Christian living at home and at work and the understanding of roles and responsibilities. It would comprise Bible Study in that light, pastoral care in the district, and seeing and planning action in the

---

43. Ibid., 6.
44. See Cattanach, "The House Church"; and Wilkie, *The Eldership Today*.
45. Orr, *The House Church*, 9–10.
46. Ibid., 3.
47. Ibid., 2.

parish and beyond. The minister would only have peripheral, occasional involvement.

Its purpose was for the building of community, for service and action, by which the Bible would come alive for ordinary people, for pastoral care of the district, but principally for "Christian people living their lives," arriving themselves at the connections between life and faith. It was thus seen as a true emancipation of each lay person for discovery:

> The vitality of the church . . . depends, in the end . . . on the particular decisions and choices we each take each day, often without our thinking about it, as parents and workers and citizens, in the particular circumstances of our particular lives in our particular world. The institutional church exists, and must exist, to provide the means of grace—the means whereby we can be helped and equipped to make these decisions and choices in accordance with the will of God . . . Only in smaller, more personal groups can we begin to help each other to see what this means for us in the particular decisions and choices of our particular lives.[48]

The Mission of Friendship and the House Church Movement were the key indications of the commitment of the Iona Community to parish mission until the early sixties, drawn from the same wellspring as Allan's model. Just as significantly, the Iona Community further inspired and then supported the development of the East Harlem Protestant Parish in New York City in the late forties and throughout the fifties. Through their involvement in the Iona Community, two young Scottish ministry students, Geoff Shaw and Walter Fyfe, were drawn to postgraduate study at Union Seminary, New York, in order to work in student placements with the EHPP. Deeply influenced by their experiences in East Harlem, Shaw and Fyfe then sought to replicate the EHPP in the most notorious slum in Glasgow, through the Gorbals Group Ministry.

## The Church on the Street—The East Harlem Protestant Parish 1948–1968

### Formation & Purpose

The East Harlem Protestant Parish ("EHPP") sought the delegation of church to a local level, by its physical re-location to storefronts on the

48. Ibid., 7.

main streets of the city. Its location was American, its inspiration lay in Scotland from the work of the Iona Community, and its church-centred concepts of mission chimed with those of Tom Allan, to whom acknowledgment was made. As the church was geographically and politically stuck in middle-class suburbs, the answer was taken to be the formation of new churches re-positioned at the heart of urban slums. Such new churches would be dedicated in theology, liturgy and social witness to the lives of those around them.

Whilst the missiology of Tom Allan and of the Iona Community sought to re-locate the *place* of contact, the *identity* of those who made contact, and the *language* and focus of the message used, by alternative means to the House Church the *physical location* of "church" would seek to bring the Gospel and liturgy to an immediate interaction with the realities of urban living.

To diminish the challenges of "cross-cultural translation," the church as institution would merge into the prevailing culture by a physical relocation to literally become part of the street. The three storefront churches and one associated church of East Harlem were complementary and united within a Protestant "parish" that was geographically defined.[49] They remained of themselves "the church" to which local people belonged, but without necessary reference for the local people back to an existing "mother church," albeit they were financially reliant on multi-denominational support in the background. Those churches were divided downwards into "agape meal" house groups, which engaged in Bible Study, prayer and discussion to form much of the liturgical, social and political agenda for the storefront congregations. The church remained as institution, but was consciously designed to be fresh, devoid of baggage and borne of its surroundings.

The period of the public prominence of Tom Allan and George MacLeod at the forefront of Scottish church life co-coincided with that of the EHPP, as did many of their common missiological goals and prior influences. Both MacLeod and Allan were to acknowledge the EHPP, MacLeod in particular as he visited East Harlem and commended those who were affiliated to the Iona Community who sought to replicate its ministry in Glasgow. Furthermore, the EHPP recognised its debt to the Community, and indeed to Allan's *The Face of My Parish*. As the historian of the EHPP,

---

49. The three storefront Churches were the 100th Street Church at East 100th St, the Church of Our Redeemer at East 102nd St, and the Church of the Son of Man at East 104th St, along with the associate Church based in an old Church building formerly comprising an Italian Protestant congregation, namely the Church of the Ascension at East 106th St. At its height, the EHPP had fifteen full-time paid staff, including pastors, administrators, a lawyer and a doctor.

Benjamin Alicea comments: "The mid to late fifties were the golden years of the EHPP. This era saw the ideal known as the Iona Community take form in an American urban ghetto. National acclaim and ecclesiastical credibility focused on this para-church ministry engaged in social action, congregational development and revitalization, theological reflection and Christian discipleship."[50]

Whilst students at Union Theological Seminary, New York City, Bill Webber and Don Benedict produced a fledgling "Proposal for a Store-Front Larger Parish System" in December 1947,[51] to begin an experimental ministry in nearby East Harlem on the other side of Central Park, starting in summer 1948. In summary of their intended method, they stated (my emphasis):

> The approach rests upon this simple hypothesis: that a team of trained Christian workers, responsive to basic human needs and thoroughly committed to the gospel of Christ as the only final answer to all human need, can identify themselves with the lives and problems of families in a disorganized city neighbourhood and build a local fellowship of people seeking together the Christian solution to their problems. *The method is to bring the church to the people where they live rather than try to bring the people to the churches.*[52]

The focus, like that of Tom Allan, would be in the regeneration of a serving church within the parish system, as reflected in the name. Benedict later recalled in his autobiography: "Whereas 'parish' might mean little to the people, we hoped to put meaning back into the word. We wanted to return to Protestantism the outgoing concept of serving everyone in a given geographical community rather than staying with the inbound idea of church as the central place of worship attracting like-minded people from anywhere."[53]

As well as a liturgy and ecclesiastical structure that was "of the street," this meant social and political action, if the church was to regain its connection with the threads of the society around it. For Webber and Benedict believed that Christianity had abandoned East Harlem to its fate, and that therefore an essential constituent element must be that "a church in these

50. Alicea, *Christian Urban Colonizers*, 201.

51. EHPP Archive, Union Theological Seminary, New York City, Box 7 and also *Union Seminary Quarterly Review*, March 1948, Vol. III No. 3, 17–23. Webber and Benedict were soon joined by Archie Hargraves as the three initial pastors of the EHPP.

52. EHPP Archive, Box 7, *The East Harlem Project for Christian Service*, March 4, 1948, 2.

53. Benedict, *Born Again Radical*, 61.

areas will be a militant, aggressive organisation, unafraid to fight for justice on economic and social levels."[54]

## Work

The storefront churches were an obvious, visual connection with the streets around—doors open, pastor available, simple Sunday worship directed to the life outside. The Gospel developed a resonance in that context, with Webber reporting: "As we dig into some of the immediate problems of human need . . . we break through into ever deeper human problems. It is then that the Gospel has its real relevance, then that it must speak to these men and women, who like the rest of us, are alienated from God and full of antagonism toward their fellowmen."[55]

The obvious and prominent location of the minsters and staff in the storefronts threw them into coping with everyday emergencies in the chaotic life of East Harlem: broken families, unemployment, welfare issues, poor education, ill health, bad housing, alcoholism and drug abuse, and police brutality. The theological, ecclesiological and liturgical response of the EHPP was based on these social circumstances, hoping to provide the platform for the people of the parish to take over the direction of those key areas. The EHPP administrator, Flossie Borgmann, later to work in Scotland for a year in 1958 to 1959 with the Gorbals Group Ministry, wrote:

> To meet these needs the Parish has tried to develop a program which ministers to the total community. The staff is convinced that only as the church has a vital concern for all of the immediate problems of daily living will the message of the Gospel come alive. They are concerned with a healing ministry, but also with a vigorous and unending effort to fight injustice. They need to provide a channel through which the people of the Parish, as citizens of a democracy, can take action to overcome the injustices from which they suffer.[56]

As regards worship, the liturgy was also to reflect the concerns of the street, seeking a responsive biblical resourcing, as Webber stated in words that would be echoed later by Ian Fraser in *Bible, Congregation and Community*: "The key word is *participation*, which implies the necessity of *recall*

54. EHPP Archive, Box 7, *Proposal for a Store-Front Larger Parish System*, 1 December 1947, 7.

55. Webber, "East Harlem Revisited," 29.

56. Box 23, EHPP Archive, Florence Borgmann 'The Church in East Harlem', *The Messenger*, October 6 1953, 8–10.

and *re-enactment*. The story of salvation must become the personal history of the worshiping congregation as it recalls in worship the mighty acts of God and as it re-enacts those events so that they become living realities, contemporary and compelling."[57]

The common ground of the EHPP with Allan and MacLeod as a matter of principle is readily apparent. Firstly, there was, like them, a diagnosis of a church whose inherent character had become hidebound in a culture alien to its surroundings; whose mission and ministry was attractional rather than incarnational; who had failed the poor and the outcast, and which had little or no concern for the human circumstances surrounding it.

Secondly, like Allan and MacLeod, a solution would still be sought *within* the church, with the rebuilding of a "missionary parish." This would also be a church of very different hue; whose purpose was to build a dynamic local community. The lives of the people of the community in integration with their faith would form the basis for mission, liturgy and social action. From the position of the clergy, the watchwords would be presence, availability and personal sacrifice. From the position of the laity, they would be biblical empowerment, personal formation and emancipation.

In these focal points, the lines of common purpose with Allan and MacLeod are illuminated, which is initially surprising when one considers the radically different geographical and cultural context, and the absence of personal contact in the early years between those forming the EHPP and their counterparts in Scotland and mainland Europe. The connections become clearer, however, when considering the influences acknowledged by Bill Webber.

## Missiological and Theological Foundations

### Mission

The story of Allan, MacLeod, Webber and the Gorbals Group is intimately interwoven. The East Harlem Protestant Parish was a remarkable "double" journey of ideas of church, ministry and mission between Europe, Scotland and the USA–initially from Scotland and mainland Europe to the USA in the formation of the EHPP, and then back to Scotland from the EHPP in the work of the Gorbals Group Ministry.

---

57. EHPP Archive, Box 22, George W. Webber, "New Wineskins of Worship," *Concern Magazine*, Vol. 4, No. 3, March 1962, 16–17.

During his time as Harry Emerson Fosdick Visiting Professor at Union Theological Seminary in the winter of 1954 to 1955,[58] George MacLeod went to the East Harlem Protestant Parish and later described it in *The Coracle* as "the most important Protestant experiment in America."[59] He wrote further: "the East Harlem Experiment claimed it was Iona that first set them thinking. If this is really so, their cerebral development is now vastly in excess of ours."[60]

Alicea identified MacLeod as "the theologian and churchman who inspired the parish."[61] Webber explained the formation and central tenets of the Community in his work *God's Colony in Man's World* of 1960, not least the Iona spiritual and economic disciplines adopted by both the EHPP and the Gorbals Group Ministry, describing the Community as "a very striking witness against the power of evil."[62] Quoting liberally throughout that work from MacLeod's *One Way Left*, he described MacLeod as a "voice of authentic prophecy, calling us back to a fresh vision of God's design."[63] Webber was further influenced by Tom Allan, correctly identifying the connection between the Iona Community "Mission of Friendship" and the Allan model.[64]

Not only did Webber become acquainted with MacLeod when he visited the EHPP, he met with Allan at Bossey, Switzerland in 1958 and 1960 at the consultations for a theology of evangelism under the auspices of the WCC, and on the former trip also visited the Gorbals Group Ministry in Glasgow.

Like Allan, Webber's other principal influences were European. He declared that "one of the most exciting developments in recent years in the Christian world has been the worker-priest movement in France,"[65] just like Allan citing the work of Godin and Michonneau.

In that context, the apparent anomaly is less stark when one realises that, as well as later feeding back to Scotland through the Gorbals Group Ministry, the EHPP took inspiration in its very existence from Allan and

---

58. From which, like Geoff Shaw after him in 1954, George MacLeod had graduated STM in 1922 following his undergraduate degree at New College, Edinburgh.

59. MacLeod, "What Do You Think of American Religion," 23.

60. The overt influence of the Iona Community on the formation and ethos of the EHPP is also noted by Ferguson, *Geoff*, 42.

61. Alicea, *Christian Urban Colonizers*, 201.

62. Webber, *God's Colony in Man's World*, 97.

63. Ibid., 154.

64. Ibid., 122.

65. See Webber, "European Evangelism and the Church in America," 155–58.

MacLeod, and from the same European missiologists and practical lay movements which had inspired Allan.

## Theology

Webber's experiences in the US Navy in the war drove him towards ministry, leading him to apply to Union Theological Seminary in late 1945 in these terms: "I feel a tremendous urge to spend my life and my full efforts in the work of the church, in dealing with the problems of people, in promoting the social gospel."[66]

This desire on Webber's part found nourishment in the teaching of Paul Tillich and Reinhold Niebuhr in his years as a Union undergraduate from 1946 to 1948. Webber cited what became chapter 15 of Tillich's *The Protestant Era*, entitled "The Protestant Principle and the Proletarian Situation," as especially influential upon his early thinking within the EHPP.

One can readily recognise Webber's later appreciation within the EHPP of Protestantism, the church and the poor from Tillich's writing, and why Webber too would later speak out against the mass revivalism of Billy Graham. Calling for a "radical laicism" as the antidote, Tillich's chapter began with an uncompromising diagnosis of the paltry attempts of Protestantism to address urban social need: "The proletarian situation, in so far as it represents the fate of the masses, is impervious to a Protestantism which in its message confronts the individual personality with the necessity of making a religious decision and which leaves him to his own resources in the social and political sphere, viewing the dominating forces of society as being ordered by God."[67]

Thus the inspiration for Webber's search, like that of Allan, was that of seeking to point *the church* in the direction of the apostolate of the laity, in order to address the gap between the church and the urban poor, to empower ordinary people in mission.

Webber interpreted the calls for world evangelisation under the ecumenical banner to include not simply proclamation (*kerygma*), but also community (*koinonia*) and service (*diakonia*). It was only in this rounded collation of the three central themes of mission that "God's Colony" would be established: like Allan reflecting a fundamental reliance on the church as agent of mission, to be a reformed, redeemed community: "By its very

---

66. George W. Webber, *Application of Admission*, Union Theological Seminary, New York, December 1, 1945, quoted by Alicea, *Christian Urban Colonizers*, 57.

67. Tillich, *The Protestant* Era, 237, 251–52.

existence, without doing anything other than being a community of God's people, the colony witnesses to the gospel.[68]

As in Geoff Shaw's example in the Gorbals Group Ministry, this entailed "the discovery that ministry had to involve unconditional acceptance." Consequently, in contrast to the popularly held approach in Scotland in the inter-war years, the "approach by way of morality was rejected, partly because it was useless, partly because it was irrelevant, but above all because the pastors slowly realised that morality with which their own faith had always been involved often stood in firm opposition to the Gospel."[69]

Mere presence by living and working in the parish, and "critical solidarity" were central. As Webber wrote, in similar terms to John Harvey's later description of the basis of the Gorbals Group Ministry: "The purpose of the colony is nothing less than to 'be there' in the midst of the real world, wherever men live and work and play. Only in being there can the colony hope to serve men at the point where their needs, frustrations, sickness, and fears emerge. The colony must intrude itself in some way into those places where men are living out the deep concerns of their lives."[70]

He recognised therefore the necessary connection in contextualization of not only knowing the gospel, but of the means and location of communication: "The Christian must not only understand fully the meaning of the gospel; he must also know about the secular world in which his life must be lived in order that the relevance of the gospel may be communicated. We dare not concentrate either on knowing the world or knowing the gospel or on means of communication, but the three must be bound indissolubly together if the secular relevance of the gospel is indeed to be a fact in our time."[71]

This further translated itself into a dislike by Webber of Billy Graham's style of evangelism in ignorance of context, promoting instead a central *Theology of the Laity*, as in Hendrik Kraemer's 1957 book of that name.[72]

## Issues and Difficulties

The advantage in an analysis of the EHPP is not only to recognise the shared ground in principle with their Scottish counterparts, and to speculate on whether their efforts to contextualise the very location and meaning

68. Webber, *God's Colony in Man's World*, 70.

69. Kenrick, *Come Out the Wilderness*, 89, 91.

70. Webber, *God's Colony in Man's World*, 82.

71. Ibid., 88–89.

72. Ibid., 134–35.

of the church can be deemed "successful," but also to see key markers of corroboration in the hindrances and challenges which such a similar model provided in a radically different cultural context.

There were problems in practice in the ministry of the East Harlem Protestant Parish which recurred with an uncanny similarity in its Scottish offshoot, and also in part with Allan's work, in particular: (a) the difficulty of bridging the cultural gap, the struggles with low formal church membership and an absence of the growth of local, lay leadership; and (b) the sometimes contradictory demands of evangelism by proclamation of the Gospel, as compared to social action in Christ's name.

### Bridging the Cultural Gap and the Apostolate of the Laity

The necessity of bridging the cultural gap with the mainly Puerto Rican and black American population of East Harlem was obvious from the start. As Benedict recalled, using language until then associated with "foreign mission": "The real function of a missionary is to make the gospel come alive within the context of the racial, social and cultural patterns of the people, and so we had to learn a new culture."[73]

Whilst studying in his Masters year at Princeton Theological Seminary in 1954 to 1955, the New College graduate Bruce Kenrick worked as a student volunteer with the EHPP. He was to return in 1960 to East Harlem to collate material for his bestselling book on the EHPP, *Come Out the Wilderness*, published in 1962.

In his Masters dissertation, Kenrick identified as the first priority in an area of urban deprivation such as East Harlem, that the church goes in:

> As much in the capacity of a learner as a teacher. It would be useless to preach the Gospel in terms which were acceptable to and, perhaps, understandable by middle-class Christians, if the bearers of the Gospel do not possess the categories of thought with which to make the Good News their own. Nor should it be the aim to hammer those same thought forms into a handpicked elite in East Harlem and reproduce an alien middle class Christian island with no power to transform the foreing waters washing its bourgeois shores.[74]

73. Benedict, *Born Again Radical*, 60.

74. EHPP Archive, Box 26, "Thesis written in 1955 by Bruce Kenrick, grad student at Princeton," 78.

The aim was for an encounter between church and people, such that the church would be changed to become more closely aligned to the culture, and the culture in turn would also re-align in accordance with the contextualized Christianity and church. In order for the "interculturation" process to take hold to produce an indigenous hybrid, there was no doubt that the element of what Webber described as "cultural intrusion"[75] by a mostly white, middle-class and educated clergy would need to be supplanted in time within the EHPP by lay leadership. Only through local, lay leadership could the strands of culture, Christianity and church be brought together, otherwise the EHPP might remain a paternalistic, "top-down" message-bearer, seeking to implant foreign concepts from one culture to another.

The demise of the EHPP was hastened by the absence of lay leadership that might have enabled its continuance, in conjunction with social changes in the urban landscape which diminished many of the attempts to build a sense of community. Knowledge of that issue was at the forefront of deliberations within the EHPP, for in the words of the pastor of the East 100th Street Church, Norm Eddy:[76] "The long-range objective is to develop a church structure simple and flexible enough so that it will be able to run itself, with its own leadership. Only then will the ideals of the Parish be able to be transmitted widely throughout our crowded city areas and be a witness to the churches everywhere."[77]

However, that objective was not realized. The local leadership did not emerge, as despite the all-encompassing dedication to the social challenges around, the numbers of lay people involved in the storefront churches, and thus the pool for local leadership, remained perilously low. By way of example, in March 1953 at the East 100th Street church where Walter Fyfe, later of the Gorbals Group Ministry, would work that winter, the average adult attendance on Sunday was about fifteen (it had been about twenty-five to thirty-five at the same time in the previous year), with only three adult men who were ". . . deeply committed to the church, and 4% of families on the block with two or more members in a church programme, which had been a specific objective."[78]

Thus, Eddy realized the need for "the developing of a church pattern fitted to the theology and social action in which we believe, but which is essentially of the people, financed, organized and run by them . . . The

---

75. As quoted by Harvey, *Bridging the* Gap, 93.

76. Norm Eddy led the ministry at that storefront following the departure of Benedict in April 1953 to Cleveland, Ohio to begin a similar ministry to the EHPP.

77. Kenrick, *Thesis*, 78.

78. EHPP Archive, Box 2, File 2, 18.

objective of the next year and a half is to crystallize a core of committed Christians and to help put them into the service of the Lord, in developing a theonomous community in the neighbourhood."[79]

The failure to achieve this goal of indigenous ownership and significant lay numbers within the institution was by the sixties to prove the undoing of the EHPP, and indeed in time of the Gorbals Group Ministry. In the case of the EHPP, the end emerged through a resurgent black consciousness in the throes of the Civil Rights Movement, which came to question why educated, white, middle-class clergy might be claiming to set the agenda in Harlem, in combination with the destruction of communities by their relocation from the slums to newly-constructed "projects," destroying the physical base and human resources of the Parish.

## Evangelism versus Social Action

This became a fundamental theological issue which split the EHPP, just as it had caused the collision of Tom Allan and George MacLeod over Billy Graham and contributed to the demise of "Tell Scotland." Unlike its progeny the Gorbals Group Ministry, the EHPP had been an overtly Christian effort from the start. Its founders viewed its role as a crucible for the development of the church elsewhere and so, again unlike the Gorbals Group, courted publicity for its operation.[80] The failure to develop the street churches numerically and to engage local leadership led to disappointment, tension and friction between the members of the group ministry, based on their varied theological appreciations of the balance between an overt evangelism by proclamation and the exercise of social action.

In practice, this focus became more difficult to emphasise as time went on. The struggle within the EHPP was highlighted most acutely by William Stringfellow, who went to work in East Harlem as a lawyer on graduating from Harvard Law School in 1956. In a mixed review in 1963 of Kenrick's *Come Out the Wilderness*, Stringfellow reflected:

79. EHPP Archive, Box 5, "A Plan for the 100th Street Church," March 15 1953, 10, by Norm Eddy, circulated to Group members.

80. Part of the avowed aim at formation in 1948 was stated as: "To explore methods of personal evangelism and small fellowship groups which may provide new techniques for Christian ministry in underprivileged areas . . . [and] . . . to provide a training center for seminary students who feel called to missionary service in the disorganized areas of the inner city"—EHPP Archive, Box 7, "The East Harlem Project for Christian Service," March 4 1948.

Those who came to the neighbourhood to establish the parish were evidently motivated and informed by simplistic (if sincere) and naïve (if wholesome) and nontheological (if humanistic) views than by regard for the truth, activity and trustworthiness of the Gospel.

[The EHPP story] continues through the struggle to differentiate secular charity from love, settlement houses from churches, ideology from theology, social planning from Christian witness and mission, ecclesiastical politics from recognition of the authority and reliability of the indigenous laity.[81]

As Kenrick recalled in the book itself, it was Stringfellow who from his arrival in East Harlem "attacked without mercy those members of the Group who were neglecting the word of God. He was rude, he was ruthless, he was rigid, and he was right."[82] The return of Letty Russell in 1958 to be the pastor of the church of the Ascension on East 106th Street led to a re-invigorated program of bible study to powerful effect.[83] However, conflict was suppressed in the name of harmony, which in Kenrick's words "led to a concentration on . . . the galvanizing of the church into action instead of helping its members to come alive with the life of Christ."[84] This absence of the banner of the Gospel contributed further to the dissipation of lay leadership within the church, leaving it further ill-equipped as a long-term proposition.

## Summary

The EHPP was the practical outworking of a Christianity that was radical, prophetic and incarnational. It sought to bridge the gap between the church and the poor, to overcome the considerable obstacles of cross-cultural communication, in a contextualization of the location of the church, and the terms and means of expression of its message. In doing so, it sought to create via experimentation and error an urban church which would translate across America and the western world. Whilst is spawned similar exploratory ministries, those offshoots were in one aspect fundamentally different: they gave up on the formation of institutional church completely in favour of forming co-operative communities. The concentration within the EHPP

---

81. EHPP Archive, Box 22, Stringfellow, Review of *Come Out the Wilderness*, 432.

82. Kenrick, *Come Out the Wilderness*, 125.

83. Ibid., 131 and 173–74.

84. Ibid., 122.

on the role of church as institution became increasingly distant from global ecumenical mission from the early sixties.

The EHPP was close in theology and ecclesiology to Tom Allan; in its adoption of "neo-orthodoxy" as against a social gospel; its primacy of the vocal expression of the Gospel in mission; its insistence on the formation of public places of worship and of "church" and congregation; its use of Bible study and teaching; its dependent relationship to the central institutions of the church, and the prominence of its ministers as clergy.

The missiological practices of the EHPP were an extension of Allan's model with the same fundamental goal—from the contextualization of Gospel and church would emerge a laity who would transform the church into a body which would more effectively radiate the Gospel amongst the people, and transform the church's life into a propagation of faith within a "missionary parish."

In the remaining concentration on the church as institution as the source and venue of return of mission, albeit radically altered in form, the Gorbals Group Ministry were to move away in practice from its intended emulation of the EHPP.

As a committed "churchman," George MacLeod's support for the Church Extension programme into the new towns of Scotland in the fifties, or a re-imagined church in East Harlem, was a natural reflection. MacLeod was less comfortable with the "para-church" community such as would develop in the Gorbals.

## The Church of the Street—The Gorbals Group Ministry, 1957 to 1978

### Introduction

If contextualization could lead to the church being physically re-located to the building on the street, and its liturgy and social outlook re-modelled accordingly, could any remaining institutional baggage not be dispensed with, so that mission would begin on the street itself?

The Gorbals Group Ministry exercised a penetrating, incarnational Christian presence as an intentional community in a Glaswegian Victorian slum then undergoing radical transformation and regeneration. Approved to proceed by the Presbytery of Glasgow in October 1957, its principal period of operation lasted until the departure of key members in 1967 to 1968. The Ministry continued until the death of Geoff Shaw, its *de facto* leader, in April 1978.

At the end of his history of the EHPP, Benjamin Alicea draws a salutary conclusion: "The EHPP is a monument to the success and failure of the main-line Protestant churches to face the challenge of ministry to the poor in American ministry, not a transferable model of urban ministry."[85] Indeed, whilst they catapulted urban ministry forward in terms of its thinking, its lasting legacy in mission, as Alicea suggests, is that "the influence of the Parish is conveyed in part by the former parish staff who now do ministry . . . the Parish was a training ground for Union Seminary field work students and graduates."[86]

Bruce Kenrick recognised that the influence of the EHPP had spread not only within the USA, but to Scotland, England and India.[87] In England, the EHPP inspired a group ministry in Notting Hill, London, after three Methodist ministers had attended UTS and volunteered with the EHPP.[88] After working in the EHPP and in Bengal from 1956 to 1959, Kenrick was part of the Notting Hill ministry, from where he co-founded the homeless charity "Shelter." In India, the Scots missionaries, George More and Dorothy More, friends of both David Lyon and Walter Fyfe, created an intentional community at Allipur, influenced by the "intense poverty that was all around us."[89]

As regards Scotland, inspired as it was by George MacLeod and the Iona Community, the EHPP welcomed in the forties and fifties as volunteers a series of like-minded young men from the Scottish theological colleges. They were mostly studying on the one-year postgraduate Master of Sacred Theology ("STM") course at Union Theological Seminary, and were then able to work on placement within the East Harlem Protestant Parish through the continuing connection with UTS of Bill Webber as a part-time professor. The Scottish students were, for the most part, also inspired by MacLeod, Iona and the worker-priests. They thus brought to Union and the EHPP a theological outlook and temperament which had been shaped by the same sources as the EHPP itself, and were ripe for its influence.[90]

85. Alicea, *Christian Urban Colonizers*, 252.

86. Ibid., 252–53.

87. Kenrick, *Come Out the Wilderness*, 194.

88. David Mason, Geoffrey Ainger and Norwyn Denny. Two of Ainger's essays are within the EHPP archive at Union Theological Seminary, New York. The experience of the Notting Hill ministry in the sixties is recounted in Mason et al., *News from Notting Hill.*

89. More and More, *This is Our Life in Central India*, 12. George More met with the Gorbals Group in Glasgow in September 1959, stressing their similarities in the Iona Community and the EHPP and proposing greater integration.

90. They included at UTS, David Lyon (1948 to 1949); Geoff Shaw and Walter Fyfe

## Formation of the Gorbals Group Ministry

Two young Church of Scotland ministers in training, Walter Fyfe of Govanhill, Glasgow and Trinity College, and Geoff Shaw of Inverleith, Edinburgh and New College, met at an SCM conference in Paris in 1951. It was there that Fyfe also encountered two "worker-priests" from the docklands of Marseilles.[91] That encounter with the French "worker-priest movement" of 1943 to 1954, together with his knowledge of the nascent EHPP, would radically change his perspective on theology, ministry and the church.

Fyfe as an undergraduate student had already decided that "the parish ministry was not for him": "Possessed of an acute mind and a love for the dialectics of political and religious thought, Walter felt the church had largely sold out on the working classes . . . At Trinity, Walter made up his mind that his future ministry would be conducted as a labourer in industry."[92]

As fate would have it, both Shaw and Fyfe were to undertake postgraduate study on the STM course at UTS in the academic year of 1953 to 1954. Fyfe had done so deliberately so that he could seek to work voluntarily within the EHPP.

The period that Fyfe and Shaw spent in New York, studying at UTS under Paul Tillich and Reinhold Niebuhr, and in particular their exposure on voluntary student attachment by working in the EHPP through Bill Webber, was to crystallize the nature of the incarnational ministry that Fyfe and Shaw were drawn towards: "It was in the crucible of East Harlem that Geoff Shaw became a twice-born man . . . the East Harlem experience constituted a revelation for Geoff. It was not simply an addition to his experience: it transformed and revolutionised his way of looking at the world."[93]

Shaw was accredited by the Church of Scotland as a youth observer to the second World Council of Churches in Evanston, Illinois in 1954. There he witnessed the affirmation at a prominent public level of the stirrings of the shift in global mission towards the ecumenical incarnational approach adopted by the Group.

"Street chapels in every street" were mooted as a way forward in Scotland following Evanston, with Stephen Neill writing in *Life and Work* in May 1954: "we have to get the Gospel back to the places where people live,

---

(1953 to 1954); Andrew Ross, (1957 to 1958); and Douglas Alexander (1959 to 1960); as well as Bruce Kenrick at Princeton (1954 to 1955).

91. Interview with Walter and Elizabeth Fyfe at Govanhill, Glasgow on 18 March 2011.

92. Ferguson, *Geoff*, 40.

93. Ibid., 39.

in simple forms, and in terms of small and manageable fellowships."[94]These "small and manageable fellowships" were being enacted within the parish structure in England, and by the Iona Community in Scotland, in the House Church Movement.

The groundswell of public interest and support for the principles of Evanston were reflected in a significant post-Evanston conference which was held at the Assembly Hall, Edinburgh in late October 1954. Shaw was appointed by the Scottish Churches Ecumenical Association as a full-time organiser in November 1954, to develop and reflect on the upsurge of public support for the Evanston principles after the conference.[95]

The excitement brought by the lay ethos of Evanston, ecumenical growth, the experiments in work/ministry and in Christian communities outwith the parish structure, and the attempts to mobilize the laity nation-wide under the umbrella of the "Tell Scotland" movement, had put "grass-roots" Christianity on the agenda and laid the foundations in Scotland for the Gorbals Group Ministry.

In that light, on their return to Scotland Shaw and Fyfe resolved to implement an EHPP ministry in Scotland, along with Fyfe's Trinity College friend, John Jardine.[96] Independently, in his work as assistant minister at Govan Old Parish Church in 1952 to 1955, as Jardine later recalled he had become "convinced that patterns different from the then congregational structures must be sought if the gospel was to be good news for people's needs especially in the inner city."[97]

Shaw, Fyfe and Jardine toured Glasgow and selected the Dickensian slum of the Gorbals area of Glasgow as the location of their ministry. The Church of Scotland had used team ministry in the "Inner Ring" prior to the war, and had financed in the post-war period two church Community Centres in Bridgeton and Anderston. However, by the mid-1950s the Church of Scotland as an institution, and the local parishes in particular, paid little attention to the social needs of the Gorbals area and tended to be staffed and were attended by members travelling into Gorbals on a Sunday from outlying districts. Jardine recalled that their goal was church structures "similar

94. Neill, "Fellowship of the Church," 114.

95. Shaw attended a meeting of the Steering Panel of the "Tell Scotland" Movement chaired by Tom Allan on 18 January 1955, and presented his report to the SCEA on 7 March 1955. Shaw wrote on "Evanston to Scotland" in *Life and Work*, March 1955.

96. And the latters" wives, Elizabeth Fyfe and Beryl Jardine. Shaw resolved to remain unmarried, and did so until he entered politics in the Seventies.

97. John Jardine, "The Gorbals Group as Seen Before and After," in "Historic Gorbals Group File," Archive of the Gorbals Group Ministry, New College Library, University of Edinburgh, GD58.

to the EHPP in an inner city area of Glasgow where the Church of Scotland was noticeably absent."[98]

They envisaged church from the "bottom up," rather than "top down": to start and end with and for the people; to begin where they were. There would be no inherited assumptions as to how the Christian faith of the Group's members should be publicly expressed.

Despite this open-endedness, the primary purpose of the Gorbals Group Ministry at its formation was clear: the creation of church and the dissemination of the gospel, where the existing structures were failing. That the model was East Harlem was overtly acknowledged in the discussions and foundational proposals of the Group.[99]

The cornerstone of the EHPP was "store-front" churches, with accessible worship and liturgy in everyday language. This was the founding intention of the Group too. Thus, in the light of the refusal of the Presbytery of Glasgow to sanction the Group in 1955, Walter Fyfe wrote in *The British Weekly* that: "In East Harlem, the meaning of "ministry" is obvious in a way that it never is in divinity college harangues about homiletics. So also is the meaning of "liturgy," for there is a very real bond of worship between the storefront communities which make up the Parish."[100]

However, it was clear from the start that, unlike the EHPP, the Group wished to distance themselves from the institutional church as it existed. Dismissing a proposal from the Presbytery to operate as a "shock-troop platoon" in three Gorbals parishes, Shaw wrote to Fyfe in April 1955: "[This] scheme is simply a mechanical device for getting more people into a congregation—it does not envisage any questioning of present church structure—it is the structures as much as the methods that we are calling into question."[101]

The Presbytery rejected the initial overture of the Group in 1955 with concerns on its relationship to the institutional church, and encouraged Shaw, Fyfe and Jardine to show their commitment to the project in their work prior to any further application. They did so in the period 1955 to 1957 by Shaw's work in youth ministry at St-Francis-in-the East, Bridgeton; Jardine as Youth Secretary of the Iona Community, and Fyfe by being locum Minster at Hall Memorial Church, Dalmarnock and beginning his future life as a "worker-priest" as a laborer in the Harland and Wolff shipyard. In

---

98. John Jardine, "The Gorbals Group as Seen Before and After."

99. The initial proposal of the Group to the Presbytery of Glasgow in 1955 stated flatly: "we acknowledge that it is inspired largely by East Harlem Protestant Parish, New York."—Archive of the Gorbals Group Ministry, 2.

100. *The British Weekly*, 1 September 1955, 7.

101. Letter within the Archive of the Gorbals Group Ministry.

the time of the Gorbals Group Ministry, Fyfe was later to work in the Dixon Blazes ironworks and the local authority Highways Department.

In seeking to rally the church behind the idea, the support of Ralph Morton, Deputy Leader of the Iona Community, was beneficial, as was the public pronouncement in their favour by George MacLeod following his visit to the EHPP, writing in *The Coracle* in March 1956:

> Of course we should have at least one counterpart experiment in Britain. We have not the racial problem but we have great areas in our larger cities where the pattern, ecclesiastical and cultural, has broken down . . . A deeper pathos is that there are men in Scotland who have worked in East Harlem, are prepared for a similar identification and to work at minimum wage in close-knit lodging, to succeed, or maybe to fail, in our differing scene. Dare we turn to them and say we are satisfied with our organisation as it is?[102]

The Memorandum by the Group on their second application to Presbytery in 1957 was again on EHPP lines: "The aim of the experiment would be to provide each small natural community (street, part street or block) with a centre of worship . . . As time went on we would hope that the centre of worship would become real in the lives of many people and that a congregation would serve this small area."[103]

Permission being obtained from Glasgow Presbytery at the second attempt in October 1957, the original members of the Fyfes, the Jardines and Shaw proceeded immediately to move into the Gorbals to begin their ministry.

As regards the involvement of clergy with the Group Ministry, for a while in the sixties the future Bishop of Edinburgh, Richard Holloway, was associated.[104] At its height in 1965, there were ten members of the Group— three Church of Scotland ministers, two wives, two schoolteachers, two social workers, including the renowned Lilias Graham,[105] and Holloway as an Episcopal priest.[106] Jardine worked as a teacher in the local school, Fyfe in industry and Shaw in running youth clubs, the latter being paid by the

102. MacLeod, "What Do You Think of American Religion?," 25.

103. Within the Archive of the Gorbals Group Ministry. It stated further that the scheme's purpose was motivated because so many in poorer areas "were outside the life of the Church."

104. See his autobiography, Holloway, *Leaving Alexandria*.

105. On her later work at Braendam, see Downie, *Stand Up Straight*.

106. Holloway, "The Gorbals Group," 38–43.

Home Board of the Church of Scotland as an "assistant minister without portfolio."

The main addition to their early ranks was John Harvey, who became a member of the Gorbals Group Ministry along with his wife, Molly. He did so full-time from 1966 to 1968, but also part-time for three years beforehand whilst a student at Trinity College and assistant minister, and for three years thereafter whilst a parish minister in the Gorbals.

Shaw had been greatly influenced at New College in 1952 to 1953 by the inaugural lectures of T. F. Torrance on Karl Barth's Dogmatics. Barth being barely mentioned where Harvey studied theology at Trinity College, Glasgow in the early sixties, Harvey brought to the Group a training in the radical theology which was to dominate world Protestant ecumenical thought and expressions of urban mission, throughout the sixties and beyond. As A. C. Cheyne has written on the theological position of the Kirk at the time: "The state of affairs around about 1960 . . . was that . . . some of the abler students of divinity were being drawn not to Barth but to the neo-liberalism of Bultmann and his interpreters at Glasgow, Ian Henderson, John Macquarrie and Ronald Gregor Smith."[107]

Based on the "de-mythologizing ethic" of a "religionless Christianity," it was a captivating mix of the incarnational living of Charles de Foucauld and the Little Brothers of Jesus, and the theology of Bultmann and Bonhoeffer.

Thus whilst we can see in Shaw, and indeed Tom Allan, the markings of a "neo-orthodox" theological education in the immediate post-war period, a fresh radical approach was emerging of which Harvey was part.

The demand to place the church centrally in its role of mission, and to rely on the church's laity for the task, had been dissipated for many of Harvey's generation. That focus attuned with Fyfe's calling to live outwith the church as a worker-priest. In practice, the Group in the sixties was further driven by the developments in world missiology between the gatherings of the Word Council of Churches in New Delhi in 1961 and Uppsala in 1968, when, under the influence of Johannes Hoekendijk and M. M. Thomas, globally the "church in missiology disappeared in the sixties like dew before the sun."[108]

---

107. Cheyne, *The Transforming of the Kirk*, 217. John Harvey is named as one of "a goodly percentage of bright students" by the Professor of Practical Theology at Trinity, Murdo Ewen MacDonald, in his autobiography *Padre Mac*, 178. Harvey was inducted as minister at Laurieston Renwick, Gorbals on 5 December 1968, and remained there until 1971 when he became the Warden of Iona Abbey. He later served as parish minister at Raploch, Stirling and at Govan Old, Glasgow, as well as being the leader of the Iona Community from 1988 to 1995 and Moderator of Glasgow Presbytery in 1998.

108. Johannes Aagard, Danish missiologist, quoted by Philip, *Edinburgh to Salvador*, 80.

## Practical Achievements of the
## Gorbals Group Ministry

The Gorbals was described in 1965 as "the worst slum in Britain and is rap-idly deteriorating. It is a sump of human degradation . . . with one of the worst over-crowding problems in Europe . . . Everywhere there is filth and rubbish: the ally of disease and vermin."[109]

In appalling social conditions, at their heart the group lived up to the passage from Luke 4:18–19 to bring good news to the poor, taken from the Iona Community and the EHPP, which formed their constitution and purpose, and was read at each weekly communion. The principles of the Gorbals Group Ministry in that light are summarised by Harvey:[110]

a. "First and foremost, to be there."[111]

The core was compassion, availability, and dedication to the people in an expression of Christ's love. Harvey's first words in the inaugural edition of the "Gorbals View" in 1967, the UK's first local newspaper which he edited, sum it all up: "We care about the Gorbals. Mainly because we live in it."[112]

b. To seek to achieve "critical solidarity" with the people.[113]

This meant not only Christian presence, but also a commitment to the discipline of shared income and economic accountability, a gathered meal once per week where decisions would be made, and communal worship and communion.

c. Social action.

What became the defining and almost overwhelming driving force of the Group was to address, alongside the people, the living conditions and social problems which they faced. Thus housing action was a key priority, as was extensive work with the young at nursery and youth level, police and court representation and political activism within the Labour Party and CND.

---

109. Christian Action, *The Gorbals 1965*, 1.

110. Harvey, "Geoff Shaw," 155–60.

111. Ibid., 155.

112. Within the Archive of the Gorbals Group Ministry.

113. In the phrase of Danilo Dolci, Italian social reformer who visited the Group, quoted by Harvey, "Geoff Shaw," 156. Sicilian priest Fr Borelli was a further significant influence.

This was realised within the Group by embracing Bonhoeffer's totem that "when Christ calls a man, he bids him to come and die."[114] It entailed a total availability for the people of the Gorbals, expressed through an open door and a commitment to care for, affirm and represent them in every manner possible. The extent of the dedication was manifested in the multitude of people passing through Shaw's flat at 74 Cleland Street seeking help, advice, answers, or shelter. Shaw's declaration that "nothing is too low for the cross" was lived out day after day. It was proved in a willingness to serve and to accept everyone unconditionally.

Holloway describes Shaw as "always there for the troubled" for whom he had "unlimited patience," exercising "a heroic commitment to what he did."[115]

It is a moving testament to Shaw that both Harvey and Ferguson cite as a source of constant inspiration a note from Shaw's diary relating to a boy described by Harvey as "wild, chaotic, but full of possibilities,"[116] who had come into the Group's orbit, of whom Shaw wrote: "Have known that he was very mixed up, and have proceeded on basis of refusal to reject, no matter how foul."

John Jardine conclusions on the work of the Group serve as an admirable assessment of its practical outcomes:

> The Group came nowhere near fulfilling the aims of the 1957 Memorandum but what it did do was worth doing.
>
> In spite of our inexperience, our many mistakes, our inconsistencies, our fierce disagreements, and our occasional arrogance, some people's lives in Gorbals were touched for the better, some unsatisfactory situations were improved, some ills were healed, some injustices were rectified.
>
> During my membership of the Group, 1957 to early 1962, I saw some local men's and women's and youngsters' potential being unlocked and developed. I saw no significant new structures involving local people, other than members of the Group, emerging. But there was a committed presence in the area, flawed but caring, in a place where the Church of Scotland was largely absent save for an hour on Sundays.
>
> The fact that the Group in Gorbals existed had an effect on the wider church outside. A witness (despite all its errors) was

---

114. From *Cost of Discipleship*, as quoted by Harvey, "Geoff Shaw," 160.
115. Holloway, *Leaving Alexandria*, 123, 125.
116. Harvey, "Geoff Shaw," 157.

being made and people were intrigued, interested and perhaps encouraged.[117]

## The Challenge of the EHPP
## and of Being the Church

The prime impetus on the formation of the Group in 1957 was to emulate the attempts of the EHPP to bring the Gospel and the church to the people. However, "in the event, no recognisable indigenous church came into being as a result of the presence of the Gorbals Group."[118]

By 1968, the unity of the Gorbals Group was beginning to dissipate, its members were leaving and its ministry had reached a watershed.[119] Recent attempts by John Harvey to initiate a form of church growth had not borne fruit.[120] Shaw was candid in his reflections in 1968 on the record of the Group in his report to the Home Mission Committee.[121] In the passage related to church and the dissemination of faith, he boldly stated that "during the ten years of the Group's existence no one has become a full member of the Church of Scotland and maintained membership over any length of time."[122] Shaw wrote of "the inevitable sense of failure that the basic faith of most of the members of the Group has not in fact been adequately shared with others outside the church."

The focus on the establishment of church, and any concept of evangelisation in any traditional sense had gone. However, to explain this, Shaw made the following doubtful contention about the original aims of the Group: "It must be stressed that in the minds of the first members of the Group the winning of people into membership of the church was never

117. John Jardine, "The Gorbals Group as Seen Before and After."

118. Harvey, "Geoff Shaw," 160.

119. John and Beryl Jardine had left in 1962. Walter and Elizabeth Fyfe left the Group in early 1967 over the abandonment of the economic discipline. Richard and Jean Holloway departed to the USA in the same year. John and Molly Harvey were to leave from full-time participation in late 1968, as John took on the charge of Laurieston Renwick in the Gorbals.

120. In Harvey's period as a full-time member of the Group from 1966 to 1968, he was engaged in attempting to initiate church in the Gorbals where it had not appeared in the prior decade of the Group. He attempted Bible study groups and small worship services. It was a near impossible task after so long. For a fuller description, see Harvey, *Bridging the Gap*, 106–7.

121. Which was judiciously edited for the 1968 official Reports for the General Assembly!

122. 1968 Report, 9, Archive of the Gorbals Group Ministry.

thought of as a prime responsibility of the Group, and this was clearly stated in early documents."[123]

In the initial goal of "bridging the gap" between the church and the poor by way of indigenous churches organically growing on the street fronts, in the admission of Harvey, "the Gorbals Group cannot be said to have succeeded."[124]

The report of the Presbytery of Glasgow of 1960, whilst endorsing the continuance of the Group for a further three years, had been the first to raise sharp questions about the development of a local, identifiable community which, in some sense, might align itself with Christianity: "They do not seem to be witnessing clearly to a definite need for corporate worship . . . while the emphasis on witnessing by sharing in life and not merely by preaching is to be welcomed, the witness of the word . . . seems to have been undervalued."[125]

In response to this report as a reflection internally within the Group, the three founders wrote on the question "Does the group truly fulfil its purpose?." Jardine reflected on the 1957 Memorandum, and accepted "an important failure" in not including "our shared group life with other people in the area," questioning whether "we are not at all sure that we really believe in the church."

Likewise, Shaw whilst energised that "we are moving towards something and should not be hurried," agreed with a failure to "fulfil purpose in so far as I find it much easier to expound implications than basic kerygma."

Fyfe, however, saw the primary need as for "obedience," such that people might see "Christ in, and through us." He believed the calling was to follow Christ's life, as "God among ordinary people, living an ordinary life, without any official purpose, backing or status." Mission and evangelism would grow from obedience by living such a life—". . . before I know whether it is possible for a worker to follow Christ, I must become a worker." Thus the group's efforts should be directed towards "being disciples—not creating disciples," doing so "as an alternative to the church pattern."[126]

Therefore, even by 1960, the theology of the Group and understanding of its own existence had developed considerably, such that God was being found and expressed more directly in ameliorating the lives of the poor, and

123. Ibid., 13.

124. Harvey, *Bridging the Gap*, 107.

125. Presbytery of Glasgow, Home Mission Committee, "Report on Gorbals Experiment in Evangelism," 1960, Archive of the Gorbals Group Ministry.

126. Within John Jardine's papers, "Historic Gorbals Group File," Archive of the Gorbals Group Ministry.

not in any attempt to form "church." As Holloway recalls the theological focus of presence and identification during his time in the Gorbals:

> The place to find [God] was among the dispossessed, among the wretched of the earth. And the idea of *presence* expressed both ends of this paradox. Henceforth, God would only be found among the poor. If you were seeking him, only there would you find him. The other end of the paradox was even sharper; if you want to make God known to the poor, don't speak to them about *him*, become poor like *them*; be *present* beside them. The flow was from word to work; form theory to practice, from theology to action.[127]

Their theology and work in the Gorbals was leading them away from the original stated aim of emulating the EHPP storefront church presence, and indeed any wider Christian fellowship. The following factors contributed.

## Contributing Factors to the Absence of a "Church" of the Gorbals Group

### Factors Related to the Model

*The jarring of the principal purposes of the group*: The conflict lay in the desire to be social redeemers and church builders, in collision with the demands of belonging to the institutional church.

This conflict proved a major impediment to clearly setting out some form of "mission statement" and core ethos. John Harvey illustrated this underlying dilemma in the light of John T. Robinson's distinction between "experimental" and "exploratory" ministries.[128] The former, as seen in the EHPP, retains ties with the central church and implies the creation of some form of congregation or community, thus being exposed to review by that church in terms of results and numbers. The latter, as exemplified by the French worker priests, however, presupposes no set forms and exercises no demands.

The Group was caught from the start between those two stools. Harvey identified this tension in the founding documents, which in his view:

---

127. Holloway, *Leaving Alexandria*, 120–21.

128. John T. Robinson, *The New Reformation*, as quoted by Harvey, *Bridging the Gap*, 81.

Reveal . . . a worrying confusion of the exploratory and the experimental in their approach, which was to have quite serious consequences later on, for it seems as if they wished to have their cake and eat it. They wanted to have the freedom to go out into the pagan world of Gorbals, confident that some form of little churches would spring up round them (and confirmed in this view by East Harlem's experience), but not at all clear what the relationship of these little churches would eventually have to the mainline churches to which the three of them belonged . . . They wanted to be explorers, but along certain well-defined lines; and they wanted to keep in touch with, and have the blessing of, their sending base, the Church of Scotland.[129]

In dealing with the overwhelming nature of social need in the Gorbals of the sixties, in "letting the world set the agenda," and in the light of the rapidly changing social and theological landscape, the Gorbals Group Ministry "began in the company of the East Harlem Protestant Parish, and eventually ended up much more in the company of the French Worker Priests."[130]

There was no agreed vision as to how "church" would arise. As Richard Holloway wrote in 1965: "In the Gorbals Group we are not very clear about where the church is being led during this "darkness of mission." We are not sure of very much. But we are here and perhaps we are waiting to become the church—waiting for the Spirit."[131]

*Ecumenism and sectarianism*: Was group-based ecumenism generally an ill-equipped missiology in a Scottish working class area of that era, in the light of sectarianism?

The Group held a healthy ecumenical understanding of the nature of sacrament, ministry, incarnational service and Christian unity,[132] but the people they sought to serve carried a cultural legacy of division which had been encouraged by both the Church of Scotland and Roman Catholic church, and which was lived out in the West of Scotland in cultural touch points such as the Old Firm football division. This had little effect on engagement with the breadth of social work undertaken by the Group, but the Group itself noted that "the point of separation comes at formal

129. Harvey, *Bridging the Gap*, 101–02.

130. Ibid.

131. Holloway, "The Gorbals Group," 43.

132. For example, in its openness to encourage the Episcopalians Richard Holloway and Lilias Graham to work in tandem within the Gorbals Group, and to admit lay people to the Group who were agnostic.

worship."[133] Put simply, sectarianism put paid to the prospect of Catholics worshipping with Protestants, and thus hindered the emergence of an ecumenical "group church."

Ian Henderson in his coruscating attack on structural ecumenism in *Power Without Glory*[134] defined the furore over the "Bishop's Report" of 1957 to 1959 as an illustration that those outwith educated circles found it difficult to thole the prospect of communing with other Christian denominations, which historically they had been taught to mistrust, in particular by the Church of Scotland of the inter-war period. Was the Group an example too of a practical ecumenism in favour within theological colleges but at odds in *praxis* not only with the sometimes reactionary conservatism of the suburban Kirk, but also in their attempts to form "church" with the working class people they sought to serve?

*Failure to evangelize?* An alternative proposition is a criticism of incarnational ministry per se, as the evangelical wing of the reformed church would consider it. The view of Donald MacLeod of the Free Church of Scotland on the failure of the Group is a classic expression of the evangelical view on the role of personal salvation in mission. He viewed the cause as derived from the missiology of the Iona Community which, in his opinion "does not believe in sin. It has room for the incarnation, but not for the atonement, and simply cannot bring itself to summon individuals (including the poor) to repentance. Terrified of proselytising, it refuses to evangelise."[135]

What this somewhat over-simplified viewing of the theology of the Gorbals Group omits is their assumption, like Allan, MacLeod and the EHPP before them, that it was only in the expression of the Gospel by social action in community that the true Gospel would come alive, and thus be made apparent to ordinary people so that they might come to faith.

## Factors Related to the Group

*Internal differences:* As John Harvey states, "from the beginning, the Group struggled, and at times fell out, over how a new form of church could grow in this rapidly disintegrating, secularised, and depressed context."[136]

---

133. Shaw, 1968 Report, 9, Archive of the Gorbals Group Ministry.

134. Henderson, *Power Without Glory*, 117.

135. In a highly controversial article to commemorate fifty years of the Iona Community, titled "Question Marks and Garbage Heaps," 24.

136. Harvey, "Geoff Shaw," 159.

The "theological and political radical,"[137] Walter Fyfe, "became irritated with suggestions that bringing in only a few church members was a shortcoming of the Group."[138] By contrast, Jardine, Shaw and Harvey all worried over the apparent "failure" to create EHPP-style storefront churches, or in any other organic form.

These differences, Shaw recognised on reflection, "underlie some of the indecisiveness of the Group in regard to the formation of some form of congregation."[139]

*The move from theology to politics by Geoff Shaw*: As for forming "church," Harvey recalls that "during the second half of his time in the Gorbals, my sense is that Geoff had moved away from expecting anything of this nature to happen."[140] Aligned with this growing disillusionment on one front was the belief for Shaw "that if it was change that God wanted for His people in the Gorbals, then the way to bring it about was not through the church, but through politics."[141] As Shaw jocularly commented, "it is not enough to feed the goldfish, you also have to change the water in the bowl from time to time."[142] This re-focusing of energies led to Shaw being elected as Councillor for Toryglen, and in time as leader of the fledgling Strathclyde Regional Council until his death in 1978.

## Factors Related to the Type of
## Ministry and to Working in the Gorbals

*The lack of engagement of local people within the Group*: As in East Harlem, the Group recognised their "cultural intrusion"[143]—that the members of the Group were highly educated and mostly middle-class. Shaw came from a wealthy Inverleith medical family and had been the Dux of Edinburgh Academy. Fyfe graduated *summa cum laude* from Union Seminary, his final paper obtaining exemplary marks from Paul Tillich. Harvey had been educated at Kelvinside Academy, Glasgow and Fettes College, Edinburgh,

---

137. Ferguson, *Geoff*, 40.

138. Ibid., 119.

139. 1968 Report, 3, Archive of the Gorbals Group Ministry.

140. Harvey, "Geoff Shaw," 160.

141. Ibid.

142. Ferguson, *Geoff*, 72.

143. In the phrase of Bill Webber, co-founder of EHPP–see Harvey, *Bridging the Gap*, 93.

and had completed a BA at Oxford University before beginning at Trinity College in 1961.

Albeit that their backgrounds flavoured many of the unsupportive contemporary responses,[144] the individuals involved did not seek to mask their prior privileges, recognising that in their "critical solidarity" they would never attain full "identification" with the Gorbals residents, particularly as they could always leave. That recognition led to a reputation for honesty and credibility, and became one of their great strengths. Donald MacLeod agreed in a rare supportive passage: "In the 1960s one of the things the Gorbals needed was a posh accent. Incarnational mission does not mean that the Christian becomes simply an ordinary, typical resident of Hutchesonstown. It means that he goes in as a Spirit-filled man (and probably a resourceful, educated one) and serves the community from the inside. That is what Christ did: and that is the model to which the Gorbals Group pointed us."[145]

As in East Harlem, one detriment of "cultural intrusion," however, was a consequent difficulty in engaging local people in membership of the group and in worship, contributing to the lack of Christian growth. As early as 1960, the necessity of that development had been highlighted to the Group by Flossie Borgmann of the EHPP: "If the aim of the Group is to create a new community free from the institutional church this demand . . . the participation of local people in policy making, and also to share in worship, sacraments, and Christian teaching."[146]

Shaw identified a possible solution in hindsight: "perhaps a greater participation of local people could have been achieved by smaller units of those Group members who have come to live in Gorbals from another area and background."[147]

*The sheer pressure and volume of work:* By "letting the world set the agenda," the absence of focus meant that those within the Group were near overwhelmed with the scale of work which came their way. This left little time to consider forming "church." As Harvey recalled: "The danger here— the danger in fact, with the whole principle of "Christian presence"—is that

---

144. The institutional Church maintained a distanced and often cynical outlook, which was clear from the outset. A view such as this from Bill Shackleton, who sought to join the Group in 1958, was common: "I knew Geoff Shaw before he was a Spartan! . . . As often happens with people from his background, Geoff seemed to try to make up for this by painful self-denial."—*Keeping It Cheery,* 79.

145. MacLeod, "Question Marks and Garbage Heaps," 25.

146. Flossie Borgmann, quoted in Harvey, *Bridging the Gap,* 104.

147. 1968 Report, 9, Archive of the Gorbals Group Ministry.

we glamorise or romanticise it. It wasn't glamorous: it was bloody hard. And it wasn't romantic either."[148]

*Knowing how to contextually communicate the Gospel:* In the absolute dedication to a fully incarnational ministry of availability, the vocabulary of church became unlearned, distant, and increasingly irrelevant. Harvey described such a difficulty in relation to the French worker-priests:

> When you cut your way out into the world from the church . . . it is not pride that keeps you silent; it is not even loyalty; you simply do not know what words to use. Your life is your statement; its living, its loving, its suffering, its failure; and almost all you have to keep you going are some water, some bread, some wine and a book.[149]

## Summary

Shaw wrote in 1968 that: "The Group has never, at any point, claimed to be providing an alternative to the Parish church system, nor to be discovering the new pattern of the church. It is not to be assumed, therefore, that the conclusions reached . . . [are] a blueprint for future developments elsewhere."[150]

Despite Shaw's disclaimer, the Group has had significant short and long term effects on church and mission. The Group foreshadowed much of the "emerging ecumenical missionary paradigm" identified in the work of David Bosch: mission as *missio Dei*; as mediating rather than proclaiming salvation; as a quest for justice; as liberation and common witness by the whole people of God; fully inculturated and contextualized.[151] The Group remained untarnished as a radical, exploratory ministry, even within the social liberation of the times.

In their social work and housing action in the name of the Gospel, the Group's impact was significant on the lives of many marginalized children and adults living in chaotic slum conditions.[152] There was often a sense of joy

148. Harvey, "Geoff Shaw," 156.

149. Harvey, *Bridging the Gap*, 91.

150. 1968 Report, 11, Archive of the Gorbals Group Ministry.

151. See Bosch, *Transforming Mission*, 349–511.

152. As teacher Elizabeth Livingston Mansill testifies: "I don't believe the Group's encounter with me was noticed . . . However *my* encounter with the Group was a life-changing experience; I encountered Jesus at work."—"Memories of 'The Gorbals Group' 1963–1966 from the Perspective of a Local Teacher," unpublished, 2006, 2, within the Archive of the Gorbals Group Ministry. In a broader social sense, the contributions of Geoff Shaw and Lilias Graham to social work policy and to the provisions on Children's Panels in the Social Work (Scotland) Act 1968 are also a lasting legacy.

and wonder within the members of the Group, as they saw their theology worked out in practice, and the positive influence which their presence had on the lives of those around them. They achieved the emulation of the ideals of the EHPP as they had sought, if not some of the practical effects.

In the initial aim of "bridging the gap" between the church and the poor by way of indigenous and vital churches organically growing from life on the street, their departure from that starting point was starkly highlighted in a report by David Rice, an American Baptist Pastor who spent part of 1968 on secondment with the Group from the Ecumenical Institute at Bossey. The crucial questions raised for Rice in the apparent inability of the Group to "be church" were twofold:

1. In what way can we *really* say that the church is present when social work alone is accomplished? Does it really matter that Christian work be a conscious thing both with the doer and the receiver?

2. Do the terms "redemption," "conversion," and "salvation" still have any meaning?[153]

The nub of these questions, as Harvey identifies, is whether *koinonia* is still an essential mark of mission, and thus of "church": "These questions the Gorbals Group, has not . . . answered, although it may have helped pose them, and others, more sharply to the church."[154]

The primary legacy of the Group goes beyond models, schemes and theological strands: the inspiring, unconditional dedication to the people in God's name. For Harvey's tribute to his late friend Geoff Shaw, read the achievements of the ministry as a whole: "For Scotland, and for Scotland's church, though, Geoff surely has much to say. About integrity. About vision. About commitment. About trusting people. About seeing where God is, and going to stand alongside him, no matter what the cost."[155]

Beyond such fervent, self-giving Christian discipleship, however, we might be drawn also to agree with William Christman that "the example of the Gorbals Group made an indelible impression upon the church and the people of Scotland,"[156] their influence resonating in Scottish missiology and ministry.[157] At the least, the Group's work is a well of understanding

---

153. Rice, "A Report on Fieldwork," 1968, 9, Archive of the Gorbals Group Ministry.

154. Harvey, *Bridging the Gap*, 108.

155. Harvey, "Geoff Shaw," 162–63.

156. Christman, "Being There," 51.

157. Christman's view is that the Group "had profound implications for the witness of the Church," directly inspiring incarnational ministry presence in disadvantaged

for contemporary practical models of urban mission: a roadmap for group ministry, incarnational living, and for pioneer ministry within the "emerging church conversation," both in triumphs and pitfalls.

As for the broader missiological vision for Scotland in the present, the rousing conclusion of Shaw and for pioneer ministry Harvey's publication *A Dead End Church?* still holds true:

> Our faith is that this is God's world—in the structures of all society, in the dark city streets, in the silent places of man's loneliness and his despair; and that there He summons His church to reflect on His love and the coming of His kingdom. Our certainty is that Christ will cleanse the world of its sickness and of its hatred; of war and of all enmity; of injustice and of destruction—if not with the church, then without it.[158]

# The Church to be Reformed by the Ecumenical Laity—Robert Mackie, Ian Fraser and Scottish Churches House

The 1950s was a remarkable and in some senses, a "golden" period for the churches in Scotland and initially at least, for ecumenism . . . The vision of the Baillie Commission had included a new drive to evangelise Scotland, which it had related to a grand ecumenical vision of the reconstruction of Scottish society in which a growing and uniting church would exercise a decisive influence across all areas of life.

—Doug Gay, 2006[159]

What if the "para-church" focus of the Gorbals Group Ministry could be elsewhere directed towards the laity of all denominations of the church institutions, such that their discovery of common ground might re-frame all of the churches from outwith?

Much of the success in Scotland of transposing the developing international, ecumenical missiology of the laity into concrete action in the late fifties was down to one of the fathers of worldwide ecumenism, Robert

areas from the Seventies onwards by such as John Millar in Castlemilk, the "community ministry" of Archie Russell in Drumchapel, Ron Ferguson in Easterhouse and Claus Clausen in Hamilton—see Christman, "Being There," 53–57.

158. Shaw and Harvey, *Dead End Church?*, 26—a passage "worthy of Bonhoeffer himself," according to Christman, "Being There," 51.

159. Gay, "Practical Theology," 142.

Mackie. Emerging from the Student Christian Movement, Mackie was the General Secretary of the World Student Christian Federation in the Forties, integral in the formation of the World Council of Churches in 1948, and latterly Associate General Secretary of the World Council of Churches in Geneva from 1949 to 1955.

Mackie's ecumenical vision reflected the focus of the times, writing in 1946 that "The ecumenical movement only has meaning in relation to the missionary movement."[160] On his return to Scotland, Mackie began to play a pivotal part in Scottish church life. Described by his friend Archie Craig as "the world's best chairman,"[161] Mackie applied his considerable organisational talents to three principal areas in the implementation of ecumenical mission and structural unity, which in combination represent the highpoint of both structural and representative ecumenism in Scotland.

Firstly, he became Chairman of the "Tell Scotland" Executive Committee, and co-ordinated the planning for the first Kirk Week for the laity at Aberdeen in August 1957, modelled on the German lay *Kirchentag,* of which Mackie had direct personal experience. The idea of "Kirk Week" within the "Tell Scotland" Movement was a reaction against the seeming distance with the laity created by the Billy Graham Crusade. "Kirk Weeks" were a recognition that theology may have become the preserve only of the academic; that the whole membership must recognise its vocation, involving education and development for both ministers and lay members; and that, in the words of Mackie's biographer, "the priesthood of all believers" had been "subverted by the ecclesiastically convenient alternative of the clericalising of further selected lay groups—such as the eldership in the Church of Scotland."[162]

In organising the first Kirk Week, Mackie experienced the same issue which stifled development of clear thinking on the role of the laity at the World Council of Churches, being the absence of lay representation in the decision-making process. He wrote to his son that the Kirk Week Executive was made up of "busy ministers," but that "it ought to be a layman's committee," lamenting that "I am fighting for lay leadership as against clerical push . . . Presbyterianism seemed to have frozen its laity in an ecclesiastical system."[163]

Despite these misgivings, the Kirk Week in Aberdeen in August 1957 was deemed a success, attended by over a thousand delegates, and providing a boost to the enthusiasm for and direction of "Tell Scotland,"

160. Quoted in Blackie, "Legacy of Robert Mackie," 23.
161. Blackie, *In Love and Laughter,* 141.
162. Ibid., 131–32.
163. Quoted in ibid., 132.

albeit temporary. The 1957 event was followed by further Kirk Weeks in Ayr and Perth.

Secondly, in an attempt to unite structural re-integration with the local church, Mackie acted in its challenging early years as Chairman of the Committee overseeing the "area of ecumenical experiment" in the new town of Livingston, West Lothian. January 1966 saw the induction of James Maitland as the Church of Scotland minister, along with the institution of an Episcopal priest, together for the first time in Scottish history. As Maitland later reflected, "something unmistakably ecumenical, something that ordinary people could see and test for themselves, had been brought into being at the grassroots of urban life in Scotland."[164]

Thirdly, and most importantly for present purposes, Mackie was integral in the formation of Scottish Churches House, Dunblane in 1960, in its initial purposes: as a dynamic attempt to not only bring more closely together those involved in seeking the integration of existing church structures, but to also to provide the forum for the investigation and resolution of social and cultural issues by groups across society, and for the church laity of all denominations to meet together in order to draw towards a common understanding of theology and the world. The hope was that in doing so the ordinary people might not only identify potential solutions to social problems, but also to re-imagine the nature of their church denominations in the future, so that the church might more truly meet the needs and concerns of the people within them.

On his return to Scotland, Mackie had become friendly with the parish minister at Rosyth, Fife, Ian Fraser. Mackie established the common ground between seven denominations for the formation of Scottish Churches House, identified the ruined row of houses in Dunblane which might serve the project, raised much of the initial funding and persuaded Fraser to become the first Warden.[165]

On graduating BD with distinction from New College in 1942, Ian Fraser refused an invitation from Professor John Baillie to apply to join the teaching staff, in order to work for two years as a prototype worker-priest in the Tullis Russell paper mill in Markinch, Fife.

Following a period as Scottish Secretary of the SCM, Fraser was called to parish ministry in Rosyth, then dominated by the Naval Dockyard, where he served from 1948 to 1960. As head of the Commission for "The Community" of "Tell Scotland," he wrote of his experiences in Rosyth in

---

164. Maitland, *New Beginnings*, 12.
165. Blackie, *In Love and Laughter*, 137.

*Bible, Congregation and Community* in 1959.[166] Doug Gay assesses the book as: "a remarkable account of a local attempt to embody the theological vision of the Baillie Commission for the post-war Church of Scotland, but in its political radicalism and its practical commitment to the empowerment of lay people it goes some way beyond that . . . It offers an inclusive vision of Christian practice which defies evangelical, ecumenical and liberal labels."[167]

Fraser's achievement in the parish was to make the Gospel come alive for the ordinary members of the church, and for that to occur through a process by which they were empowered to achieve for themselves the biblical insights necessary to interpret the relationship of the Gospel to the everyday, and to utilise Scripture and their faith as a living guide to their future path.

As Fraser wrote in 2011 in an introduction to a reprint of the book, "the whole church became Bible-based. That gave members a fresh appreciation of what church and ministry should be, and led them to live in the light of that discovery. I would call this basic factor "Bible resourcing" rather than Bible study."[168] Thus he could write: "It has been one of the highlights of my life to hear people speak together about the real circumstances with which they daily have to contend, out of their rooting in the Bible."[169]

Over a dozen years, Fraser had brought the elders to a point where they could identify "the relevance of biblical insights to developments in the dockyard," and indeed the whole congregation to "the relevance of the scriptures to what they had to work through in the different pressures and opportunities life presented."[170]

He had done so by a process of integrating scripture to the "business" of the church courts, by allowing the lives and biblical insights of ordinary members to play a role in liturgy in "participative worship" whereby "the real pressures of life" are "continually woven into the fabric," with the minister "instructed by the congregation out of their immersion in the world."[171] Above all, Fraser recognised his role in the relationship with the laity as one of encourager and inspirer: "The gifts given by the Spirit need to be identified, matured and effectively deployed. That is the first responsibility of those of us who are ordained. Our ministry is auxiliary to the main

---

166. On Fraser's ministry in Rosyth, see also chapter 4 of Ian Cranston, *I've Seen Worse: Glimpses of Ian Fraser*.

167. Gay, "Practical Theology," 179.

168. Fraser, *Bible, Congregation and Community*, 2nd ed., 9.

169. Ibid., 36.

170. Ibid., 10.

171. Ibid., 20–21.

ministry of the church. It exists to bring the ministry of God's people into play, nourishing it, equipping it."[172]

In all of his work in Rosyth and following, Fraser was clear that mission was an integrated work of "proclamation" both in word and deed, by the whole people of God immersed in the life of the world. His manifesto for the church expressed in 1959 still bears well in the present era:

> The business of the church in the world is to proclaim him. Proclamation is not simply a work of the ordained ministry, nor is it simply a matter of words . . . Proclamation belongs to the ministry of the whole church. Christ is made known by words wherever members willingly combat untruth, and interpret their faith as need requires and opportunity offers. He is made known wherever the Christ-like deed confirms words and clothes them with reality. These two, words and deeds, go together, form a single testimony. He is made known where there is self-sacrificial love. Proclamation is a total activity, the whole membership making Christ known at every point in its common life—when it is conscious of making him known and when it is not, when it is speaking and when it is silent. Wherever members of the church are in the world, there is the place of witness.

Contextualization was essential for Fraser to the "proclamation" of the whole people of God: "For the proclamation to be made, the language and lessons of the world must be learned. The church must take serious account of the world's life. The context which disciplines it is as inescapably given as the revelation which masters it. It has no language with which to speak but that which is common currency in the world. It must be immersed in the traffic of men."[173]

The process of integrating "the language and lessons of the world" with the Gospel and the churches was central to the vision for Scottish Churches House. Writing on the eve of his departure as Warden in 1969, Fraser set out its purpose and achievements since its inception in 1960 as:

> Something more than an earnest endeavour towards cooperation between Christians. It represents an act of faith that God has something urgent to give us to do when we are willing to learn it together—a new shape for His church.[174]

172. Ibid., 12.

173. Ibid., 60.

174. Fraser, *Scottish Churches' House*, 1. Gay notes that Scottish Churches House was consciously styled on the German Evangelical Academies referred to in chapter 3—"A Practical Theology," 147, 151.

Its goal therefore was not simply a place for friendly discussion, but a forum for an earnest attempt between ordinary lay members of denominations as well as their leaders to more fully address the problems of the world with the Gospel, and to provide a new direction for the structures of the churches themselves. In implementation of that goal, as one of three types of "consultation" which the House hosted constantly throughout the sixties, as Gay notes, "a series of lay consultations were instituted under the heading 'sharing the Gospel.' These meetings held two or three times a year aimed to educate and empower lay people to take part in ecumenical debates and consultations about the order and mission of the church, both in Scotland and globally."[175]

For Fraser, this recognition of the primacy of the laity in all consideration of mission was essential for the development of a theology of the laity, and of the content of direct, local action. It would point the way ahead for the church, both for unity between denominations, and for mission itself: "Much too little attention is paid to the significance of the fellowship of Christians in localities . . . Much more emphasis needs to be placed on the coming together of Christians at the grass roots, as a sign and promise of the coming great church. This coming together could also offer a testing-bed for forms of the church."[176]

There is now, regrettably, no obvious forum in Scotland like Scottish Churches House for the formation of a "de-clericalized lay theology" which tempers and transforms our institutional decision-making. The venues that opened for that purpose, for the most part in the period 1945 to 1960, to allow the meeting, discussion and training of lay people in mission and unity have been closed. St Ninian's, Crieff founded by D. P. Thomson in 1958 for the training of lay people in mission and evangelism was shut by the General Assembly in 2001; Community House of the Iona Community in Clyde Street, Glasgow, has also gone; the Scottish Churches Open College closed in 2003; and Scottish Churches House was closed in January 2012 and is now a hotel.

The widespread closure by the Scottish churches of the avenues for the laity in which to find voices to contribute to the major issues of mission and unity, and the confidence to carry them out, may be a hindrance to the vitality and future vibrancy of the churches themselves. That is certainly the view of the former Warden of Scottish Churches House, Alastair Hulbert who believes that the churches are "symbolically closing down a channel

---

175. Gay, "Practical Theology," 174.
176. Fraser, *Let's Get Moving*, 33–34.

through which living water has flowed, by which the laity has irrigated the church with its imagination and creativity."[177]

With their dissipation and closure, the arm of the institution, and the authority of the clergy in theological and missiological argument, has become re-asserted. The stifling of the oxygen of a wider debate has diminished the possibility of, and any real interest in, closer co-operation and communion, whilst Tom Allan's "greatest lesson" that effective mission flows only from co-operative unity, and *vice versa*, has proved impossible to teach.

Meanwhile, there has been a gradual dissipation of the voice of ecumenism at grass roots level to a whisper. Ian Fraser wrote in 1969, "Livingston should not simply be a beacon, but a torch thrust into ready undergrowth to start a forest fire."[178] Instead the Livingston Ecumenical Parish, as Sheilagh Kesting, the Head of Ecumenical Relations in the Church of Scotland since 1993, comments, "is a swear-word in some quarters of the Church of Scotland—the experiment that failed. It is held up as a warning to others who might want to follow suit."[179]

Using Hulbert's distinction, "representative ecumenism," between those at levels of power and influence within the Scottish churches, persists in a fashion. However, "participative ecumenism," the engagement of local people in dialogue, action and theology has waned. The stark reality is that the bodies founded for lay training and engagement at the height of international, ecumenical enthusiasm for the laity have closed through lack of numbers. Why are they not so interested anymore? Hulbert's view is regretful of the decline and the resulting stasis, ascribing it to: "a lamentable loss of ecumenical vision amongst church people . . . Nowadays, the majority of church members have been shaped either in a conservative evangelical setting where world mission, ecumenism and visible unity are not seen to be important, or in a merely denominational setting which gives no opportunity to form deep and trusting friendships outside it."[180]

Despite the functioning of Action of Churches Together in Scotland to at least maintain cross-denominational communication at the local level, the type of exchange between lay people at the grassroots level that Ian Fraser envisaged for the benefit of the churches, or that formed the *raison d'être* of Scottish Churches House, is mostly gone.

---

177. Hulbert, *The Hint Half Guessed*, 181.

178. Fraser, *Let's Get Moving*, 33–34.

179. Kesting, "Being Ecumenical in Scotland Today," 15.

180. Hulbert, *The Hint Half Guessed*, 181.

# Conclusions on the Five
# Streams of Missiology

It is hard to escape the conclusion that lay people have become marginalised by accident or design. What has certainly departed is the concentration on the importance of their role in mission and unity, and thus any impetus towards their engagement and training for the tasks those challenges might involve. They are no longer venerated as they were in the fifteen years after World War II: as the powerhouse that would revolutionise the church internally, that would break out to fully communicate the Gospel in every breath of life, and would provide the impetus and means of unity across the denominations, whether organic or conciliary. It was an attempted revolution in the democratization of the churches, but it has run its course.

Understandably in the present stasis, missiological excitement is centred not on how the lay people of the church can change the institution and society, but on side-lining the institution altogether, and by implication and effect, those marooned with it. It is focused upon "emerging church" or "Fresh Expressions," whose ethos excludes institutionalisation. Mission is expected to "emerge" on its own terms. The challenge is to seek to integrate the missiological insights of "Fresh Expressions" within the outlook of the institutions, to reform their very essence, and the role of the laity within them, as Fraser had envisaged. The alternative is to be content with managed decline.

There remains a large pool of resource in the laity within the mainstream denominations. Despite their diminishing numbers and heightening age-profile, they may be the last hope of institutional survival for the churches, if they are to continue to play a significant part in the *missio Dei*. Maybe the future does lie in a graceful death of institutional Christianity in Scotland, and a gradual re-birth from the "bottom up" as envisaged by all of the protagonists in this story. Whilst they still retain potential, however, in their human and financial resources, perhaps it is worth a concerted effort, for one last time, to re-invigorate institutions such as the Church of Scotland, in a way that Allan, MacLeod, Webber and Fraser intended.

The resource that was identified in the period of 1945 to 1970 to do so, common to all models of contextual mission, was to bring the life and faith of ordinary people to the fore, identified as the future of mission and unity. Has their day passed? There must still be a remnant of hope now for the utility of the ordinary people who still invest large proportions of their time, finance and faith in the furtherance of the institution. Before the time is passed, it would require soon a diversion of some of the church's energies from being expended in cost-cutting rationalization.

Is a "call to mission" amongst the laity of the church realistic at all, when the laity are diminishing, would need to be inspired to action, and have been so distanced over the past half century from ideas of what mission might constitute? When everything is rejected by one side or another, nothing can be done concertedly in the name of mission, and inaction results. Church members might be hard pressed to come to a working definition of mission and what it means practically in his/her parish. There remains a common misconception that the purpose of "mission" is to increase the numbers in the parish church, and that the means of "mission" are grand-scale events; very much a revivalist "Call to Church" concept close to the mission of the thirties, married to the Christendom ideal, unaware of developments in *missio Dei* theology. Not many talk about mission, or are being trained in it; and ordinary people are not being empowered to exercise it.

So if such an endeavor is indeed worthwhile, what needs to be recaptured? It would be a re-alignment of trust, confidence and investment of time, energy and money in the lives, theology, training and witness of ordinary church members. It may be time to seek to re-ignite in their Christian lives a sense of the relevance for them, and for the church, of mission and unity from the ground upwards.

The diagnosis of the ailment facing the institutional church was near identical in all models considered in this book—that it had long ceased to be representative of ordinary people in their goals and aspirations, in their daily struggles in life, family and work, and in their social and political outlook. The solution was to be found in the re-planting of the place of Christianity at the heart of society.

From the first phase of the Iona Community until the mid-sixties, the church might seek to re-vitalize the Gospel outwith the building on a Sunday morning through visible presence and cell communities in the streets of the parish; at work and in people's houses.

From the EHPP, the church as institution might seek to re-align its core understanding towards the contextual flows of the world in its immediate midst; of adapting structure and hierarchy so that its form might be visibly present and more greatly defined by life outside.

From the Gorbals Group Ministry, there is a sense of the church as institution letting go of all structures which might hinder the process of lay encounter and the formation of Christian community, allowing contextualized forms of "church" to develop and grow without pre-determined models being imposed, or "results" being anticipated.

Ian Fraser and Scottish Churches House point towards a "bible re-sourcing" of the laity to allow their fuller "proclamation," and the re-opening of avenues by which their common ground might "irrigate" the churches.

Taking the five streams of post-war mission together that have been identified and discussed in chapters 2 to 5, where do the Christian encounters in mission of the laity and clergy with the ordinary people in Scotland in 1945 to 1970 direct us now for theologies of the church, the laity and the people?

The essence of the issues for the church that result might be summarised thus—"re-make or re-model?"

As for "re-make," the majority of the book has focused on the work on the work of Tom Allan and internationally on the mobilization of the laity within the church in the forties to sixties. The laity were viewed as boosting and developing mission *through* the church, with mission being exercised partly as a means of purging and redeveloping of the church itself. Lay movements were either held under the umbrella of the church, or fed back *into* the church.

The "apostolate of the laity," if the correct sociological and missiological foundation is identified and applied for mission in the present day, retains at least the potential to purge or re-energize the church, break down the clergy/laity divide, and re-align a culture of passivity and conservatism to one at the forefront of a "missionary parish," as Allan had intended.

In the alternative of "re-model," Allan has been set in historical context through a reflection on the work of the Iona Community, the Gorbals Group Ministry, derived from the East Harlem Protestant Parish; and of Robert Mackie, Ian Fraser and Scottish Churches House. They were attempts of laity and clergy to engage with the world on its own terms by recasting the church and re-forming its structure from beyond, or in simply by-passing it altogether.

Laity and clergy were seen as boosting and developing mission *outwith* the present institution. They sought to purge and redevelop the whole concept of what "church" might be. "Church" was a prospective project rather than a fixed and unerring entity, being a work in progress depending on the movement of the people and the Spirit. "Church" was thus expressed either by the people influencing the clergy, as in East Harlem and the early ideas in the Gorbals, or by consciously rejecting any stylized form in favour of living within the community as an implanted cell or group, as in the worker-priests and the later Gorbals, the latter having no intention of feeding back into the pre-existing institution. Alternatively, Scottish Churches House sought to be a lay "seed-bed," out of which would grow new forms of ecclesial entity and structure.

Once more, the potential persists, subject to appropriate focus and empowerment, for ordinary people to act in mission outwith the structures of the church, such that there may be a re-imagining from the communities they encounter of the form that "church" might take; "emerging" communities acting as a "church before the church" as the Student Christian Movement once was.

In all of the streams, there is one constant that persists—that the lives and theologies of lay, church people, or ordinary people on the street, must take centre-stage if a process of contextualization is to gather pace. As Ralph Morton wrote in 1953, in words that bear equal resonance now: "The day of the professional evangelist is past, at least when he stood apart as the exponent of faith to men. It is only through personal contact that men outside will be won. The members of the congregation are the agents of mission."[181]

Paul Lakeland recently wrote: "There is a certain irony, as peculiar as it is revealing, to the fact that theology is almost bereft of sustained reflection on the history and theological significance of these "laity," over 95 per cent of the members of the Christian church through the ages. Theologically speaking, the Christian laity have been all but invisible for most of the last fifteen hundred years."[182]

There are two major expressions of lay commitment since the heady times of the sixties which have sprung up ecclesially, almost by definition outwith the boundaries of the church, where the laity has once again taken prominence. There has been a dissolution of the laity/clergy divide, the voice of each member being heard, and the laity being called to act as key to the construction of the form and content of community. They are further examples of "church before the church," from which the institution can readily learn in relation to the role and gifts of the laity.

The first is what is variously described as "basic ecclesial communities," or "base communities," emanating from Latin America but spreading throughout the developing world, and reviewed extensively in the mid-Eighties within Protestantism by Guillermo Cook[183], and in Catholicism by Leonardo Boff.[184] In Scottish perspective, a key agent in their identification and lionization was Ian Fraser, working in the seventies for the World Council of Churches, travelling around the world making contact with such communities.[185] This was also, in essence, the nature of the Gorbals Group Ministry—as ministers in the form of laity, seeking to form a basic Christian gathering.

181. Morton, *Evangelism in Scotland Today*, quoted in Shannon, *Tom Allan*, 10–11.

182. Lakeland, "The Laity," 511.

183. Cook, *The Expectation of the Poor*.

184. Boff, *Ecclesiogenesis*.

185. A subject on which Fraser has written extensively, in publications such as *Living a Countersign: from Iona to Basic Christian Communities*; and *Many Cells, One Body: Stories from Small Christian Communities*.

For Bosch, "their significance lies in the fact that the laity have come of age and are missionally involved in an imaginative way."[186] The claim of Boff, however, takes matters much further—as the necessary practical step to implement all of the well-stated talk on the lay apostolate since the Second World War, and a recapture by the laity of their rightful inheritance:

> The basic church communities are helping the whole church in the process of declericalization, by restoring to the People of God, the faithful, the rights of which they have been deprived in the linear structure. On the level of theory, theology itself has already gone beyond the old pyramid. But it is not enough to know. A new praxis must be implemented. This is what the basic communities are saying. They are helping the whole church to "re-invent" itself, right in its foundations. Experiment is gradually confirming theory, and inspiring in the church-as-institution a confidence in the viability of a new way of being church in the world today.[187]

Whatever the veracity of his claims for such communities, Boff was correct in his insistence that the words of scholars and church hierarchy in relation to laity emancipation had to be followed by concrete action, learning from such outposts of a "new way of being church today."

The formation and development of "basic ecclesial communities" by lay people was a precursor in the nature of its structure and personnel to the contemporary "emerging church" movement in the West. In the absence of a fuller consideration of their ecclesiology and theology, for present purposes it may be to sufficient to side with Doug Gay in his sympathetic assessment of the "re-mixing" of ecclesiology in the light of the "emerging church" movement, when he points to the predominance of lay involvement in the setting up of such groups. For Gay, "the emphasis on lay activism and involvement is one of the low church Protestant distinctives that was valued and held to by at least the first generation of those who developed the emerging project," arising from "the free church, evangelical and charismatic roots of many of its founders and activists."[188]

The desire of the church as institution, as Gay puts it, "to hug emerging groups and embrace the currents of renewal they represented"[189], may lead to a destructive pressure to conform to certain constituents which the institution insists upon doctrinally, but may also illuminate for the church

---

186. Bosch, *Transforming Mission*, 473.
187. Boff, *Ecclesiogenesis*, 259.
188. Gay, *Remixing the Church*, 76.
189. Ibid., 78.

the action it must take to reform. Gay thus concludes that "this disturbing supplement that we have been taught to call "the laity" has reasserted itself in the emerging church conversation in ways that call for further theological reflection, if it is not simply to have been a supplement suppressed."[190]

The experience of lay empowerment and prominence within "basic Christian communities," the "emerging church" conversation, in Tom Allan's congregations and those of the EHPP, and in the participative ecumenism of Scottish Churches House and the "lay" ministry of the Gorbals Group, offers direction markers as to where that merged pathway might lie.

Such directions require nourishment by the institutional church, accepting that the Christian faith and not the church might be the ultimate beneficiary, for as Werner expresses it:

> The tension between church and mission is related to the basic tension between the church as a charismatic and spirit-filled reality, and the church as a safeguard for the continuity of the tradition of the Gospel that needs institutional shape. Signs of renewal in missionary presence, therefore, involve the affirmation of lay initiative networks and missionary minorities–in many cases, far outside the institutional churches–which are trying to live in accordance with the values of the Gospel, and are seeking new and daring forms of inculturating Christian faith.[191]

The future may lie in the promotion of lay enterprises to form new ventures and communities, and for the institutional church in turn to learn and adapt from their example.

Despite their varying emphases, the work of Tom Allan, George MacLeod, Scottish Churches House and the Gorbals Group Ministry were all attempts at promoting and establishing a lay, ecumenical witness in word and deed at the forefront of the re-energization of Christianity in Scotland, and towards the desired integration of Christianity with the lives of the people.

The four key Scottish streams and one American which have been considered in the preceding chapters flowed from common springs. They were intermingled, co-dependent and sometimes mutually supportive. They occurred almost in a lineal progression, both in missiological and chronological terms, from "accommodation" via "contextualization" towards "inculturation," as "breakouts" from the pre-war exposition of standardised mono-cultural Christianity.

---

190. Ibid., 78–79.
191. Werner, "Rediscovering a Missionary Understanding," 144–45.

"Inculturation," however, is a tentative, ongoing process. All theologies challenge and enrich each other. Mission being essentially dialogical, there must be a "giving and receiving." The ultimate goal which did not come to immediate fruition in any of the streams was the end result described by Bosch as "interculturation"—the creation of an indigenous Christian faith hybrid by the meeting of cultures.

Within those concurrent flows of development in the expression of "contextualization," however, there are elements of all of the models considered in chapters 2 to 5 which retain a depth and resonance for present purposes, in particular when further filtered through current missiological frameworks. Indeed, there are aspects within the models which, had length permitted, would have merited further consideration to also critique and develop those frameworks.

In conclusion, therefore, we look now towards the key points from the preceding chapters, directing a path towards a recovery of the "apostolate of the laity" in mission. However, to meaningfully transpose the missiology of 1945 to 1970 to the present will require not only analysis of the successes and failings from the tensions of the models of Allan and his contemporaries, but also a re-configuration through a filter of present day global missiological thinking, so that aspects definitely "of their time" might remain there.

# 6

# Adapting the Mission of Allan and His Contemporaries to the Present

If it is true...that the entire life of the church is missionary, it follows that we desperately need a theology of the laity—something of which the first rudiments are now emerging. But also, such a theology is only now becoming possible again, as we are moving out of the massive shadow of the Enlightenment. For a theology of the laity presupposes a break with the notion, so fundamental to the Enlightenment, that the private sphere of life has to be separated from the public.[1]

—David Bosch, 1991

T HE PRECEDING CHAPTERS HAVE considered the practical "successes" of the missiology of Tom Allan, turning thereafter to the lessons of all five streams, in the journey towards the recovery of the laity in mission. Drawing all of their work together through the lens of current global missiology, a framework for future mission by the laity will now be offered.

The first section of this chapter will therefore look to identify a present-day missiological framework which might offer a lens through which to analyse and assess their work, so that the appropriate pathways in the current landscape might become more apparent.

Aspects of that analysis will provide a platform by which the Scottish missiology considered in chapters 2 to 5 can be streamlined and refreshed. Derivations and principles will then be drawn from the work of the Scottish missiologists of the immediate post-war period in the final part of the chapter, to be translated from their time to our own.

---

1. Bosch, *Transforming Mission*, 472.

# Present-Day Missiology

## Introduction

Is there any way to conceive of mission beyond secularization, using the work of Allan and his contemporaries? Taking the premise that the journey through the missiology of Tom Allan and his Scottish contemporaries might survive sociological changes and the passage of history to lead us towards the primacy of the laity in mission, with Gospel and church contextualised in everyday experience, the next step is to locate global missiological foundations that can more properly focus such assertions, and help to transpose them from that era to the present.

What missiological lens might be employed to retrieve something of the vitality of that model in those circumstances, cutting through the barrier that the social revolution and institutional decline has presented between ourselves and those former times?

Proceeding from the broad guidelines of lay empowerment and contextualization in the exercise of mission to which this book is inclined, inherent within identification of relevant aspects for this day of Tom Allan and his contemporaries are foundational definitions of "mission" and "evangelism," and further missiological building blocks, in the concepts to follow in this section. They are non-exclusive and necessarily selective. They are set out at this stage in their own terms in short compass, in the belief that they are directly applicable to what has gone before, and form a framework for the final conclusions to follow.

## "Glocalization," Global and Local— Why is *Local* Mission Pertinent Now in the Social Circumstances of the West?

Why bother to concentrate on *the laity* of the local church in engagement with the world? Why not mobilize the clergy to reproduce large-scale national mission such as the "Tell Scotland" campaign; or look to further common unity and agreement on the nature and theology of mission, to then be implemented worldwide in international organizations such as the World Council of Churches or the Lausanne Movement?

The Protestant ecumenical vision of the twentieth century is slowly dying. The hope of consensus for high-level structural unity amongst denominations, or mutual dedication to a shared global conception of what might constitute "justice, peace and the integrity of creation," is married to ideals whose precepts are fast eroding. The focus, instead, must now be upon the local, where the laity of the church have the prime advantage in the exercise of their faith.

The inculturation of Gospel and church within Western civilisation has developed over many centuries. In the period of early Christianization, in the words of Antonie Wessels, "it took on the colour of its environment," and thus "related to existing holy places, times, persons and stories."[2] There developed a solidity over more recent centuries of the marriage bond of Christendom and rational modernity, in their concurrent global spread throughout Western empires. The dilemma now is that in the West "the two projects are beginning to run out of power."[3]

In a 2001 article, the Dutch missiologist Bert Hoedemaker marked the direction of Christian mission in the displacement and fragmentation of culture that marks "late modernity" in Western Europe.

Hoedemaker began by identifying the complicity of "Christianization" in Western Europe with the processes of "modernization": through (a) the desire to conquer complexity with universal rationality; (b) the creation of global stability by applying universal concepts as normative supra-culturally, such as unified models of Christianity or human rights, in contrast to a local inculturation process; and (c) in the close connection between a Kantian elevation of the autonomy of the individual and the evangelical process of personal conversion, to be initiated through persuasive, rational discourse.[4]

In the need to apply standard universal norms, the "common motivation" of the "syntheses" of Christianization and modernization was "the containment, the taming of local, plural religion in an overarching cultural system," in order to define religion "from the point of view of some 'centre.'"[5]

Inevitably, the process assumed a power ethic, and was intrinsically bound to imperial and diplomatic strength, because "it draws the world into the Western historical narrative,"[6] implying that the imposition of a strain of Christianity inculturated in Western Europe, and founded upon its social structures, is the will of a universal God and should be imposed elsewhere.

The boon for Christianity in Western Europe in its relationship with the process of modernization has been, as Hoedemaker puts it, "a certain

2. Wessels, "Inculturation of Christianity in Europe," 36.

3. Hoedemaker, "Mission beyond Modernity," 212. See also the in-depth consideration of issues of the global and the local in late modernity by Schreiter in *Constructing Local Theologies* and *The New Catholicity*.

4. Hoedemaker, "Mission beyond Modernity," 213.

5. Ibid., 215.

6. Ibid., 213.

freedom of development and self-assertion, and in some cases the semblance of public significance."[7] In few countries has this been more marked than with the Church of Scotland. In modernity, the Church of Scotland was unfettered to express its will in civic society; its doctrinal opinion in matters of private morality took centre stage in politics and education; its views were widely disseminated through the media; and its leaders were accepted as cohorts in the power élite which ran the country. No-one told the Church of Scotland what to do, but its voice was heard and respected when it chose to tell others.

The problem now is adroitly summarised by Hoedemaker, as rationality has turned against religion in the late modern setting: "The synthesis . . . is constituted on the basis of a rationality that suspects religion and seeks to contain it. In other words, *in so far as religion supports and confirms the modern synthesis, it is suicidal* (my emphasis)."[8]

The backlash of rationality against religion is manifested in two principal directions: "first in the sense of emancipation, of liberation from dogma and superstition considered to be a hindrance to the development of autonomous reason, then in the sense of a systematic functionalism that prides itself on its ability to organize life without reference to the transcendent."[9]

A rebellion against the "meta-narrative" and the re-assertion of personal autonomy in decision-making thus undermines the three major streams of twentieth-century global ecumenism: firstly, that there might be one message (Christocentric ecumenical mission of the fifties); secondly, one universal social ethic over-riding different cultural viewpoints (ecumenical mission for justice and peace of the sixties); or, thirdly, that visible structural unity could still be possible in global pluralism (ecumenical structural aspirations for one church).

If such meta-narratives are increasingly unworkable, this may mean "the surfacing of types of religion that disregard the limits placed on them by modernity."[10] Therefore, whilst the future may be religion of the "remainders, the loose ends and the reservoirs,"[11] it is religion which might survive the tensions of the *global* only by maintaining its distinctive, *local*, inculturated identity.

What, however, *is* the *local*? It is no longer simply constructs such as a geographical "parish" or social institutions. The task of closely defining the

7. Ibid., 219.
8. Ibid.
9. Ibid., 214.
10. Ibid., 222–23.
11. Ibid., 223.

"culture" of a prevailing geographical area or demographic group in Western Europe has become nigh impossible with the disparity and displacement of inter-relationships amongst people who otherwise live in close proximity. This has been the ironic counter-force of instant global communication, as well as the result of world migration and fluidity of employment which have mixed urban society as never before. Whilst one may still feel some sense of connection in community and corporate responsibility with those living in the immediate vicinity, the churches in Scotland no longer serve as the social glue which provides a focus of community-building, and nor, indeed, do social clubs, political parties or trade unions. An individual is as likely to form a common bond with those who share a passion worldwide for a form of online gaming, a musical genre, or a sexual preference. The result is, in Dale Irvin's words, that "life on the street and the culture of streets take on intensely new configurations of inter- and cross-cultural experience and meaning."[12]

Missiological reflections on "inculturation" and "cross-cultural translation" once would have been the preserve of large North American missionary societies, or pan-global denominations such as the Roman Catholic church, in considering territorial journeys outwards from a Westernized cultural base to Africa or Asia. The same reflections are now directly applicable to the everyday and the ordinary; to a church trying to make sense of the world around it. They apply to multi-faceted daily encounters with individuals who may span a variety of "micro-cultures" and can no longer be "pigeon-holed" according to sex, class, race, neighbourhood or occupation. A generic attempt now to relate, for example, to "white, (notionally) Protestant, working-class, West of Scotland males" is increasingly meaningless, as the validity of the assumptions that those indices would conjure under modernity in relation to social standing, cultural preferences, and human association is dissipating.

The defining words for future religion in Western society are, therefore, that communities of faith will be plural, disparate, culturally individual and especially "local." "Local," in this sense, however, does not just mean the immediate geographical surroundings ("the parish"), but also encompasses the "micro-cultures" which those within the immediate geographical area more commonly inhabit.

If "local" mission is therefore pertinent in the social circumstances of the West, how does that particularly engage the laity of the church? The laity are uniquely placed in their avenues of access to the "micro-cultures" in which they reside or participate, either geographically or though identity

---

12. Irvin, "The Church, the Urban, and Global Mission," 179.

formed by common interest. It is only through the lives of individuals and small groups that cultural connections might be made, and the divide between private and public realms crossed. Any attempt by a large institution such as the church to establish reciprocity with the "local" and the individual is fraught with potential ambiguity and misalignment—the key is relationship in community.

How then, would a vision of emerging "local" communities of faith survive the processes of globalization, secularism and post-modernization, in contrast to those Christian projects that are welded to modernity? The interaction for Hoedemaker must be through a process of "glocalization,"[13] whereby there is a forming and undoing of the "local," in conversation with the "global." In other words, rather than modernism imposing one dominant form of culture or religious viewpoint from the general to the particular, the movement is the reverse: the particular locality forms an interactive space with the general, and is thus open to reflection and self-reformation at local level in the light of the insights of the general.

Thus, for Hoedemaker, "in the situation of glocalization, to put it very succinctly, *rationality is global, religion is local.*" This combination serves to undermine any attempt at the over-arching imposition of religious norms: "What remains of modern synthesis is pulled apart in local, plural religion on the one hand and global, secular rationality on the other. *Globalization itself diminishes the necessity of the containment of religion.*"[14]

But is Christianity not reliant at its core on a global outlook? If one is to retain a concept of an identifiable "Christian tradition," what is still required is "a master image of how all local manifestations of Christian faith belong together."[15] Hoedemaker suggests that the path may lie in the engagement by local Christian communities with each other in the search for common identity, whereby: "Ecumenism will then mean the creation of networks in which a critical testing takes place of whatever presents itself as "Christian faith" across the world, and in which a common memory is both constructed and maintained."[16]

Therefore, for Hoedemaker, "mission is the effort to localize and actualize the promise that God is constructing *one* heaven and earth for a *diverse* and *pluriform* humanity.[17]

13. A concept which Hoedemaker takes from Robertson, "Glocalization," 9–34.
14. Hoedemaker, "Mission beyond Modernity," 228.
15. Ibid., 229.
16. Ibid., 230.
17. Ibid., 231.

In other words, as Andrew Walls expresses the connection, there must be an identification of a necessary but essential tension between the operation of an "indigenizing principle" by which Christians will associate with the "particulars of their culture and group," in conjunction with a "pilgrim principle" associating them with influences outwith their culture as a "universalizing factor."[18]

Globalization in the modern context has not produced a unified worldwide consensus in Protestantism by amalgamating the varied geographical or theological cultures on common ground, or even formed the appropriate context by which such a consensus might be forged. Nor, indeed, has it opened the door to forms of unification with the Roman Catholic church. Now the time is passing with the twilight of the modern enterprise where such consensus or unification might be achievable.

If Hoedemaker is correct in his assertions that the old global ecumenical conciliar Protestant and Orthodox vision inspired by the lay movements of the nineteenth century, drawn from the Edinburgh International Missionary Conference of 1910, and reaching its peak in the immediate post-war period, is doomed to extinction because it is intrinsically mired in modernist propositions which are disappearing from global view, and that any new conception must respect the process of "glocalization"; then in the writer's proposition, "local," lay, ecumenical, contextual theology and mission *praxis* which is informed in critical reflection with the "global," becomes one of few viable future visions which might involve the institutional churches.

## "Cross-Cultural Translation" and "Interculturation"— How Do We Recognize the Crossing of Boundaries, and What Does This Mean for Theology and Mission?

In the compulsion of participation in the *missio Dei*, and in recognition of the "local" informed by the "global," what Gospel have we to express in this context? Is there receiving as well as giving?

The error from which Tom Allan sought to depart was the assumption under an "accommodation" of culture in the "home mission" of the inter-war years and the post-war rural and island campaigns of D. P. Thomson, that Scotland was essentially Christianised and thus mono-cultural. This led to the fallacy that an irreducible core of cultural and theological norms fell to be parachuted into any given surroundings irrespective of

18. Walls, *The Missionary Movement*, 9.

the context. Thus the process of "becoming a Christian" was to involve the supplanting of the cultural and theological assumptions of the donor, over against the recipient.

The drive of the "New Evangelism" of the post-war decade, from the landmark of the Baillie Commission onwards, accepted that such "top-down" enforcement was no longer viable, because of the distance that had emerged from inner faith to outward life, of the Gospel from the community, of the laity of the church from their fellows outwith, and of the theology of the church from the social and political ills of the nation.

If the "culture" to which aspects of faith were to be contextualized was now to be of the utmost importance in setting the agenda for mission and Christian life, then it had to be properly identified in its particular locality. Allan's solution was "visitation evangelism" and the parish survey. In that process, Scotland of the fifties maintained some definitive and identifiable cultural distinctions. "The parish" could be roughly reduced to a bounded set, given that the fluidity of movement in society was lesser than the present day, and the familial bonds within a strong, local community were more evident. The surveys of "visitation evangelism" could thus identify with some certainty the target cultures of the parish by uncovering only location and expressed nominal Christian denomination: alternative ethnicity, religious faith other than Christianity or overt atheism were the exception, and social class could be more readily defined by the very look of the area.

In the present era, any attempt at a broad one-dimensional Gospel expression across a nation like Scotland, or a limitation to contextualization by stamping a "cultural label" within a small, defined geographical area such as a parish boundary, has become more difficult and artificial.[19]

The gulf between church and world which Allan identified, and by which his model partially foundered, has widened considerably over the past half century in contemporary Scotland; a situation replicated across Western Europe and North America. It would be a mistake to conclude that the culture of the institutional church automatically attunes with any surrounding culture; or perhaps it is better considered that it is simply a "micro-culture" of itself, one of many. The present church institution begins its attempts at cross-cultural mission at a disadvantage: its very "churchiness" of assumed language, norms of behaviour and educated liturgy is a somewhat pale reflection of many of the present micro-cultures of society.

How then can the church in a particular locality hope to translate a Gospel hidebound in "churchiness" to those in the laity's wider sphere of

19. "In no more than two decades Scotland has gone through such profound transformations that, in some important aspects, it is barely recognizable as the same place."—Paterson, Belchhofer, and McCrone, *Living in Scotland*, 149.

influence within "micro-cultures" of society? It might start by the simple recognition of the problem: that the cross-cultural experience is at the heart of the expression of the Gospel, both for the giver and the receiver, and that the Gospel is never enacted in word or deed in a vacuum without the imposition of the culturally acquired inflexions of the giver, in terms of language, norms of behaviour, ecclesiology, and biblical exegesis.

In that recognition within our present existence as part of a multiplicity of "micro-cultures" in a "late modern" Western society such as Scotland, just as Allan, Benedict and Fraser realised, the parallels of the past worldwide missionary experience from the West in a cross-cultural context can be drawn.

The cross-cultural missionary movement from the fifteenth century onwards, so closely related to the European colonial age, had, as David Smith notes, an "unintended consequence," through its effect to "open channels of knowledge and communication which would challenge European assumptions and liberate Christianity from its identification with the culture of the Western world."[20]

For Western culture, "the discovery of peoples and cultures outside Christendom, and the gradual realisation that these alternative world-views posed previously unheard of questions for theology, was deeply challenging for a church so long conditioned by the thought and culture of Europe."[21] For the first time in a millennium, Western Christian theology and ecclesiology had to face the reality of cultural and religious pluralism.

The experience that Vincent Donovan describes in Africa with the Masai in the Seventies in *Christianity Re-Discovered* is, in its essence, the discovery of the necessity for bi-lateral dialogue in the future of Christian mission. It envisages a radical exchange, a mutual growth and development by the birth of a new theological and cultural creation through the meeting of a Gospel conditioned in the donor's culture with the culture of the recipient, through which theological insight on new grounds for both can burst forth and flourish.

Thus for Lamin Sanneh the notion of a "dynamic equivalence" between cultures in the missionary engagement entails that: "Mission as translation makes the bold, fundamental assertion that the recipient culture is the authentic destination of God's salvific promise and as a consequence, has an honored place under the 'kindness of God' . . . By drawing a distinction

---

20. Smith, *Mission after Christendom*, 15.

21. Ibid.

between the message and the surrogate, mission as translation affirms the *missio Dei* as the hidden force for its work."[22]

At the immediate practical level, Donovan recognised that in his Gospel encounter with the Masai his role was one of learner as well as teacher, with both sides leading towards a higher understanding and enlightenment of the contextual relevance of Christ: "Going back and forth among these pagan communities week by week, I soon realized that not one week would go by without some surprising rejoinder or reaction or revelation from these Masai. My education was beginning in earnest."[23]

As Spencer comments, "this was not, then, a one-way street for mission: there was significant traffic in both directions. Donovan was bringing the gospel to share with the Masai but the language and idioms open to him were those of the Masai, and these were forcing him to rethink and recast his understanding of the Gospel."[24]

The mistake of a literal, fundamentalist approach in the application of what might be characterised as a "simple faith" acquired by a reading of the "plain language" of the Bible is a failure to recognise the differing cultural inflexions and relativity of the transmission of Scripture. Firstly, the transmission of Scripture is influenced by the prevalent culture in the initial drafting of the books of the Canon. Secondly, it is influenced by the cultural context in which those engaged in mission have previously acquired faith themselves, and its effect upon their appreciation, and application to their surroundings, of the meaning of Scripture. Thirdly, there are the contrary cultural contexts of the recipient in the process of transmission, meaning that the way in which the recipient comprehends a transmitted Gospel message is crucial. This encounter inevitably involves the clash of the culturally affected Gospel of the missionary, already formed at an oblique angle to the recipient, with the assimilation of that message within a second culture context, whose modes of comprehension will be influenced by often entirely separate norms.

A realization that this is a theological cross-fertilisation process brought about by genuine dialogue would recognise, as David Bosch expresses it, that "inculturation can never be a *fait accompli*" but instead engages as a "tentative and continuing process."[25]

In the relationship of the laity of the institutional church with the "micro-cultures" of society in Scotland and other developed nations of the

---

22. Sanneh, *Translating the Message*, 62.

23. Donovan, *Christianity Re-Discovered*, 41.

24. Spencer, *SCM Study Guide to Christian Mission*, 162.

25. Bosch, *Transforming Mission*, 455.

West, just as in the encounter of missionaries from one region of the world with another in the past and present, heed must be taken of the necessity of dialogue between church theology and the culture in which it is exercised, and the consequent exchange that occurs through that "tentative and continuing" process. In Bosch's words:

> The relationship between the Christian message and culture is a creative and dynamic one, and full of surprises. There is no eternal theology, no *theologia perennis* which may play the referee over "local theologies." In the past, Western theology arrogated to itself the right to be such an arbitrator in respect to Third-World theologies. It implicitly viewed itself as fully indigenized, inculturated, a finished product. We are beginning to realise that this was inappropriate, that Western theologies (plural!)—just as much as all the others—were theologies in the making, theologies in the *process* of being contextualized and indigenized.[26]

If ever a Western theology had the right to assume that it was safely rooted as a contextualised, inculturated whole, cognizant and reflective of the culture within which it stood, then those times have now surely passed. Whereas a strident ecclesiology and Christian dominance within state education once exercised control over the formation of the cultural norms, morals and expectations of a Western nation such as Scotland, and therefore in a sense "church theology" could be said to have reflected those norms almost by creating them, the past half-century has eradicated that power and influence.

Therefore, the laity exercising "local" Western mission must re-learn the contextual relevance of the Gospel, both in the "culturization of Christianity" and the "Christianization of culture." A marked effort of the church as institution through the laity to embark on such a voyage of bi-lateral exchange to the "micro-cultures" which they inhabit is of the essence—an essential requirement if the Christian church in Scotland and beyond is not destined to dwindle further in decline.

Once there is the fundamental realization that acquired theologies remain "*in the process* of being contextualized and indigenized," then it may follow that the old fallacy of mission by "God-Church-World" might finally be dispensed with, some sixty years after Willingen and the formation of *missio Dei* theology. If the idea can be dismissed that acquired faith must be transferred as a unitary object, intact and in its entirety, over the territorial frontier by "going out" to "those beyond" to "convert" not only to Christ

26. Ibid., 456.

but also to our cultural sub-set, then it may further be recognised, as Bosch crucially describes, that "what we are involved in is not just inculturation but "interculturation," or an "exchange of theologies."[27]

In genuine dialogue with local culture, the old language of occupation from a vertical pathway of deliverance of the Gospel to those "unreached" may be replaced "first by bilateral and then by multilateral relationships."[28] It is then that the Christian churches and their laity might "discover, to their amazement, that they are not simply benefactors, and [those in society] not merely beneficiaries, but that all are, at the same time, giving and receiving, that a kind of osmosis is taking place."[29]

If mission then is to be carried out by the laity, in participation within the *missio Dei*, in the "local" situation, recognising cross-cultural translation and seeking "interculturation," what are the core requirements of such "mission"?

Flowing from such observations, there are certain key definitional concepts from recent missiological works which are complementary to the consideration in this chapter of the place of the laity within *missio Dei* theology, and in the process of cross-cultural mission. They serve as the ethos of what "mission" might then entail.

## "Prophetic Dialogue"— A Definition and Foundation of Mission?

What is the "mission" to be focused upon that local laity might exercise to the "micro-cultures" in which they live? Is it simply the oral proclamation of the Gospel for evangelistic purposes? What sort of engagement should occur? Mere contact, or good works, or something deeper?

### Definitions of "Mission" and "Evangelism"

As to "what is mission?," the following broad definition of "mission" is offered by the writer: "the audible or visible expression of the Gospel in word or deed relative to others which seeks to inductively inspire, through the further movement of the Holy Spirit, an interculturation of cultures and theologies, whereby there emerges a relationship of faith in others in their

---

27. Ibid., 456.
28. Ibid.
29. Ibid.

context with God, and/or the contextual advancement of His Kingdom of love, justice and peace."

The definitional distinctions of the World Council of Churches in 2000 are further adopted as guideposts:

a. "Mission" carries a holistic understanding of the proclamation and sharing of the good news of the gospel by word (*kerygma*), deed (*diakonia*), prayer and worship (*leiturgia*), and the everyday witness of the Christian life (*martyria*); teaching as building up and strengthening people in their relationship with God and each other; and healing as wholeness and reconciliation into *koinonia*—communion with God, communion with people, and communion with creation as a whole.

b. "Evangelism," while not excluding the different dimensions of mission, focuses on explicit and intentional voicing of the gospel, including the invitation to personal conversion to a new life in Christ, and to discipleship.[30]

Thus "evangelism" is not fully equated with "mission," but is a subset of the broader means and methods of "mission," each of which bear equal validity and purpose. It is towards such an holistic definition of "mission" that the present study is directed.

### Framework Concepts:
### "Bold Humility" and "Prophetic Dialogue"

As to the mode of mission in present and future, in a classic exposition of the mindset and attitude which must inform the exercise of mission, Bosch wrote:

. . . we regard our involvement in dialogue and mission as an adventure, are prepared to take risks, and are anticipating surprises as the Spirit guides us into fuller understanding. This is not opting for agnosticism, but for humility. It is, however, *a bold humility—or a humble boldness*. We know only in part, but we do know. And we believe that the faith which we profess is both true and just, and should be proclaimed. We do this, however, not as judges or lawyers, but as witnesses; not as soldiers, but

30. *Mission and Evangelism in Unity Today* (2000), para 7, World Council of Churches, *You Are the Light of the World.*

as envoys of peace; not as high-pressure salespersons, but as ambassadors of the Servant Lord.[31]

As noted before, the language of "paradigms" used by Bosch to define changes in mission over time is not without its difficulties, insofar as it might pre-suppose that shifts between "paradigms" in mission are readily identifiable, or that any era is not, of necessity, an amalgam of ideas that may fit both the emerging and preceding paradigm, as has been seen in the work of Tom Allan in his "tale of two paradigms." Therefore, their utility as solid definitional structures through which to form the future of mission, rather than analysing the past, is called into question.

Following from Bosch, rather than utilising a framework of developing and overlapping paradigms to conceive of the potential direction of emerging missiology, in his 1996 essay "The Gospel as Prisoner and Liberator of Culture,"[32] the missiologist Andrew Walls offered instead two "constants" from the history of Christianity which might underlie the foundations of mission, no matter the age, theological or cultural outlook, and thus serve as necessary marks of any present missiological construct.

The primary constant is one of Christology in that "the person of Jesus called the Christ has ultimate significance,"[33] a focus with which Allan would have readily agreed. The secondary constant relates to ecclesiology, in the sense, as Bevans and Schroeder later described it, that Christians "will always see themselves as a community that is nourished and equipped for its work in the world by both word and sacrament," thus maintaining an emphasis on "the constant use of the Bible; the sacramental significance of Eucharist and baptism; and a consciousness of continuity with Israel."[34]

In their formative work on a theology of mission from 2004 entitled *Constants in Context: A Theology of Mission for Today*, comparable in its breadth and depth to Bosch's *Transforming Mission*, the American Roman Catholic missiologists Stephen B. Bevans and Roger P. Schroeder supplemented Walls's two constants of Christology and ecclesiology with four more of their own. They argued that the approach taken to the six constants in answering the questions raised by them has historically determined, and will determine, the expression of mission in all epochs and contexts:

---

31. Ibid., 489.
32. Walls, *The Missionary Movement*, 3–15.
33. Ibid., 6.
34. Bevans and Schroeder, *Constants in Context*, 33.

1. Eschatology, and the issue of to what extent the church is called upon to participate in the attempted fulfilment of the Kingdom of God on earth;

2. Salvation, and the focus of the church's preaching either upon inner spiritual purity, or transformation by wholeness and holistic healing;

3. Anthropology, with the determination of Christianity of the human condition and its value or otherwise; and

4. Culture, as a vehicle or obstruction for the communication of the Gospel.[35]

The basis of Bevans and Schroeder's work is thus formed around the six "constants."[36]

Bevans and Schroeder proceeded in the main body of *Constants in Context* to examine how the questions raised by the six constants have been answered in the history of theology and mission in each period. They sought to do so under each of three broad categorisations of "types of theology" on a spectrum from "orthodox/conservative," to "liberal" to "radical/liberation theology," whereby "every attitude in mission can be seen as a logical consequence of a distinct perspective that is characteristic of one of the three."[37]

Bevans and Schroeder's further novel contribution in the concluding section of *Constants in Context* was to begin to develop a concept of "prophetic dialogue" as an over-arching determinative, or "paradigm," with the potential to underpin and help define all elements in the future of mission where the "types of theology" relate to the "constants," describing: "a synthesis that would serve well as an underlying theology of mission for these first years of the twenty-first century and the third millennium. We propose to call this synthesis *prophetic dialogue*."[38]

As they later indicated, taking the "types of theology" and the "constants," Bevans and Schroeder's bold conception in the final chapter was to establish "prophetic dialogue" in relation to what they viewed as the six essential elements of the practice of mission (as opposed to Bosch's thirteen "elements of an emerging ecumenical paradigm") that their work had identified. Thus, "prophetic dialogue" could be seen as an: "*overarching umbrella* for an understanding of the various elements in the practice of mission—*witness and proclamation; liturgy, prayer and contemplation; justice, peace and the integrity of creation; interreligious dialogue; inculturation;*

35. Ibid., 34.
36. See ibid., 72.
37. Ibid., 35.
38. Ibid., 348.

*and reconciliation.* Each of these components can be understood from a 'dialogical' perspective and each can also be understood from a perspective of "prophecy."[39]

What is mission as "dialogue"? It is to reflect the perfect Triune nature of God, such that the church "not only gives itself in service to the world," but also "learns from its involvement." As to the manner of the "dialogue" with the world, "just as the Triune God's missionary presence in creation is never about imposition . . . , mission can no longer proceed in ways that neglect the freedom and dignity of human beings. Nor can a church that is rooted in a God that saves through self-emptying think of itself as culturally superior to the peoples among whom it works."[40]

As Kritzinger gracefully expresses it in a later article considering "prophetic dialogue" as a concept, the goal is a "transformative encounter" on both sides, as "when the praxis of a community starts resonating with the music of the Gospel, it gets improvised or remixed in surprising ways."[41]

What is the "prophetic" element? Bevans and Schroeder expanded in detail on the overarching theme in *Prophetic Dialogue: Reflections on Christian Mission Today* in 2011.

In that work, they developed the concept of speaking or acting dialogically in "mission as prophecy," in the following senses of the word "prophecy":

a. "speaking forth without words: witness"—meaning that "as Christians live a life of vital community, of community service, of ecological integrity, of shared prayer that is beautiful and inspiring to visitors, they speak forth without words what the gospel is and what human life might be if the gospel is lived authentically."[42]

b. "speaking forth with words: proclamation"—as "they proclaim the message of the Reign of God . . . by telling the world about Jesus."[43]

c. "speaking against without words: being a contrast community"—being "profoundly countercultural," the church "offers a different vision of the world than what is the natural drift of society . . . leading a simple life, standing for peace and justice, learning to forgive people who have offended us . . . learning to serve and not be served . . . these are

---

39. Bevans and Schroeder, *Prophetic Dialogue*, 2.

40. Ibid., 348.

41. Kritzinger, "Mission in Prophetic Dialogue," 39.

42. Bevans and Schroeder, *Prophetic Dialogue*, 44.

43. Ibid., 44–45.

all prophetic actions in a world that envisions success as being self-centred and having power over others."[44]

d. "speaking against in words: speaking truth to power"—to speak out against any form of injustice.

"Prophetic dialogue" is indelibly linked for Bevans and Schroeder to what they term "the spirituality of inculturation," by which we exercise "mission in reverse" in "reverence for the other, learning from our hosts, being vulnerable."[45] It is "where agents of inculturation need to live on the boundary . . . between Christianity and other religions, between Christianity and local culture, between orthodoxy and superstition, between authentic and inauthentic syncretism."[46]

In conclusion, Bevans and Schroeder offer the following summary of "prophetic dialogue":

> Mission is not constituted by one or the other, but by both working together. There may be some situations in which *dialogue* may be the only way that Christians can continue to witness to the truth of their faith. Certainly, Christians must always respect the cultures, religions and contexts in which they live, and the peoples among whom they work. The basic attitude must be one of dialogue. On the other hand, there may be situations–when Christians are asked about their faith, as they live in a non-Christian or secular society, or when they find themselves in situations of grave injustice—when a clear, *prophetic* proclamation of and witness to the gospel is necessary. Like mission itself, prophetic dialogue is multifaceted. It includes respect, being open, on the one hand, and on the other the courage to live out and speak the truth—albeit gently (1 Pet. 3:15)—in prophecy.[47]

To place "prophetic dialogue" as a mode of mission in the context of all missional considerations, Kritzinger summaries the various necessary impulses in considering mission as follows:

> Mission is . . . *missio Dei* (motivation, direction)

> Mission as . . . dimensions of mission (broadness, inclusivity)

> Mission through . . . pastoral circle, praxis matrix (contextual dynamics)

44. Ibid., 46.
45. Ibid., 88–89.
46. Ibid., 97.
47. Ibid., 154–55.

Mission *with* . . . transformative encounters (mutuality, complexity)

Mission *in* . . . prophetic dialogue, bold humility (ethos, spirituality)[48]

The final section of the book will seek to draw together the framework of Bosch, Walls and Bevans and Schroeder, and apply it to the main body of this work. In short summary of the above, any means of "mission *in* . . ." must recognise shifting social circumstances for which the notion of "paradigms" may provide a starting point if not an ending; the six "constants" of Walls, Bevans and Schroeder must always be present no matter which of the three types of theology may refer to them; the six essential elements of mission must be recognised, and throughout mission must be applied to "dialogical" relationships and "prophecy" in the sense of "speaking forth" and "speaking against."

It is in this fertile ground that we shall now move towards conclusions on the work of Tom Allan and his fellow missiologists who form the centrepiece of the present book, who exercised, exemplify and illuminate the concepts of which Bevans and Schroeder now write, and who offer concrete references of modes of success and failure in doing so.

## Derivations and Principles

The final conclusions thus bring together all of the strands considered to garner principles that might assist in that search for direction in mission, offered for a Western nation such as Scotland, and for broader application where the context permits. Their pertinence to the present day and a framework for applying those models has been set out in selective, foundational aspects of present global missiology and sociology. The principles to follow are therefore filtered through those global considerations, such that they might resonate as potential building blocks appropriate to present late modern mission in the West, raising fundamental issues, but also, of necessity, acting as signposts only for reflection and development in the "local" context. They are offered as a perception of "the confluence of streams," from the tributaries both of the vibrant Scottish missiology of the immediate post-war period, and of the signs, symbols and ideas of the present-day context.

The following principles are, therefore, collated by the writer as being derived directly from the missiology and mission practice of Tom Allan

48. Kritzinger, "Mission in Prophetic Dialogue," 36.

from chapters 2 to 4, in comparison and conjunction with the four models of mission within chapter 5, being the Iona Community, East Harlem Protestant Parish, the Gorbals Group Ministry, and Robert Mackie, Ian Fraser and Scottish Churches House, and in the light of the missiology set out in the present chapter. In order to avoid constant repetition, specific reference to the sources in the preceding chapters has not been made in relation to each principle: given that each principle finds common ground in the models, or, if not, the source of the principle ought to be apparent from a reading of the preceding chapters.

Therefore, in my view, the ground that has been travelled in this book leads to the following principles for future mission.

## The Underlying Missiology

Mission is set in the context of the *missio Dei*, of the movement of "God-World-Church."

Mission is christological, in that throughout its history it has been focused in the expression in word and deed of the Gospel of Jesus Christ, and in the role of his meaning and teaching in an appreciation of the world that has been and is to come.

Mission is "trinitarian," in the sense of participation in the relationship of the Triune God in engagement in the formation of community in his image, and in harmonious inter-relationship.

"Mission" is "holistic" and involves any action which furthers the tripartite relationship in communion with God, people and creation. "Mission" may include any or all of the following: *kerygma, diakonia, leiturgia, martyria,* teaching, healing, and reconciliation into *koinonia.*

If "mission" is holistic, "evangelism" is specific. It is a sub-set of all of the above elements of "mission," focused on oral proclamation as *kerygma,* involving a call to conversion and discipleship.

Mission is central to all Christian expression and to the very existence of the church. Mission in exercise of the *missio Dei* must recognise that there is church because there is mission; it is of the DNA of the church; that mission *is* the agenda, the fundamental reality of the Christian life.

Mission is a core value of the church, but is only expressed in the power of the Triune God, not simply by the ingenuity or dynamism of our individual or collective efforts. The church is sent under the *missio Dei* for the mission within the world of the Son and Spirit through the Father. The concept of the *missio Dei* admitting through its intrinsic looseness extremes of church-centrism or "humanization," the secure judgment is that the church and its members are the only self-conscious agents of the Kingdom, without their ecclesial community being necessarily equated with it.

The church and laity must therefore seek (a) to adapt the structures of the church; (b) to listen to the world; (c) to realise that the whole world is the "mission field"; and (d) be renewed themselves and in community as a living sign of the Kingdom. They live and share, engage and act and serve contextually in seeking to emulate the incarnation of Christ. The laity move in the world not as conquerors but in solidarity; not in search of territorial acquisition, but in faith, offering love and seeking reconciliation.

Why ought particular attention be paid to the local and the lay in the exercise of the *missio Dei* in present circumstances?

Christianity became an inherent constituent in the myths and stories of the Western civilisation narrative. There was a strong marriage bond between Christianity and rational modernity. Religion in the present "scientific worldview" operates within the private realm where the "heretical imperative" has free reign, in which realm only it is acceptable to raise the question "why?" By contrast, the permissible goal within the public realm is a rational search for a consensus on unadulterated "fact," exclusively considering issues of "what?" and "how?"

In the late modern/postmodern era, there has been a secular backlash against the truth meta-narratives of religion, in a call for emancipation and in the exercise of a systematic functionalism. Christian mission lies at the friction point where it seeks to encroach within the public sphere at a level beyond the compartmentalised or the advisory, that might by the words and actions of ordinary people offer critique or condemnation upon presupposed public "fact." There is once more a sense of "bridging the gap" cross-culturally, not only between church and world, but between belief system and public norm, to challenge and confront untruths and injustices.

The impossibility of imposing globally one ethic or message now endangers the ecumenical hope of structural unity and worldwide evangelisation. In that light, the type of religion which might emerge or persist is that which cannot be tied to the modernist enterprise—communities of faith which are plural, disparate, individual and, ultimately, "local." However, "local" is not defined simply within a geographical sub-set, as imposing a mono-cultural stamp is now fraught with imprecision, if it were ever valid. Instead, "local" relates beyond a defined geographical boundary, into boundaries of personal identity.

Therefore, the notion of "parish" in the present context must be less of a defining entity for the exclusivity of areas of control, and more simply a bureaucratic convenience to divide wider resources. The "re-churching" of a definable, geographical parish is an unrealistic aspiration, and therefore the church must be prepared to seek the proliferation of small Christian groups around its location.

In the light of Christianity's universal claim, and in the necessity of communication and mutual support between such Christian communities, one route may be to recognize the importance of "glocalization"—the global in conversation with the local; the "indigenizing principle" in conversation with the "pilgrim principle" as a "universalizing factor."

That may entail a "creation of networks" which might "critically test" the faith of each other—thus one heaven and earth for a diverse and pluriform humanity.

The laity, as individuals or collectively, are uniquely placed to exercise mission as "pilgrims" in such circumstances, in their everyday contact with "the local," whether it be geographically within a parish boundary, or in their interactions with the "micro-cultures" of identity which form their own lives. They are in a unique position to relate such "local" manifestations to the universalising global claims of Christianity.

"Local," lay, ecumenical, contextual theology, ecclesiology and mission *praxis*, in dialogical connection with the global, is a future vision which might involve an institutional church.

## The Place of the Laity

The church must move away from a reversion to "revivalism"—"call to church" mission which continues to rely only on the performance of the ordinances of religion within a church building.

The answer to inspire the laity towards formation for mission is not mass evangelism either—"Crusades" are likely to undermine rather than encourage a lay-based model, lead to division and make little sustainable difference in adherence, the vitality of congregations or Christian "conversions."

The laity cannot remain "frozen in the ecclesiastical system." The future of mission lies with the laity in the slow, patient, organic growth of Christian communities, both within the pre-existing structure of the church and without. Only the laity can engage continuously at every level with the world: everyone is thus a minister, a "worker-priest" and an evangelist.

The "donor" of the Gospel must have credibility and relevance: in a cross-cultural encounter, the Gospel is best represented by the laity of the existing church, acting in their everyday lives at home, work and leisure; or by clergy acting almost as "worker-priests" within the recipient culture.

Therefore, "the place of the lay person is decisive," albeit "resourcing" and the abrogation of control is required from the minister in the parish context. Common to all models considered, the fundamentals are that the laity as the whole people of God hold the key; and that in order for lay mission from the institution to have any prospect, the Gospel and church must be contextualized; rooted, present and reflected in the everyday. There should be an interactive process of the gearing of laity and the regeneration of the church, such that both might move towards a more dynamic *koinonia*.

This recognizes the sometimes parlous state of the present church in its clergy/laity divide and hierarchical structures of decision-making, its separation and distance from the world, reflective of a super-imposed culture; *semper reformanda*, always requiring to be reformed. The church must change internally and in mission—'structural fundamentalism" has no future. A local fellowship might, however, develop to radiate and illuminate the Gospel, both in its internal practices and in the implementation of mission *praxis*.

The laity should be empowered for mission: whether it be in a quasi-military sense by developing an élite squad amongst the laity, the "congregational group," to begin mission in the parish that would in turn exhibit the true *koinonia* which the church and parish could emulate; or in "laity formation," by a "bible resourcing" of the laity to integrate the everyday with the word of God, such that the issues and problems of the world become the problems of the Christian community and of God.

To do so, the place of the laity within the structural model of the church as institution needs to be re-considered, in particular the eldership as formalizing and elevating lay involvement without responsibility for mission, and lay training being mostly focused on fulfilling the tasks of clergy within the church and not missional ones. Decisions on the direction of such "laity formation" need to be taken by the laity and not the clergy.

## The Exercise of Mission

If the laity thus have a crucial role in "local" mission in conversation with the global, how should they recognise their context, in terms of the crossing of cultural boundaries? What Gospel have they to give? Are they receiving as well as giving?

Every encounter is "cross-cultural," every Gospel reading and application reflects the cultural inflexions of the donor, as does every Gospel reception. Mission must recognise the differing cultural backgrounds of both the Gospel, the donor and the recipient, and take heed of their interaction. Thus, "inculturation" of the Gospel is a "tentative and continuing process."

Mission is exercised as much as the learner as the teacher, forcing us to rethink our own understanding of the Gospel. True "dialogue" across cultures entails a two-way process of mutual inter-relationship and growth towards a new theological and cultural creation; an "interculturation."

In that interaction, under what paradigm of mission should the laity act?

Mission should be carried out "in bold humility" in our present late modern era, at a time of what is tentatively described as part of a "paradigm shift" towards an "emerging paradigm," as yet unestablished.

There are six "constants" recognised to have been present in Christian mission in the past two millennia that must persist—Christology, ecclesiology, eschatology, salvation, anthropology and culture.

There are, furthermore, six essential elements of mission now to which any concepts must relate—witness and proclamation; liturgy, prayer and contemplation; justice, peace and the integrity of creation; interreligious dialogue; inculturation; and reconciliation.[49]

The synthesis may lie in the concept of "prophetic dialogue," which provides "an underlying theology of mission for these first years of the twenty-first century."

The "basic attitude" of mission is "dialogue" in a mutual exchange, with no assumption of power or cultural superiority.

"Prophecy" entails "courage to live out and speak the truth, albeit gently." "Dialogue" can be "prophetic" in four senses—(a) "speaking forth without words: witness"; (b) 'speaking forth with words: proclamation"; (c) "speaking against without words: being a contrast community"; and (d) "speaking against in words: speaking truth to power."

At its core, mission in "prophetic dialogue" involves "the spirituality of inculturation," in "reverence for the other" as we continue to "live on the boundary."

In the exercise of "prophetic dialogue" in mission, a ministry of marked presence is vital, by living there or being integral within a "local" community.

The starting point is always "contact": in the past era by visitation evangelism, now by identifying the intersections of the church community and the broader community in the parish.

---

49. For "mission as reconciliation" as the foundation for future mission, see the extensive work on the subject by Robert Schreiter, e.g., Schreiter and Jørgensen, eds., *Mission as Ministry of Reconciliation.*

As mission is contextual, its content should draw from religious and theological tradition and personal influence to bear the mark of authenticity, but be reflective as a sign of the times.

The movement of the laity in mission is towards "identification" or "critical solidarity" with the struggles around them. It is to bring Christianity to the people, and not the people to the church. It is the process whereby we "share in God rather than attempting to observe God."

The missiology to be expressed must recognise that religion is not simply an inner, private matter of the soul, but must be embodied. It is to serve *everyone* in the community in social and political action, regardless of race, class or religion. The message must be holistic in its terms, encompassing the whole of life in the detail of the everyday and the mundane, not in "grandstand" preaching for conversion, but addressing the life and needs of the immediate context.

Mission involves both identification with all strands of humanity and a relationship with God. Thus, centrally, mission involves *both* the "participation in the struggles for justice" and "sharing the knowledge of the kingdom." A one-dimensional "single-issue" approach to mission, concentrating solely on a particular facet, will not suffice. Local mission is resolutely "both/and," through "every God-given method," looking towards both personal conversion and social commitment.

Nonetheless, it must be ensured that the foundation of the Gospel is articulated in undertaking mission, whilst expressing a concurrent social witness. The church thus engages with the Gospel in the whole of life: it seeks the integration of the economic and social to the personal, spiritual experience. Mission thus seeks expression in church buildings, in the street, in shop-fronts and in the home. It wears its Christianity "on its sleeve."

"Dialogue" entails mission by a humble and penitent church, conscious of where it has come from and who it serves. Mission must be "in bold humility," that the world is scarred by the immediate past failures of the church to offer appropriate contextual engagement or to recognise surrounding social realities, and therefore will have to be slowly convinced that its present perception of the church as institution is misplaced, and that the church can indeed activate the goals outlined in a relevant and respectful manner.

Therefore, the approach of "morality" is rejected. The character required is of unconditional acceptance of others, and of self-giving. Liturgy and worship is to be relevant to the language and issues of the world in the immediate locale.

Common difficulties begin at successfully addressing the heart of the problem identified, which is bridging the cultural and theological gap between the church and the world. "Cultural intrusion" in mission creates an ongoing tension, which necessitates the urgent formation, growth and continuing activity of a "local" group who will assume control and direction within their "local" community, otherwise proto-church and mission might peter out. Efforts at forming Christian community may be hampered by social circumstances, such as sectarianism.

Within those exercising mission, there is further a recurrent problem in reconciling division within a group in any expression of mission, between those who see its purpose simply as either personal evangelism or as social action, and not "both/and." Unless those visions can be reconciled with some clarity, any larger-scale endeavor is significantly hampered.

Likewise, there is a need to clarify some form of relationship in mission undertaken by a small, lay group with the mother institution, and as part of that clarification to consider whether the group might be permitted to become *esse* or must remain *bene esse* of the church. The solution may lie in the institutional church sponsoring and supporting such movements, but being willing to allow experimentation to develop, grow independently and potentially fail, learning in its own practice from such triumphs and struggles, and not seeking ownership of either.

To overcome institutional reaction and apathy may be central to effectiveness. The engaged laity should be ready for resistance by those other lay members determined to maintain the sanctification of the established norms, being exercised against, firstly, themselves, secondly, against those "incomers" who are unaware or unwilling to accept those norms, and, thirdly, against any attempt to disturb those norms in the re-alignment of the focus of the church as community.

Participative ecumenism across denominational divides is a given for the exercise of "prophetic dialogue." Mission is ecumenical in outlook and encourages contact and action in conjunction with pre-existing denominations, to embrace ecumenical respect and co-operation.

All mission must "walk the tightrope," avoiding theological extremes that would draw the community into a "holy huddle," never turning away from the world in its midst. Allegiance in mission to cliques and closed fraternities should be avoided. Like-minded contemporaries within the church, whether at ministerial or lay level, must be willing to engage fully together by setting aside differences in theological nuance.

It must be recognised that this may all have to be achieved in a sometimes uncomfortable marriage between the "old" and the "new."

At a personal level, there is the difficulty of knowing what to say or do, given a learned, cultural vocabulary of Christianity. There is a need to become more theologically articulate, in order to contextualize models of mission to the local situation, along with dedication and commitment.

## The Goal of Mission

Mission is a voyage of empathy and self-giving, towards a bi-lateral exchange seeking "interculturation," an intermingling of theologies to create "a kind of osmosis"; a new hybrid of theologies and cultures.

Gospel and culture are thus interactive, and the goal of mission is the creation of a symbiotic union which becomes expressed in local theologies of the people and an indigenous "church." The key questions are therefore: how does the Gospel speak to these people, in this place, in this age, within this culture?

The exercise of mission, transcending all "paradigms" and "constants," is an interaction of one human with another, whether that be in a form of oral proclamation or simply by the unexpected gift and exercise of God's love. In other words, a mutual exchange is established with a learning and growing process occurring between the two participants, carried out in respect and trust avoiding the danger of proselytism, whereby the local and contextual, the common material that is apparent in humanity and circumstance, is infused with insight from the Gospel.

Thus establishing "dialogue" is central to all models—seeking to "bridge the gap," to reach out by setting aside the assumptions of power and knowledge which might come with clericalization and institution, looking to learn in the encounter as well as teach, to see where God is already active in the world and to take part.

Mission will seek "rayonnement," by which the Gospel will propagate and proliferate through the lives and witness of ordinary people, seeking a constant re-iteration of mission of engagement and service.

The goal is for small, local, organic growth of Christian communities, of "living cells," or at least the breaking down of the present institution into smaller units which can be near-autonomous. A key purpose of mission is thus "to foster the multiplication of local congregations," gatherings of true *koinonia* expressing faith, word and sacrament, but not necessarily by the building up of existing congregations, nor by the identical replication of structures.

The divergent culture of "church" and "world" must be addressed, in a movement away from the sanctification of an enclosed, traditional church community and the perception of set, unerring values. Any emerging Christian communities must be created out of the culture and remain of the culture. Their form and leadership must become more fully indigenous, led and developed by the people of that culture, not only to ensure "contextualization" and the longer-term continuance of the community, but also to avoid norms of power and "cultural intrusion" and to promote the stripping away of Christianity from the acquired culture of the donor. Its theology may be freshly formed by a meeting of its expression by the donor, and the reaction in cultural context of the recipient. The desired outcome is to form new "interculturated" Christian expressions of the nature of the gathering and inter-relationship of Christians.

The donor should thus seek to withdraw as much as possible once lay participation has begun: "light the touch paper and retire." The presence of the donor, and any position of power in their retention and dissemination of knowledge, ought to persist only in the period of the introduction of the Gospel and the provision of theological tools for local hermeneutics. Thus the indigenous form of "inculturated" Christianity might be left to develop within the previous receiving culture; avoiding dependence on the cultural reading of Christianity as an institution, the control of development, or the imposition by that institution of a received set of ecclesiological, missional, doctrinal, liturgical or governmental norms.

"Church" in whatever form must seek to be an all-inclusive entity, drawing from a breadth of social groupings, or at least relate to a broader universality. The "local" is paramount, but must connect with and be informed by the "global."

A re-vitalized institutional church may still hold a role as a hub for such development, but not of necessity. It should engage with and learn from the missiological strands of "emerging church"—the institution may be fed from outwith. The Student Christian Movement, "basic ecclesial communities" and "emerging church" have formed "church before the church." They set the tone for the institution in a form of the empowerment which would assist in breaking the lay/clergy divide, allowing a voice, and placing the laity at the forefront of the community, whilst understanding contextuality, embracing difference and finding common ground for broader development. They, in turn, provide models for the nature of community which the church laity might seek in mission.

## Conclusion

With those principles, is there a single model which has been encountered that could be held up as having best fulfilled the basic criteria? Reverting the focus at the conclusion to Tom Allan, attention returns to his ministry at St

George's Tron from 1955 to 1964. The model Allan which implemented at that time was of the laity as the whole people of God, acting in unity in the name of Christ, being present and available to all, thus:

- Being overt in their compassion;

- Being active in the community;

- Exercising social concern and a radical, outspoken social commitment;

- Giving priority to the poor and lowly;

- Providing them concurrently with physical refuge and spiritual hope;

- Expressing the Gospel, both in word and deed; and

- Doing so in a manner which relates only to their specific context, at that time in that place, but in recognition of points of wider conjunction.

Like Allan's model, mission in those terms now would also be rooted in its own tradition, local context and be characterized not only by personal influences, but also a deep personal grasp of theology, and by a renewed vigor and confidence. It would be all-encompassing in its scope, content and places of engagement, as Allan set out: "The mission of the church is concerned not only with the man, but with the world in which the man lives, and is committed to bringing the light of God to bear upon the whole of life. This can only be accomplished in a continuing engagement with the world at every level-within which engagement every 'method' of evangelism, explored and yet to be explored, has a part to play."[50]

Above all, it would begin to express the utmost assurance in the expectation, as did Allan, that the process of exercising mission might be startlingly transformational for ordinary people, especially the unloved and despairing, as Gospel, church and world come together in a dynamic interaction.

Who could doubt that the *missio Dei* would then be encountered to dramatic effect? As Tom Allan wrote, "as if Christ who raised Lazarus from the dead, can't raise an alcoholic from the gutters of Buchanan Street."[51]

50. Allan, *Agent of Mission*, 3.

51. AA6.5.7, *EC*, c.1959, Article 1.

# Bibliography

Aisthorpe, Steve. *The Invisible Church: Learning from the Experiences of Churchless Christians*. Edinburgh: Saint Andrew, 2016.

Alicea, Benjamin. "Christian Urban Colonizers: A History of the East Harlem Protestant Parish in New York City, 1948–1968." PhD diss., Union Theological Seminary, 1988.

The Papers of Tom Allan (19 boxes), New College Library, University of Edinburgh, Archive AA6.

Allan, Tom. *The National Conference of United Churchmen: The Company of the Committed*. Elgin House, Canadian Keswick, June 1963. Three-LP set of program highlights, produced by Berkley Studio and distributed by The United Church of Canada, Toronto, Ontario.

———. *The Agent of Mission: The Lay Group in Evangelism; Its Significance and Task*. Glasgow: "Tell Scotland" Pamphlet, 1954.

———. "The All-Scotland Crusade: Preparation and Expectation." *Life and Work*, March 1955, 57–58.

———. *The Congregational Group in Action*. Glasgow: "Tell Scotland" Pamphlet, 1955.

———, ed. *Crusade in Scotland: Billy Graham*. London: Pickering & Inglis, 1955.

———. *1808–1958: One Hundred and Fifty Years of Worship and Witness*. Glasgow: St George's Tron, 1958.

———. "Evangelism in Scotland." *Christianity Today* 1.7 (1957) 14–16.

———. "Evanston and Tell Scotland: The Mission to Those Outside." *Life and Work*, August 1954, 195–96.

———. *The Face of My Parish*. London: SCM, 1954.

———. *An Open Letter to a Layman*. Glasgow: "Tell Scotland" Pamphlet, 1954.

———. "The Place of the Layman." *Christianity Today* 2.1 (1957) 8–10.

———. *The Secret of Life: Six Broadcast Talks*. Glasgow: Henry Munro, 1950.

———. *The "Tell Scotland" Movement and Billy Graham*. Glasgow: "Tell Scotland" Pamphlet, 1954.

———. *To Be a Christian*. Glasgow: United Christian Witness, 1957.

———. "Truth that Sings." *Scottish Journal of Theology* 3 (1950) 439–42.

———. *Why I Believe*. Crieff: St Ninian's, 1963.

Allan, Tom, and Henry B. Meikle. *"Tell Scotland" Movement*. Recording of Interview at Aberdeen, 31 October 1954. William Smith Morton Library, Union—PSCE, Richmond, Virginia.

Amaladoss, Michael. "The Trinity in Mission." In *"Mission Is a Must": Intercultural Theology and the Mission of the Church*, edited by Frans Wijsen and Peter Nissen, 99–106. Amsterdam: Rodopi, 2002.

Arnal, Oscar L. *Priests in Working-Class Blue: The History of the Worker Priests (1943–1954)*. Mahwah, N.J: Paulist, 1986.

Baillie, Donald. "The Place of the Iona Community." *The Coracle* 19 (January 1951) 8–11.

Bardgett, Frank. "D. P. Thomson and the Orkney Expedition—a 'Tell Scotland' Case Study." *Records of the Scottish Church History Society* 40 (2010) 185–228.

———. "Missions and Missionaries: Home." In *Scottish Life and Society: A Compendium of Scottish Ethnology*, vol. 12, *Religion*, edited by Colin MacLean and Kenneth Veitch, 479–517. Edinburgh: Donald, 2006.

———. *Scotland's Evangelist: D. P. Thomson; A New Biography*. Edinburgh: Handsel, 2010.

———. "The 'Tell Scotland' Movement: Failure and Success." *Records of the Scottish Church History Society* 38 (2008) 105–54.

BBC Television. *Meeting Point in a City Centre*. Broadcast on 26 March 1961 (40 mins. duration). DVD held at AA6.7.1, The Papers of Tom Allan, New College Library, University of Edinburgh.

Bebbington, David W. *Evangelicalism in Modern Britain: A History from the 1730s to the 1980s*. London: Unwin Hyman, 1989.

Benedict, Don. *Born Again Radical*. New York: Pilgrim, 1982.

Bevans, Stephen B., ed. *A Century of Catholic Mission: Roman Catholic Missiology 1910 to the Present*. Oxford: Regnum, 2013.

———. "Mission in Britain Today: Some Modest Reflections and Proposals." *Holiness: The Journal of Wesley House Cambridge* 1 (2015) 161–76. http://www.wesley.cam. ac.uk/wp-content/uploads/2015/10/02-bevans.pdf.

———. *Models of Contextual Theology*. Maryknoll, NY: Orbis, 1992; revised and expanded, 2002.

———. "What Has Contextual Theology to Offer the Church of the Twenty-First Century?" In *Contextual Theology for the Twenty-First Century*, edited by Stephen B. Bevans and Katalina Tahaafe-Williams, 3–17. Eugene, OR: Pickwick Publications, 2011.

Bevans, Stephen B., and Roger P. Schroeder. *Constants in Context: A Theology of Mission for Today*. American Society of Missiology Series 30. Maryknoll, NY: Orbis, 2004.

———. *Prophetic Dialogue: Reflections on Christian Mission Today*. Maryknoll, NY: Orbis, 2011.

Bisset, Peter. *The Kirk and Her Scotland*. Edinburgh: Handsel, 1986.

———. "Kirk and Society in Modern Scotland." In *Religion, State and Society in Modern Britain*, edited by Paul Badham, 51–65. Texts and Studies in Religion 43. Lewiston, NY: Mellen, 1989.

———. "Training for Evangelism: National Resources for Local Mission." In *Local Church Evangelism: Patterns and Approaches*, edited by David F. Wright and Alastair H. Gray, 113–21. Edinburgh: Saint Andrew, 1987.

———. "William Franklin Graham." In *Dictionary of Scottish Church History & Theology*, edited by N. M. S. Cameron, 376. Edinburgh: T. & T. Clark, 1993.

Blackie, Nansie. *In Love and Laughter: A Portrait of Robert Mackie*. Edinburgh: Saint Andrew, 1995.

———. "The Legacy of Robert Mackie." *International Bulletin of Missionary Research*, January 1997, 20–23.

————, ed. *A Time for Trumpets: Scottish Church Movers and Shakers of the Twentieth Century*. Edinburgh: Saint Andrew, 2005.

Blakey, Ronald S., ed. *The Church of Scotland Yearbook 2007/8*. Edinburgh: Saint Andrew, 2007.

Blythe, Stuart. "Open-Air Preaching: Performing Beyond the Walls." In *Worship and Liturgy in Context: Studies and Case Studies in Theology and Practice*, edited by Duncan B. Forrester and Doug Gay, 246-58. London: SCM, 2009.

Boff, Leonard. *Ecclesiogenesis: The Base Communities Reinvent the Church*. Translated by Robert R. Barr. Maryknoll, NY: Orbis, 1986.

Bonhoeffer, Dietrich. *The Cost of Discipleship*. Translated by R. H. Fuller. London: SCM, 1948.

————. *Letters and Papers from Prison*. Edited by Eberhard Bethge. London: Fontana, 1959.

Borgmann, Florence. "The Church in East Harlem." *The Messenger*, October 6, 1953, 8-10.

Bosch, David. *Transforming Mission: Paradigm Shifts in Theology of Mission*. American Society of Missiology Series 16. Maryknoll, NY: Orbis, 1991.

Boyd, Robin. *The Witness of the Student Christian Movement: 'Church Ahead of the Church'*. London: SPCK, 2007.

British Council of Churches. *Evanston Essentials*. London: British Council of Churches, 1954.

Brown, Callum G. *The Death of Christian Britain: Understanding Secularisation, 1800–2000*. London: Routledge, 2001.

————. "'Each Take Off Their Several Way'? Protestant Churches and Working Classes in Scotland." In *Sermons and Battle Hymns: Protestant Popular Culture in Modern Scotland*, edited by Graham Walker and Tom Gallagher, 69–85. Edinburgh: Edinburgh University Press, 1990.

————. *Religion and Society in Scotland since 1707*. Edinburgh: Edinburgh University Press, 1997.

————. *Religion and Society in Twentieth-Century Britain*. Harlow, UK: Pearson Longman, 2006.

Brown, Stewart J. "The Campaign for the Christian Commonwealth in Scotland, 1919-39." In *Crown and Mitre: Religion and Society in Northern Europe since the Reformation*, edited by W. M. Jacob and Nigel Yates, 203–21. Woodbridge, UK: Boydell, 1993.

————. "From Godly Commonwealth to Iona Community: Christian Visions of Scotland 1929-49." In *Scotland to Slovenia: European Identities and Transcultural Communication*, edited by H. W. Drescher and S. Hagemann, 71–88. Frankfurt am Main: P. Lang, 1996.

————. "Presbyterians and Catholics in Twentieth-Century Scotland." In *Scottish Christianity in the Modern World*, edited by Stewart J. Brown and George Newlands, 255–81. Edinburgh: T. & T. Clark, 2000.

————. "The Social Ideal of the Church of Scotland during the 1930s." In *God's Will in a Time of Crisis: A Colloquium Celebrating the 50th Anniversary of The Baillie Commission*, edited by Andrew R. Morton, 14–31. Edinburgh: CTPI, 1994.

————. "The Social Vision of Scottish Presbyterianism and the Union of 1929." *Records of the Scottish Church History Society* 24 (1990) 77–96.

Bryant, Chris. *Possible Dreams: A Personal History of British Christian Socialists*. London: Hodder & Stoughton, 1996.

Burleigh, J. H. S. *A Church History of Scotland*. Oxford: Oxford University Press, 1960.

Burnham, George. *Billy Graham: A Mission Accomplished*. Edinburgh: Marshall, Morgan & Scott, 1955.

Cameron, Lewis L. L. *Opportunity My Ally*. London: James Clarke, 1965.

Cattanach, W. D. "The House Church." *The British Weekly*, 26 July 1956, 5.

Cheyne, A. C. *The Transforming of the Kirk: Victorian Scotland's Religious Revolution*. Edinburgh: Saint Andrew, 1983.

Christian Action. *The Gorbals 1965*. London: Christian Action, 1965.

Christman, William G. "Being There." *Theology in Scotland* 2 (1995) 45–60.

Church of England. *Mission-Shaped Church: Church Planting and Fresh Expressions of Church in a Changing Context*. London: Church House, 2004.

Church of Scotland. *Call to Church: The Book of the Forward Movement of the Church of Scotland*. Edinburgh: The Church of Scotland Offices, 1931.

———. Commission for the Interpretation of God's Will in the Present Crisis. *God's Will for Church and Nation*. London: SCM, 1946.

———. Committee on Evangelism. *Into All the World: A Statement of Evangelism*. Glasgow: McCorquodale, 1946.

———. *Reports to the General Assembly: Report of the Home Board*. Edinburgh: Wm Blackwood, 1946–69.

Congar, Yves. *Lay People in the Church: A Study for a Theology of the Laity*. Translated by Donald Attwater. London: Geoffrey Chapman, 1957.

Cook, Guillermo. *The Expectation of the Poor: Latin American Basic Ecclesial Communities in Protestant Perspective*. American Society of Missiology Series 9. Maryknoll, NY: Orbis, 1985.

Cranston, Ian. *I've Seen Worse: Glimpses of Ian Fraser*. Larbert: Cranston, 2011.

Davidson, Nevile. *The Parish Church*. New Evangelism Series. Edinburgh: The Church of Scotland Offices, 1947.

Davie, Grace. *Religion in Britain since 1945: Believing without Belonging*. Oxford: Blackwell, 1994.

Davison, Andrew, and Alison Milbank. *For the Parish: A Critique of Fresh Expressions*. London: SCM, 2010.

Devine, T. M. *The Scottish Nation, 1700–2000*. London: Allen Lane, 1999.

Dinwiddie, Melville. *The Layman at Work*. Glasgow: "Tell Scotland" Movement, 1960.

———. *Religion by Radio: Its Place in British Broadcasting*. London: Allen & Unwin, 1968.

Donovan, Vincent J. *Christianity Rediscovered*. 2nd ed. Maryknoll, NY: Orbis, 1982.

Downie, Elaine. *Stand Up Straight: The Story of Lilias Graham and Braendam's Families*. Glasgow: Braendam Link, 2003.

Doyle, Ian B. "I Remember Tom Allan." *Life and Work*, March 1986, 25.

East Harlem Protestant Parish Archive (33 boxes), held by the Burke Library, Union Theological Seminary, Columbia University, New York City.

Ellul, Jacques. *The Presence of the Kingdom*. Translated by Olive Wyon. London: SCM, 1951.

Falconer, Ronald. *The Kilt beneath My Cassock*. Edinburgh: Handsel, 1978.

———. *Message, Media, Mission: The Baird Lectures 1975*. Edinburgh: Saint Andrew, 1977.

Ferguson, John F., ed. *When God Came Down: An Account of the North Uist Revival 1957–58*. Inverness: Lewis Recordings, 2000.

Ferguson, Ronald. *Chasing the Wild Goose: The Iona Community*. London: Collins, 1988.

———. *Geoff: The Life of Geoffrey M. Shaw*. Gartocharn: Famedram, 1979.

———. *George MacLeod*. London: Collins, 1990.

Papers relating to William Fitch collated by David Stay and Mary Stay, held by Revd. Prof. A. T. B. MacGowan.

Fitch, William. *Enter Into Life*. Grand Rapids: Eerdmans, 1961.

Finlay, Richard. *Modern Scotland: 1914–2000*. London: Profile, 2004.

Flett, John. *The Witness of God: The Trinity, Missio Dei, Karl Barth, and the Nature of Christian Community*. Grand Rapids: Eerdmans, 2010.

Forrester, Duncan. "Theology in the Shadow of War: The Baird Lectures as Contextual Theology." Baird Lecture, 31 October 2007. http://www.clydeserver.com/bairdtrust/pdfs/2007/Baird%20Conference%20-%20Duncan%20Forrester.pdf.

Forsyth, Alexander. "The Apostolate of the Laity: A Re-discovery of Holistic Post-War Missiology in Scotland, with Reference to the Ministry of Tom Allan." PhD diss., University of Edinburgh, 2014.

———. "The Missiology of Tom Allan for Today." *Theology in Scotland* 21 (2014) 45–58.

———. "Walking the Tightrope: The Missiology of Tom Allan for Today." *Practical Theology* 4 (2011) 227–45.

Fraser, Ian M. *Bible, Congregation and Community*. London: SCM, 1959.

———. *Bible, Congregation and Community*. 2nd ed. with introduction by author. Ferndale: Ian Fraser, 2011.

———. *Let's Get Moving: A Plea for Church Revolution in Scotland*. Edinburgh: The Scottish Churches Council, 1969.

———. *Living a Countersign: from Iona to Basic Christian Communities*. Glasgow: Wild Goose, 1990.

———. *Many Cells, One Body: Stories from Small Christian Communities*. Geneva: WCC, 2003.

———. *People Journeying: A Source-Book and Record of the Work of Scottish Churches' House, 1959–69*. Dunblane: The House, 1969.

———. *Reinventing Theology as the People's Work*. Glasgow: Wild Goose, 1980.

———. *Scottish Churches' House: Its Origins and Story*. Dunblane: Scottish Churches' House, 1969.

Free Church Monthly Record. "The Record Meets Eric Alexander." August 2009, 6.

Fyfe, Walter. "All Kinds of Talk about Evangelism: And Another Action." *The British Weekly*, September 1, 1955, 7.

Galbraith, Douglas, ed. *The Church of Scotland Yearbook 2015/16*. Edinburgh: Saint Andrew, 2015.

Gallagher, Tom. "Protestantism and Politics." In *Sermons and Battle Hymns: Protestant Popular Culture in Modern Scotland*, edited by Graham Walker and Tom Gallagher, 86–111. Edinburgh: Edinburgh University Press, 1990.

Gammie, Alexander. *Dr John White: A Biography and a Study*. London: James Clarke, 1929.

Gay, Douglas C. "A Practical Theology of Church and World: Ecclesiology and Social Vision in 20th Century Scotland." PhD diss., University of Edinburgh, 2006.

———. *Remixing the Church: Towards an Emerging Ecclesiology*. London: SCM, 2011.

Gibbs, Mark, and T. Ralph Morton. *God's Frozen People: A Book for and about Ordinary Christians.* London: Collins, 1964.

———. *God's Lively People: Christians in Tomorrow's World.* London: Collins, 1971.

Girvan, Adam. "Religion in Newmilns." In *Historical Aspects of Newmilns,* 86–96. Newmilns and Greenholm Community Council, 1990.

Godin, Henri G., and Yvan Daniel. "France a Missionary Land?" In Maisie Ward, *France Pagan? The Mission of Abbé Godin,* 63–191. London: Sheed & Ward, 1949.

Archive of the Gorbals Group Ministry, New College Library, University of Edinburgh, Archive GD58 (full archiving pending).

Archive of the Billy Graham Collection, Wheaton College, Wheaton, Illinois, USA.

Harvey, John. *Bridging the Gap: Has the Church Failed the Poor?* Edinburgh: Saint Andrew, 1987.

———. "Geoff Shaw." In *A Time for Trumpets: Scottish Church Movers and Shakers of the Twentieth Century,* edited by Nansie Blackie, 152–63. Edinburgh: Saint Andrew, 2005.

———. "What There Is to See." In *Seeing Scotland, Seeing Christ,* 70–75. Occasional Paper no. 28, Centre for Theology and Public Issues. New College: University of Edinburgh, 1993.

Harvie, Christopher. *No Gods and Precious Few Heroes: Scotland 1914–1980.* London: Arnold, 1981.

Havea, Jione. "The Cons of Contextuality . . . Kontextuality." In *Contextual Theology for the Twenty-First Century,* edited by Stephen B. Bevans and Katalina Tahaafe-Williams, 38–54. Eugene, OR: Pickwick Publications, 2011.

Heard, James. "Inculturation—Faithful to the Past: Open to the Future." In *Generous Ecclesiology: Church, World and the Kingdom of God,* edited by Julie Gittoes, Brutus Green, and James Heard, 61–77. London: SCM, 2013.

Henderson, Ian. *Power Without Glory: A Study in Ecumenical Politics.* London: Hutchinson, 1967.

———. *Scotland: Kirk and People.* Edinburgh: Lutterworth, 1969.

Highet, John. "The Churches." In *The Third Statistical Account of Scotland: Glasgow,* edited by J. Cunnison and J. B. S. Gilfillan, 713–50. Glasgow: Collins, 1958.

———. *The Churches in Scotland Today.* Glasgow: Jackson, 1950.

———. "The Protestant Churches in Scotland: A Review of Membership, Evangelistic Activities and Other Aspects." *Archives des Sciences Sociales des Religions* 8 (1959) 97–104.

———. *The Scottish Churches: A Review of Their State 400 Years after the Reformation.* London: Skeffington, 1960.

Hoedemaker, Bert. "Mission beyond Modernity: A Global Perspective." In *Christian Mission in Western Society: Precedents, Perspectives, Prospects,* edited by Simon Barrow and Graeme Smith, 212–34. London: CTBI, 2001.

Hoekendijk, Johannes C. "The Call to Evangelism." *International Review of Missions* 39 (1950) 162–75.

———. "The Church in Missionary Thinking." *International Review of Missions* 41 (1952) 324–36.

———. *The Church Inside Out.* London: SCM, 1967.

Holloway, Richard. "The Gorbals Group: An Experiment in Service." In *Changing Frontiers in the Mission of the Church,* edited by Barry Till, 38–43. London: SPCK, 1965.

————. *Leaving Alexandria: A Memoir of Faith and Doubt*. Edinburgh: Canongate, 2012.

Hulbert, Alastair. *The Hint Half Guessed: Mission, Ecumenism and Other Holy Things*. Edinburgh: Reid, 2008.

Hull, John M. *Mission-Shaped Church: A Theological Response*. London: SCM, 2006.

Irvin, Dale T. "The Church, the Urban, and Global Mission: Mission in an Age of Global Cities." In *International Bulletin of Missionary Research* 33 (2009) 177–82.

Papers of Jessie Margaret Strathdee or Johnston (1925–2008), daughter of John Strathdee, Elder, Treasurer and Session Clerk of St George's Tron Parish Church, held at The Mitchell Library, Glasgow, Ref TD 1800, Box 31.

Johnston, Ronald, and Elaine McFarland. "'Out in the Open in a Threatening World': The Scottish Churches' Industrial Mission 1960-1980." *International Review of Social History* 55 (2010) 1–27.

Johnstone, H. Martin. "Towards a Practical Ecclesiology for Urban Scotland." PhD diss., University of Glasgow, 2005.

Kenrick, Bruce. *Come Out the Wilderness*. London: Collins, 1962.

————. *The New Humanity*. London: Collins, 1958.

Kernahan, A. Earl. *Adventures in Visitation Evangelism*. New York: Revell, 1928.

————. *Visitation Evangelism: Its Methods and Results*. New York: Revell, 1925.

Kernohan, R. D. "Postscript: The Kirk since 1929." In John Buchan, *The Kirk in Scotland*, 138–67. Dunbar: Labarum, 1985.

Kesting, Sheilagh. "Being Ecumenical in Scotland Today." *Theology in Scotland* 13 (2006) 5–16.

Kirk, J. Andrew. *What is Mission? Theological Explorations*. London: Darton, Longman & Todd, 1999.

Kraemer, Hendrik. *A Theology of the Laity*. London: Lutterworth, 1958.

Kritzinger, J. N. J. (Klippies). "Mission in Prophetic Dialogue." *Missiology: An International Review* 41 (2013) 35–49.

Kung, Hans, and David Tracy, eds. *Paradigm Shifts in Theology*. Edinburgh: T. & T. Clark, 1989.

Lakeland, Paul. "The Laity." In *The Routledge Companion to the Christian Church*, edited by G. Mannion and L. Mudge, 511–23. London: Routledge, 2008.

Lamb, John Alexander, ed. *Fasti Ecclesiae Scoticanae*, vol. 9, *1929-1954*. Edinburgh: Oliver and Boyd, 1961.

Lennie, Tom. *Glory in the Glen: A History of Evangelical Revivals in Scotland, 1880-1940*. Fearn: Christian Focus, 2009.

Lyon, David. *How Foreign is Mission?* Edinburgh: Saint Andrew, 1995.

————. *In Pursuit of a Vision: The Story of the Church of Scotland's Relationship with the Churches Emerging from the Missionary Movement in the Twenty-Five Years from 1947 to 1972*. Edinburgh: Saint Andrew, 1998.

————. *Why Missions Today?* Issues of the Church 3. Edinburgh: Saint Andrew, 1978.

MacDonald, Angus, ed. *A Fraction of His Image*. Glasgow: Washington Irvine, 1965.

MacDonald, Catriona M. *Whaur Extremes Meet: Scotland's Twentieth Century*. Edinburgh: John Donald, 2009.

MacDonald, Donald Farquhar MacLeod, ed. *Fasti Ecclesiae Scoticanae*, vol. 10, *1955-1975*. Edinburgh: Saint Andrew, 1981.

MacDonald, Murdo Ewen. *Padre Mac: The Autobiography of the Late Murdo Ewen MacDonald of Harris*. 2nd ed. Isle of Lewis: Islands Book Trust, 2008.

MacLean, Colin. "Marvellous New Trumpets: The Media 1920s–2001." In *Scottish Life and Society: A Compendium of Scottish Ethnology*, vol. 12, *Religion*, edited by Colin MacLean and Kenneth Veitch, 413–78. Edinburgh: Donald, 2006.

MacLeod, Donald. "Question Marks and Garbage Heaps." *Life and Work*, August 1988, 21–25.

MacLeod of Fuinary and Iona Community, The Papers of George MacLeod, National Library of Scotland, Edinburgh, Acc. 9084.

MacLeod, George. "Modern Evangelism with Particular Reference to Scotland." Recording of speech at Union Seminary, New York, 2 January 1955. William Smith Morton Library, Union—PSCE, Richmond, Virginia.

———. *Only One Way Left: Church Prospect*. Glasgow: The Iona Community, 1955.

———. *We Shall Rebuild*. Glasgow: The Iona Community, 1946.

———. "What Do You Think of American Religion?" *The Coracle* 28 (March 1956) 9–26.

MacLeod, Hugh. *The Religious Crisis of the 1960s*. Oxford University Press, 2007.

Macwhirter, Iain. *The Road to Referendum*. Glasgow: Cargo, 2013.

Magnusson, Sally. *A Shout in the Street: The Story of Church House in Bridgeton*. Edinburgh: Saint Andrew, 1991.

Maitland, James. *Caring for People—the Church in the Parish*. Glasgow: Tell Scotland, 1954.

———. *New Beginnings: Breaking through to Unity; Early Years in Livingston's Ecumenical Parish*. Edinburgh; Saint Andrew, 1988.

Mantle, John. *Britain's First Worker-Priests*. London: SCM, 2000.

Marwick, Arthur. *The Sixties: Cultural Revolution in Britain, France, Italy, and the United States, c. 1958—c. 1974*. Oxford: Oxford University Press, 1998.

Mason, David, et al. *News from Notting Hill: The Formation of a Group Ministry*. London: Epworth, 1967.

McCrone, David. *Understanding Scotland: The Sociology of a Nation*. 2nd ed. London: Routledge, 2001.

Michonneau, Georges. *Revolution in a City Parish*. London: Blackfriars, 1949.

Moltmann, Jürgen. *The Church in the Power of the Spirit*. Translated by Margaret Kohl. 1977. Reprint, Minneapolis: Fortress, 1993.

More, George, and Mary More. *This is Our Life in Central India*. London: Edinburgh House, 1962.

Morton, T. Ralph. *Evangelism in Scotland*. Geneva: World Council of Churches, 1954.

———. *Evangelism in Scotland Today*. Glasgow: "Tell Scotland" Pamphlet no. 2, 1954.

———. "The House Church: The Next Step or a First Step?" *The Coracle* 28 (March 1956) 1–8.

———. *The Household of Faith*. Glasgow: The Iona Community, 1951.

———. *The Iona Community: Personal Impressions of the Early Years*. Edinburgh: Saint Andrew, 1977.

———. *Missionary Principles for the Home Front*. Glasgow: Iona Youth Trust, 1944.

Moyes, Andy. "The Face of My (Missionary) Parish." *Life and Work*, August 1990, 16–17.

Muir, Augustus. *John White*. London: Hodder & Stoughton, 1958.

Murray, Stuart. *Church after Christendom*. Milton Keynes, UK: Paternoster, 2004.

Neill, Stephen. "Fellowship of the Church Must Begin on the Street." *Life and Work*, May 1954, 113–14.

————. *On the Ministry*. London: SCM, 1952.

Neilson, Peter. *Church on the Move: New Church, New Generation, New Scotland; An Emerging Profile*. Glasgow: Covenanters, 2005.

Newbigin, Lesslie. "Can the West be Converted?" *International Bulletin of Missionary Research* 11 (1987) 2–7.

————. *Foolishness to the Greeks: The Gospel and Western Culture*. Grand Rapids: Eerdmans, 1986.

————. *The Household of God*. London: SCM, 1953.

————. *Unfinished Agenda*. Geneva: WCC, 1985.

North Kelvinside Parish Church, Glasgow, Minutes of the Kirk Session, 1946–1953.

Orr, David C. *The House Church*. Glasgow: The Iona Community, 1961.

Paterson, Bill. *Tales from the Back Green*. London: Hodder & Stoughton, 2008.

Paterson, Lindsay, et al. *Living in Scotland: Social and Economic Change since 1980*. Edinburgh: Edinburgh University Press, 2004.

Perrin, Henri. *Priest-Workman in Germany*. Translated by Rosemary Sheed. London: Sheed & Ward, 1947.

Philip, T. V. *Edinburgh to Salvador: Twentieth Century Ecumenical Missiology*. Delhi: CSS & ISPCK, 1999.

Pollock, J. *Billy Graham: The Authorised Biography*. London: Hodder & Stoughton, 1966.

Pugh, Martin. *State and Society: A Social and Political History of Britain since 1870*. 3rd ed. London: Hodder Education, 2008

Raiser, Konrad. *Ecumenism in Transition: A Paradigm Shift in the Ecumenical Movement?* Geneva: WCC, 1991.

————. "Profile of the Laity in the Ecumenical Movement." In *A Letter from Christ to the World: An Exploration of the Role of the Laity in the Church Today*, edited by Nicholas Apostola, 12–22. Geneva: WCC, 1998.

Read, David. "The British Churches: Another Sign from Scotland." *The British Weekly*, 27 May 1954, 7.

Reid, Harry. *Outside Verdict: An Old Kirk in a New Scotland*. Edinburgh: Saint Andrew, 2002.

Rice, David Arthur. "A Report on Fieldwork with The Gorbals Group Ministry." Presented to The Sixteenth Graduate School, Ecumenical Institute, Céligny, Switzerland, 1968, within the Archive of the Gorbals Group Ministry.

Riddell, J. G. *What We Believe*. Edinburgh: Church of Scotland, 1937.

Robertson, Roland. "Glocalization: Time–Space and Homogenity–Heterogenity." In *Global Modernities*, edited by M. Featherstone, Scott Lash, and Roland Robertson, 25–44. London: Sage, 1995.

Robinson, John T. *Honest to God*. London: SCM, 1963.

————. "The House Church and the Parish Church." *Theology* 53 (1950) 283–89.

Ross, Cathy, and Stephen B. Bevans, eds. *Mission on the Road to Emmaus: Constants, Context and Prophetic Dialogue*. London: SCM, 2015.

Sanneh, Lamin O. *Translating the Message: The Missionary Impact on Culture*. American Society of Missiology Series 13. Maryknoll, NY: Orbis, 1989.

Scherer, James A., and Stephen B. Bevans, eds. *New Directions in Mission and Evangelization*. Vol. 1, *Basic Statements 1974–1991*. Maryknoll, NY: Orbis, 1992.

Schmidt, Leigh Eric. *Holy Fairs: Scotland and the Making of American Revivalism*. 2nd ed. Grand Rapids: Eerdmans, 2001.

Schreiter, Robert J. *Constructing Local Theologies*. Maryknoll, NY: Orbis, 1985.

————. *The Ministry of Reconciliation: Spirituality & Strategies*. Maryknoll, NY: Orbis, 1998.

————. *The New Catholicity: Theology between the Global and the Local*. Faith and Cultures Series. Maryknoll, NY: Orbis, 1998.

————. *Reconciliation: Mission and Ministry in a Changing Social Order*. Boston Theological Institute Annual Series 3. Maryknoll, NY: Orbis, 1992.

Schreiter, Robert, and Knud Jørgensen, eds. *Mission as Ministry of Reconciliation*. Regnum Edinburgh Centenary Series 16. Eugene, OR: Wipf & Stock, 2013.

Shackleton, Bill. *Keeping It Cheery: Anecdotes from a Life in Brigton*. Glasgow: Covenanters, 2005.

Shannon, Bill. *Tom Allan: In a Nutshell*. Edinburgh: Handsel, 2000.

————. "Tom Allan (minister)." http://en.wikipedia.org/wiki/Tom_Allan_(minister).

Shaw, Geoffrey, and John Harvey. *A Dead End Church? Study Guide for the Eighteenth Scottish Christian Youth Assembly*. Falkirk: SCYA Steering Committee, 1966.

Shenk, Wilbert R. "The Mission Dynamic." In *Mission in Bold Humility: David Bosch's Work Considered*, edited by Willem Saayman and Klippies Kritzinger, 83–93. Maryknoll, NY: Orbis, 1996.

Simpson, James A. "Faith and Works." *Life and Work*, October 1990, 19–20.

Skreslet, Stanley H. *Comprehending Mission: The Questions, Methods, Themes, Problems, and Prospects of Missiology*. American Society of Missiology Series 49. Maryknoll, NY: Orbis, 2012.

Small, Mabel. *Growing Together: Some Aspects of the Ecumenical Movement in Scotland 1924–1964*. Edinburgh: Scottish Churches Council, 1975.

Smith, David. "The Culture of Modern Scotland as the Context for Christian Mission: A View from Over the Border." *Theology in Scotland* 5 (1998) 55–70.

————. *Mission After Christendom*. London: Darton, Longman & Todd, 2003.

Smith, Ronald Gregor. *The New Man: Christianity and Man's Coming of Age*. London: SCM, 1956.

————. *Secular Christianity*. London: Collins, 1966.

Somerville, Anastasia. "Renewal in the Church, Social Reconstruction and a Community on Iona: The Origins and Development of George MacLeod's Christian Social Vision in 1930s Scotland." PhD diss., University of Aberdeen, 2010.

Southcott, Ernest. *The Parish Comes Alive*. London: Mowbray, 1956.

Spencer, Stephen. *SCM Study Guide to Christian Mission: Historic Types and Contemporary Expressions*. London: SCM, 2007.

Stewart, James S. *A Faith to Proclaim*. London: Hodder & Stoughton, 1953.

————. Review of *The Face of My Parish*, by Tom Allan. *The Expository Times* 55 (November 1954) 63.

Still, William. *Dying to Live*. Fearn, UK: Christian Focus, 1991.

Storrar, William F. "Liberating the Kirk: The Enduring Legacy of the Baillie Commission." In *God's Will in a Time of Crisis: A Colloquium Celebrating the 50th Anniversary of The Baillie Commission*, edited by Andrew R. Morton, 60–72. Edinburgh: CTPI, 1994.

————. *Scottish Identity: A Christian Vision*. Edinburgh: Handsel, 1990.

————. "A Tale of Two Paradigms: Mission in Scotland from 1946." In *Death or Glory: The Church's Mission in Scotland's Changing Society; Studies Honouring the Contribution of Dr Geoffrey Grogan to the Church*, edited by D. Searle, 54–71. Fearn, UK: Christian Focus, 2001.

Stringfellow, William. Review of *Come Out the Wilderness*, by Bruce Kenrick. *Christian Century* 3 (1963) 431–32.

Sunquist, Scott W. *Understanding Christian Mission: Participation in Suffering and Glory*. Grand Rapids: Baker, 2013.

Tell Scotland Archive, within the papers of Scottish Churches' House/Action of Churches Together in Scotland, New College Library, University of Edinburgh.

Templeton, Elizabeth. *God's February: A Life of Archie Craig 1888–1985*. London: BCC/ CCBI, 1991.

Thomas, Norman E., ed. *Classic Texts in Mission and World Christianity*. American Society of Missiology Series 20. Maryknoll, NY: Orbis, 1995.

———, ed. *Readings in World Mission*. Maryknoll, NY: Orbis, 1995.

Thomson, D. P. *Aspects of Evangelism*. Crieff: Research Unit, 1968.

———. "The Diary of My Life." Transcribed by Frank Bardgett. http://www.bardgett. plus.com/Scotlands_Evangelist/The_Diary_of_My_Life.html.

———. *Dr Billy Graham and the Pattern of Modern Evangelism*. Crieff: St Ninian's, 1966.

———. *Harnessing the Lay Forces of the Church*. Crieff: St Ninian's, 1958.

———. *Personal Encounters*. Crieff: Research Unit, 1967.

———. *We Saw the Church in Action*. Crieff: n.p., 1954.

Thomson, P. D. *Parish and Parish Church: Their Place and Influence in History*. London: Thomas Nelson, 1948.

Tillich, Paul. *The Protestant Era*. Translated by James Luther Adams. Chicago: University of Chicago Press, 1948.

Torrance, James. *Worship, Community and the Triune God of Grace*. Carlisle, UK: Paternoster, 1996.

Visser 't Hooft, W. A. "Notes on the Relevance of the Main Theme for the Sections," 16 July 1954, World Council of Churches Archive, Geneva, Box 32.006, File 4.

Voillaume, René. *Seeds of the Desert: The Legacy of Charles de Foucauld*. London: Burns & Oats, 1955.

Walls, Andrew F. *The Cross-Cultural Process in Christian History*. Edinburgh: T. & T. Clark, 1996.

———. *The Missionary Movement in Christian History: Studies in the Transmission of Faith*. Maryknoll, NY: Orbis, 1996.

Watson, David. *Social Problems and the Church's Duty*. London: A. & C. Black, 1908.

Webber, George W. *The Congregation in Mission: Emerging Structures for the Church in an Urban World*. New York: Abingdon, 1964.

———. "East Harlem Revisited." *Union Seminary Quarterly Review* 5 (1949) 25–29.

———. "European Evangelism and the Church in America." *Christianity and Crisis* 10 (November 1958) 155–58.

———. *God's Colony in Man's World*. New York: Abingdon, 1960.

———. "New Wineskins of Worship." *Concern Magazine*, March 1962, 16–17.

Weber, Hans-Ruedi. "On Being Christians in the World: Reflections on the Ecumenical Discussion about the Laity." In *A Letter from Christ to the World: An Exploration of the Role of the Laity in the Church Today*, edited by Nicholas Apostola, 30–46. Geneva: WCC, 1998.

———. "The Rediscovery of the Laity in the Ecumenical Movement." In *The Layman in Christian History*, edited by Stephen Charles Neill and Hans-Ruedi Weber, 377–94. London: SCM, 1963.

Werner, Dietrich. "Evangelism from a WCC Perspective." *International Review of Mission* 96 (2007) 183–203.

———. "Rediscovering a Missionary Understanding of the Church in the West: Observations from Germany." In *Ecumenical Missiology: Contemporary Trends, Issues, and Themes*, edited by Lalsangkima Pachuau, 129–46. Bangalore: United Theological College, 2002.

Wessels, Antonie. "The Inculturation of Christianity in Europe." In *Christian Mission in Western Society: Precedents, Perspectives, Prospects*, edited by Simon Barrow and Graeme Smith, 31–49. London: CTBI, 2001.

Wickham, Edward. *Church and People in an Industrial City*. London: Lutterworth, 1957.

The Papers of John White, New College Library, University of Edinburgh, Box 95.

Whiteman, Darrell L. "Contextualization: The Theory, the Gap, the Challenge." *International Bulletin of Missionary Research* 21(1997) 2–7.

Whyte, James. Preface to New Edition of *The Face of My Parish*, by Tom Allan. Glasgow: Loudon, 1984.

Wilkie, George D. *The Eldership Today*. Glasgow: The Iona Community, 1960.

Wolfe, J. N., and M. Pickford. *The Church of Scotland: An Economic Survey*. London: Chapman, 1980.

World Council of Churches, Library & Archives, Geneva, Switzerland, Boxes 26.19.10, 32.001, 32.4, 42.4.099, 42.4.100, 213.14.15.

World Council of Churches. *Centres of Renewal: For Study and Lay Training*. Geneva: WCC, 1964.

———. *The Church's Witness to God's Design: An Ecumenical Study*. London: SCM, 1948.

———. *Evangelism: The Mission of the Church to those Outside her Life*. London: SCM, 1954.

———. *Evanston Report*. London: SCM, 1954.

———. *Laici in Ecclesia: An Ecumenical Bibliography on the Role of the Laity in the Life and Mission of the Church*. Geneva: WCC, 1961.

———. *Laity Formation: Proceedings of the Ecumenical Consultation, Gazzada (Italy), September 7th –10th, 1965*. Rome: Arti Grafiche Scalia, 1966.

———. *Mission and Evangelism: An Ecumenical Affirmation*. Geneva: WCC, 1983.

———. "Mission and Evangelism in Unity Today." *International Review of Mission* 88 (January–April 1999) 109–27.

———. *Signs of Renewal: The Life of the Lay Institute in Europe*. Geneva: WCC, 1957.

———. "A Theological Reflection on the Work of Evangelism." *The Bulletin* 5.1–2 (November 1959) Geneva: WCC.

———. *You Are the Light of the World: Statements on Mission by the World Council of Churches 1980–2005*. Geneva: WCC, 2005.

Yates, Timothy. *Christian Mission in the Twentieth Century*. Cambridge: Cambridge University Press, 1994.

# Index